D1595840

Conspiracy Theory in Film, Television, and Politics

Gordon B. Arnold

Westport, Connecticut
London

Library of Congress Cataloging-in-Publication Data

Arnold, Gordon B., 1954–
    Conspiracy theory in film, television, and politics / Gordon B. Arnold.
        p.   cm.
    Includes bibliographical references and index.
    ISBN: 978–0–275–99462–4 (alk. paper)
    1. Conspiracies—United States.   2. Motion pictures and television—United States.
3. Popular culture—United States.   4. Political culture—United States.   I. Title
HV6285.A76   2008
001.9—dc22   2008019904

British Library Cataloguing in Publication Data is available.

Library of Congress Catalog Card Number: 2008019904
ISBN: 978–0–275–99462–4

First published in 2008

Praeger Publishers, 88 Post Road West, Westport, CT 06881
An imprint of Greenwood Publishing Group, Inc.
www.praeger.com

Printed in the United States of America

The paper used in this book complies with the
Permanent Paper Standard issued by the National
Information Standards Organization (Z39.48–1984).

10 9 8 7 6 5 4 3 2 1

Contents

Preface   vii

Acknowledgments   xi

Chapter 1: Conspiracy Theory in the American Imagination   1

Chapter 2: The Red Menace and Its Discontents   19

Chapter 3: Conspiracy in the New Frontier   43

Chapter 4: Shock and Upheaval   65

Chapter 5: Scandal and Skepticism   89

Chapter 6: Vision and Re-Vision   113

Chapter 7: A New Age of Conspiracy   133

Chapter 8: Belief and Disbelief   159

Notes   173

Bibliography   181

Index   185

Preface

Since the middle of the last century, many movies and television productions with a conspiracy theory theme have appeared on screen. They constitute an important part of American popular culture history. The story of how and why this happened and what it means is the primary focus of this book.

The conspiracy theory, in many forms and guises, has been one of the most recognizable and durable themes in American culture since the middle of the twentieth century. It is a thoroughly familiar concept in modern life. Yet, the term "conspiracy theory" implies different things to different people. For some, conspiracy theory reveals the true causes of events. For these people it may, as one writer noted, even constitute their "normal way of thinking about who they are and how the world works."[1] Others see such ideas as little more than anxious or paranoid reactions to a troubled world.[2] Still others see conspiracy theory as a little bit of both—a mixture of fact and fiction, of realism and paranoia.

Whatever a person thinks about specific conspiracy theories—whether one believes them or not—there is little doubt that they represent a significant current in American popular and political culture. Dealing with topics as far-flung as the assassination of John F. Kennedy and captured extraterrestrial aliens, they have attracted much attention. They have inspired a host of fiction and nonfiction books, articles, movies, television productions, and other material for popular consumption.

Indeed, there is no doubt that conspiracy theory has emerged as a mass phenomenon, and there are many avenues that might be taken to uncover the story of its development. This book aims to investigate the evolution of conspiracy theory as a powerful cultural narrative. To accomplish this, one might examine its presence in any of the popular arts. But although the conspiracy theme can be found in many forms, perhaps none of its manifestations has been as prominent as its appearance in popular movies and television. That is the avenue that is taken here.

Indeed, popular films—and later, television series—have been among the most reliable indicators of American cultural tendencies over the past century. Whether such productions feature realistic portrayals of life or more fanciful and fantastic screen visions, the popular film of an era provides a window into the hearts and minds of that era. Film and television reflect public perceptions and help shape them; they provide some insight into what people are thinking about and the ways in which they perceive various topics. Hope, anxiety, pride, fear—these emotions and more are the staples of the screen. How they appear in a narrative and are interpreted by an audience tells us something important.

It is not unusual that portrayals of conspiracy and intrigue have found a lasting place on the screen. Throughout American history, some people have been drawn to the belief that conspiracies have shaped major events. Such ideas are usually embraced most strongly by only a fraction of the population. At times, however, conspiracy theories capture the interest of a much wider public. This is especially so when everyday life is interrupted by a national trauma—an assassination, a surprise attack, or an unforeseen constitutional crisis. In such instances, conspiracy theories hold the allure of explaining unforeseen developments, especially those with complex and vaguely understood causes and backgrounds. Some of these cases, it is true, do involve a genuine conspiracy. In many other cases, the emergence of strong belief in a conspiracy theory—that a sinister plot is responsible for the given traumatic event—seems to run counter to available evidence. In still other instances, the role of conspiracy remains unsettled and can depend upon how precisely the term is defined.

In the period since the end of the Second World War, American culture has provided a fertile breeding ground for a very wide variety of conspiracy theories, touching on an astonishing range of topics. Conspiracies have been blamed for assassinations, coups in foreign lands, attempts to establish one-world government, deceptions about the alleged truth regarding unidentified flying objects, and a multitude of perceived efforts to manipulate an American public that is simply trying to go about daily life.

As the following chapters show, it is not simply that there have been a number of conspiracy theories over this time, as impressive as that number might be. Rather, when observed through the mediums of film and television, it becomes apparent that the conspiracy theories, as well as the underlying cultural mood that they express, have undergone major change over the decades. Simply put, a conspiracy theory that is widely available in the culture today (as, for example, might be the case of various 9/11 conspiracy theories) tells us something very different about popular and political culture than a typical conspiracy theory from the early Cold War does about that time.

With all of this in mind, this book treats the progression of films and television productions dealing with conspiracy theory themes as a rich stream of data, as cultural artifacts with a story to tell about the way that the conspiracy theory idea penetrated and resonated with the American public. In considering many screen productions, the chapters aim to set each of the works discussed into the context of their times in order to show the unfolding, long-running conspiracy theory story line that runs through the past six decades of the American experience.

THE APPROACH OF THE BOOK

In the period covered in this book, thousands of films and television productions were created. Directly or indirectly, a substantial number of these are either influenced by, or have something to say about, the development of the conspiracy theory narrative in American culture. This raises the question of which productions to include in the study.

In preparing the following chapters, it was necessary to identify which of those many productions would clearly and accurately reflect the main thrust of conspiracy theory's evolution in America culture. The list of movies and television productions discussed in the chapters was developed using a few guiding principles. Beyond evidence of a conspiracy theory or closely related theme, many of the productions discussed here were selected because they were either widely disseminated or evoked a strong response from the audiences, particularly at the time of first release. In a lesser number of cases, works that failed to effectively reach or influence a mass audience, but were noteworthy for some other reason in the evolution of the conspiracy theory theme, are also considered.

Since the purpose of the study is to reveal the development of this theme, the artistic merit of the works discussed is, for these purposes, much less important than a given work's role in spreading and reinforcing the theme among the general public. While many of the films here enjoy first-rate critical reputations, others have substantially weaker reputations. Indeed, some are usually relegated to the footnotes of media history.

But regardless of a production's critical reputation, a movie or television show that successfully reaches a broad audience and that holds its attention for even a short while can have an important impact on popular and political culture. After all, a film is no less significant in terms of its effect on a culture because it is branded a simple entertainment, rather than a work of high art. *Rambo* was hardly a film garnering the admiration of film critics, for example, but its wild popularity in the mid-1980s reveals much about the attitudes and mood of the American public at that time. Popularity is not everything, of course, but deep penetration of a production into the public's consciousness and mindset is important. Familiarity has a function in popular culture.

The book does not assume that readers will have seen each of the films and television productions that are discussed. For that reason, many of the works are summarized. Although it would have been possible to mention only those specific parts of productions that applied to the main theme under discussion, movies and television series are experienced as wholes, not as parts. Thus, to help readers who are unfamiliar with these works more fully understand how the broader argument applies to a given movie or television show, the text often provides overviews to entire works, rather than simply small parts of them.

In order to establish the historical contexts in which the conspiracy theory theme developed, the following pages also provide a very brief summary of major national and international events that had an impact on the story. It is a necessarily brief and selective exposition. Indeed, this aspect of the text is intended simply to establish this historical framework, with the hope that readers looking for a more thorough explanation of this important period will consult one the many other fine books that have been produced about this subject.

A word about conspiracy theories themselves is also in order relative to the text. This investigation takes individual conspiracy theories as social "facts," that is, as ideas that some people take to be true whether or not they really are. People act and make sense of the world based on what they believe is the truth. One might agree or disagree with the belief, but it is the belief itself, rather than independently verified validation of it, that is important. Therefore, readers will not find defenses or refutations of the various theories in these pages. Many other fine works exist that explore this aspect of conspiracy theory, but here the focus remains on the power of an idea, not in questions about the literal truth of an idea.

AUDIENCE

This book is aimed at several audiences. The first and most obvious of these consists of those nonspecialist readers who are interested in conspiracy theory as a general phenomenon in the period since World War II. Beyond this, readers with interests in American cultural history generally, and the history of film and television, more specifically, may find useful information in these chapters. In addition, readers with interest in aspects of political history may find the text to be a useful supplement to standard accounts of the era. Finally, movie and television buffs may find information about specific works that will heighten their appreciation of the many films and series discussed throughout the text.

Acknowledgments

Many people were directly or indirectly instrumental in the preparation of this book. Of special note are past and present students in my film history and other courses at Montserrat College of Art. Their curiosity and creativity about many things prompted me to ask many of the questions that were instrumental in conceiving and conducting the research for this project. Their energy and enthusiasm are a constant source of inspiration.

Also at Montserrat, I have enjoyed the support of many fine colleagues. Library director Cheri Coe and public services librarian Lisa Batchelder were helpful, as always, especially in tracking down background material that was important in the preparation of the manuscript. My colleagues in the liberal arts provided an ideal climate for getting the work done. I also thank Laura Tonelli, dean of the college, for her efforts in creating a warm and collegial atmosphere in which one can teach and write successfully.

Many libraries contributed their service and resources to my efforts in completing the book. In addition to the library at Montserrat College of Art, I give special thanks to the Westborough Public Library, Northborough Public Library, Boston Public Library, Lancaster Public Library, Marlborough Public Library, the O'Neill Library at Boston College, and the Worcester Public Library.

I also am grateful to the editorial team and staff at Praeger for their interest and commitment to this project, with special recognition of Dan Harmon, my most helpful editor. The final months of the project were greatly facilitated by Sweety Singh at Aptara Corporation.

Finally, I thank my family for their support and understanding during the months of research and writing.

Conspiracy Theory in the American Imagination

Conspiracy theory is a staple of American popular culture, with a particularly strong presence in film and television. But conspiracy theory's frequent appearances on screen reveal something about American society that extends beyond the walls of the movie theater or living room. Indeed, it has penetrated the American consciousness. To explore this powerful theme, this chapter examines the evolution of conspiracy theory in film and television to consider what this says about American life and politics.

Despite its durability as a cultural and political theme, conspiracy theory has not been a static notion. Rather, its portrayal in popular culture and in politics has constantly changed, and so has its meaning. What this idea tells us about American life and culture shifts from one era to the next. Once, the term "conspiracy theory" was synonymous with fear and paranoia. Now, this same term might just as easily prompt a shrug or dismissive glance.

The term "conspiracy theory" evokes more than scheming and manipulation, which have frequently appeared throughout human history. Instead, conspiracy theory suggests something larger, something that encapsulates a specific worldview. To amplify this point, writer Daniel Pipes draws a useful distinction between what he classifies as *conspiracies* as opposed to *conspiracy theories*. Conspiracies, according to Pipes, are those "commonplace" real-world phenomena in which people clandestinely engage in "various sorts of criminal conspiracy such as bribery, racketeering, price fixing, and drug trafficking."[1] They are mostly mundane and ordinary. Conspiracy theory, on the other hand, has broader implications. It evokes an uneasy state of mind characterized by "the fear of a nonexistent conspiracy." In other words, it is "a perception" that is not necessarily based on an underlying reality.[2]

Whatever the interpretation, conspiracy theory has deeply penetrated American thought.[3] For some people, it is a framework that explains the reality of the modern world. For others, it is not much more than contemporary folklore, a general theme underlying much popular storytelling.[4] Still others see it as something in between.

Regardless of a person's attitude about it, though, conspiracy theory in the early twenty-first-century imagination extends beyond the fringes of American life. A popular motif, in which shadowy figures and clandestine machinations imperil the hapless public, the conspiracy theory vision of reality has a considerable presence in the mainstream.

Indeed, the far reach of conspiracy theory as a cultural phenomenon is not simply the result of advocacy by its true believers, although a substantial core of people harbors at least some of its ideas. But committed conspiracy theorists—those who make that belief central to their interpretation of the world around them—remain in the minority. Rather than the true believers, then, it is people with more tentative, sometimes even casual, interest in conspiracy theory that have pushed the idea from the fringes into the mainstream, to new levels of acceptance and respectability. But they did not do this alone.

Indeed, the conspiracy theory worldview has catapulted into the mainstream with the help of other forces, as well. One was the development of a willing political culture in which seemingly any idea that promotes one's cause, however implausible, is embraced. In such a culture, conspiracy can be a profoundly useful idea to attack one's political foes. After all, conspiracies are hidden and undercover by definition and so lack of evidence is not necessarily a problem, especially if the idea is heavily promoted by enemies with an agenda. In the court of public opinion, the case for conspiracy can be made as easily with innuendo as evidence, and on many occasions, it has.

Another force that brought the conspiracy theory theme to new heights of attention is at once more obvious, yet seemingly benign. It is the barrage of film and television productions with the conspiracy theory themes. Beginning just after World War II, there was an explosion of such productions. Dovetailing with the political and cultural climate of the times, they reflected society's genuine fears. But they did more than reflect. By their sheer number and sensory bombast, they also helped influence American ideas and attitudes about the subject. Looking at the prominent presence of conspiracy theory in American life a half-century later, it is sometimes hard to tell which parts of the phenomenon have been shaped by historical events and which parts have been shaped by movie and television fictions. Whatever the reasons, and whichever way it is interpreted, there is no denying that the conspiracy theory idea is firmly planted in the American consciousness. It has not always been so.

Indeed, though there were some exceptions, for much of American history conspiracy theory existed mainly at the margins of American culture. And while in some respects conspiracy theorizing was a populist phenomenon, at times broadly reflecting the attitudes and prejudices of the day, serious adherents of such theories were relatively few. To be sure, persons or groups representing minority racial, political, ethnic, or religious groups were too often regarded as the potential enemies of those in the majority, but such thinking only rarely manifested itself in organized theories of conspiracy. Successful conspiracies, after all, require intelligence, careful planning, and organization, and those in the majority were often unwilling to admit that members of other groups could possess such traits.

Sometimes, of course, there are genuine conspiracies, often involving a limited set of specific objectives revolving around crime—organized crime is at its base conspiratorial in this commonplace sense—or an attempt to manipulate circumstances in a quest for power, as in the Watergate scandal. Moreover, ordinary people recognize that a real conspiracy can have terrible consequences. A leader could be assassinated or a criminal enterprise could run rampant.

But the grander, more global type of intrigue and subterfuge, which is usually suggested by modern idea of conspiracy theory, has often been harder to imagine. It is more difficult to believe that groups could clandestinely co-ordinate the complex, large-scale workings of entire governments, or that the members of such groups could keep such an enterprise secret long enough to change the trajectory of human affairs. Indeed, large-scale conspiracy theories generally seemed too complex to work and involved too many people to keep secret. For much of American history, such ideas were usually far removed from the everyday experience of here and now to have sufficient allure to hold the general public's interest for very long.

Conspiracy theories have made their way slowly but inexorably into the world of everyday experience.[5] In the modern United States, this impulse can be traced back to the general paranoia about communism that emerged with the Cold War in the late 1940s. It grew and transformed over subsequent decades, reaching a peak in the late 1990s. It was at that time, for example, that Hillary Clinton responded to lurid accusations about her husband having an inappropriate relationship with a White House intern by claiming the accusations were the product of a "vast Right-wing conspiracy." At that moment, it was clear that the conspiracy theory mindset had come out of the shadows, even among political elites.

Over the past several decades, the public developed a strong fascination for speculations of this sort. Such ideas are now encountered everywhere from the seat of government to the living room sofa. Unquestionably, conspiracy theories somehow have become thoroughly interwoven into the colorful tapestry of American life. Once the province of the marginalized, the paranoid, or the political extremist, the words "conspiracy theory" are now uttered by ordinary citizens, usually without eliciting much notice. To the ordinary person, the term seldom refers to a literal or criminal conspiracy, but rather to a generalized worldview in which ordinary folks are constantly the targets of spin, manipulation, and deception.

This is a new way to think about conspiracies, bearing only a superficial resemblance to the way the idea of conspiracy was usually interpreted in the past. The increasing pervasiveness of the conspiracy idea has been accompanied by a paradoxical shift in perceptions about it. Although the conspiracy theory impulse can now be found throughout American culture, few people take it very seriously. Conspiracy theory is sometimes used as a pejorative label for ideas that other people think are outlandish.

This is not to say that these ideas are insignificant, however. Americans may not have succumbed to the fear and paranoia that the victims of conspiracy exhibit in many fictionalized accounts, but along with the public's constant exposure to the idea has come a change that may be just as important. At the same time conspiracy theories have become more prominent and accepted in the mainstream, many Americans have become significantly more cynical about the central institutions of their society than was the case just a few decades ago.

Many writers and researchers have noted the strong allure of conspiracy theories in modern America.[6] One study of residents in New Jersey found that a majority believed at least some conspiracy theories were probably true.[7] In another example, researchers examined suspicions among African-Americans about a racially motivated conspiracy involving HIV/AIDS, rumors of which have been circulating for many years. The 2002 report found that about a quarter of their sample agreed with the statement, "HIV/AIDS is a man-made virus that the federal government made to kill and wipe out black people." Another quarter of the sample said they were undecided about it. The study is only one demonstration of how comprehensively conspiracy theory ideas have penetrated modern life.[8]

Although many conspiracy theories have ardent advocates, most people have a more blasé attitude about them. This is not to say that the ideas are rejected out of hand. Instead, conspiracy theory ideas are sometimes accepted as semi-plausible alternatives to ordinary accounts of the world. But they are just as often viewed as entertaining diversions—side-shows in the media-saturated circus of modern life.

Thus, conspiracy theories have been accepted by the general public not as face-value descriptions of the real world, but rather as emblems of a stance. They have been absorbed not literally, but metaphorically. They are part of a worldview in which the individual has little power against enormous external forces, sometimes seen, sometimes not. The confluence of rising cynicism and the mainstreaming of the conspiracy theory theme in the United States is an important development.

Once, the suggestion of conspiracy was something that people would likely dismiss out of hand or else fearfully accept as a type of truth-speaking. Today, however, it is often the case that the suggestion of conspiracy doesn't raise much reaction at all. It would be easy to argue that conspiracy theory is presently so thoroughly interwoven into the American mainstream that it often scarcely draws notice. Conspiracy theories have been aired in books, magazines, films, television and, more recently, the Internet, usually finding an audience without much difficulty. Yet, it would be hard to argue that Americans, as a whole, are significantly more fearful and anxious about sinister cabals and organized subterfuge than in the past. It is seldom observed how odd a development this is.

There is something about conspiracy theory that appeals to many people. It has an allure in the busy, complex, and often chaotic world that emerged in the latter part of the twentieth century and that continues today. Intentionally or not, American entertainment media has aggressively promoted the conspiracy theory theme since the 1950s in a succession of movies and television shows. This theme, which can easily be molded to fit within a number of popular movie and television genres, was quickly embraced by the public. It has proven to be as remarkably durable as it is adaptable. Conspiracy theory has appeared in political thrillers, murder mysteries, science fiction, and other genres across the entertainment media and for audiences of all ages. It is hard to imagine that many people escape exposure to the theme given the ubiquity of film, television, and video in modern life.

On screen, as elsewhere in contemporary culture, conspiracy theory is found in a wide array of incarnations, from works and discussions deal-ing with the world's most pressing affairs to the trivialities of everyday life. Just as a person need not look far before finding an assortment of such theories on topics such as war, assassination, September 11, and the AIDS epidemic, other examples can be found on matters that seem insignif-icant by contrast, such as the outcome of a football game. Unquestion-ably, the penetration of conspiracy theory into American life is deep and far-reaching.

Although many people today regard conspiracy theory as a delusional way of thinking about world affairs, at times there has been at least some factual basis for such beliefs. To be sure, there have been many occasions in which conspiracies, or something closely resembling them, have been at work. De-spite the excesses of the McCarthy period, for example, there were, in fact, Soviet spies working to steal America's secrets and undermine its prestige. And later, during the Watergate crisis of the 1970s, government officials did clandestinely attempt to influence electoral politics and thwart the discovery of misdeeds. These and other actual conspiracies do present situations wor-thy of public scrutiny. In corporate America, too, there have been attempts to hide known dangers to public health and safety. Cases such as these give pause to reasonable persons to be sure.

Often, however, people encounter conspiracy theories in forms that seem less connected to demonstrably real situations. Indeed, experience reveals that the fear of conspiracies does not require that they be proven beyond a reasonable doubt. American history is littered with examples of alleged conspiracies that fall into this category. Fraternal groups, such as the Freemasons, and religious orders, such as the Jesuits, have been the targets of such thought at various times in American history. Further afield from the mainstream, white supremacist groups have spawned extravagant, racially based conspiracy theories. Others have suggested a global One World Government conspiracy, having ancient origins and involving the Illuminati, the British royal family, Jewish bankers, the Rockefeller family, and many others. Less politically charged, devotees of the unidentified flying object (UFO) phenomenon have suggested massive government plots and cover-ups.

Still, as much as the public has been exposed to, and at times shown an appetite for material positing that conspiracies lie at the heart of various events, such ideas are very often not taken seriously. Indeed, as popularly construed in the 2000s, the label of "conspiracy theory" is frequently taken to indicate an unhinged and implausible view.

INTERPRETING CONSPIRACIES AND CONSPIRACY THEORIES

In the past, analyses have often viewed conspiracy theory impulses as evidence of clinical paranoia. Looking at the conspiracy theory mindset in this way, it appears as a dysfunctional psychological state. Persons and groups drawn to conspiracy theory views are likely to be unstable, then. And they are likely to be found at the fringes of society.

Over the past fifty years, however, newer ways of thinking about the conspiracy theory impulse have emerged, which delegate psychological factors to a lesser role. Over time, a view slowly emerged that suggested disaffection from the political realm plays an important part in the willingness of people to accept the speculations of conspiracy theory.[9]

After World War II, however, fears of conspiracy became more prominent. This gradually attracted the notice of writers interested in understanding current impulses in American society. After the assassination of John F. Kennedy in 1963, the conspiracy theory worldview seemed to be increasing. Pondering this phenomenon, historian Richard J. Hofstadter published a groundbreaking study of the topic the following year. His "The Paranoid Style in American Politics,"[10] which appeared in the influential *Harper's* magazine (and later in book form), brought the topic of conspiracy as a political phenomenon to wide attention. Though still couching it in the language of paranoia, Hofstadter's new analysis introduced a more political reading.

Hofstadter's conception of what he called the "paranoid style" was the "sense of heated exaggeration, suspiciousness, and conspiratorial fantasy,"[11] which he saw in parts of the political world. People with this worldview, in Hofstadter's analysis, see the world in terms of good and evil, but more than that:

> The paranoid's interpretation of history is distinctly personal: decisive events are not taken as part of the stream of history, but as the consequences of someone's will. Very often the enemy is held to possess some especially effective source of power: he controls the press; he has unlimited funds; he has a new secret for influencing the mind . . . [and] he has a special technique for seduction . . . .[12]

Hofstadter's "paranoid" was clearly obsessed with a conspiracy theory outlook on life.

Hofstadter noticed that the tendency toward a conspiracy theory worldview was often found among people with extreme right-wing views, but he realized that this impulse was much broader than that. Indeed, what was true when he wrote his essay is even truer today; the conspiracy theory mindset is distributed across American life. Equally at home among liberals, conservatives, and political agnostics, it knows no bounds.

Although widely dispersed, conspiracy theory still draws relatively few strongly devoted advocates. To the extent that they are sympathetic to this outlook, most people seem to identify with only part of what conspiracy theories say. And so while many Americans may believe, as public opinion polls suggest, that a conspiracy was involved in the assassination of John F. Kennedy, they do not necessarily believe that a vast conspiracy is controlling modern events. As a literal worldview, conspiracy theory is well known, but for the most part it has only been accepted in a piecemeal, superficial way.

Indeed, there is a paradox in the contemporary place of conspiracy theory in American consciousness. Although often dismissed as a literal way to understand the world, a significant part of the conspiracy theory worldview—especially with regard to its skeptical and cynical aspects—has nonetheless made its way into mainstream attitudes. Elements of the conspiracy theory mindset appear to have contributed to the rise in American politics over the past several decades. Interestingly, screen media during the same period have steadily advanced conspiracy theory themes, promulgating a cultural milieu in which individuals are vividly portrayed as unwitting victims of a variety of scheming forces.

The conspiracy theory theme has been aggressively marketed to the public by the movie and television industry, which has treated the subject in a long string of screen productions featuring this theme. Conspiracy theory has received substantial airing throughout popular culture,[13] and its exposition in visceral screen media has played a significant role in it as a cultural theme.

This book examines the role of film and television appearances of conspiracy theory themes in the contexts of the times during which they appeared. The purpose here is less on the internal aesthetic quality of these productions and more on the productions as cultural artifacts, which were shaped by their times and which concurrently helped to shape the public's mood and opinion.

When thinking about conspiracies and conspiracy theories, it is immediately apparent that a wide range of material is involved. Some of it is pedestrian, local, and even boring. In other instances, however, the topic is truly shocking, having implications that are as large as they are inescapable. Of course, although some discussions of conspiracy are grounded in the real world, others seem, to most people, to be flights of fancy or perhaps even clinically paranoid. Complicating matters is the fact that in the modern, media-saturated world, the different variants of conspiracy—real and imaginary, small-scale and global—have become intertwined, and elements from different versions have crept from one to another.

GLOBAL CONSPIRACY

The most ardent conspiracy theory advocates often claim that conspiracy is a widespread, maybe even all-encompassing, facet of contemporary existence. It is not what Daniel Pipes classified as the "petty" conspiracy with "limited aims," but rather a "world" conspiracy with malicious goals that are grand and overarching.[14] The global conspiracy, then, is similar to what Frank P. Mintz called conspiracism, a belief system that "serves the needs of diverse political and social groups in the United States and elsewhere. It identifies elites, blames them for economic and social catastrophes, and assumes that things will be better once popular action can remove them from positions of power. As such, conspiracy theories do not typify a particular epoch or ideology."[15]

In recent decades, the public's appetite for news and stories about conspiracies revolves around those that are huge and global. Their far-flung reach is expansive not only in geographical terms, but also sprawled across many dimensions of modern human experience. The global conspiracy is a near total conspiracy, which is said to so permeate our experience that it dominates our lives, mostly without our knowledge, and exerts enormous control over our destinies. Such conspiracies may bring together political, social, and scientific efforts to shape our lives for the benefit of someone, or even something, other than ourselves.

To some, in fact, it defines modern life. In the extreme variants of conspiracy theory, layer upon layer of conspiracies mask a supposedly underlying truth that is deeply hidden from ordinary people. Aside from the shadowy conspirators, only a few believers are aware of the deception. Even in cases where it is suggested that evidence of the conspiracy is lying in plain view—as supposedly in the case of the Freemasons, who have long been subject to conspiratorial rumors—it is only the believers that recognize the plot and the danger. This is a profoundly exceptionalist worldview, requiring complex mental gymnastics just to keep track of the conspiratorial web that surrounds the believers at every turn.

In the extreme cases, then, with everyone else either part of the conspiracy or duped by it, the believers can trust no one but other believers. (Even then, of course, there are questions.) All of society's institutions are, therefore, questionable. Official accounts mask hidden truths, in matters ranging from UFO sightings to international political developments. Of course, the mass media in all its guises is not thought to be immune to this deep-seated skepticism, as they also are seen as either part of the plot or oblivious to it.

For many people, however, the extreme form of conspiracy theory still seems like either paranoia or a joke. Yet, frequently people are willing to listen to often complex hypotheses of extreme conspiracism. Ordinary people encounter these most extreme forms of conspiracy theory not directly, but are instead bombarded with them in the entertainment media. The enthusiastic fans of the popular 1990s television series *The X-Files*, for example, waded through a sea of overlapping, intertwining theories. Added to the mix was a steady stream of quasi-documentary exposés, especially popular on several cable networks, which purport to set the record straight on conspiracy subjects as varied as UFOs and extraterrestrial alien abductions and the Kennedy assassination.

CONSPIRACY THEORY ON SCREEN

For the past half-century, in fact, extreme variants of conspiracy theorizing have been a reliable staple across the entertainment forms of the mass media. Their most popular home has been in many movies and television productions. As history has progressed from the age of the Cold War and McCarthyism to the complexities of the post-9/11 world, so, too, have many conspiracy theory screen productions made their mark in popular culture.

Conspiracy fears are scattered throughout the generations of American history, but the phenomenon dramatically accelerated after World War II.[16] In the postwar era, the conspiracy theme reverberated not only through American politics, but in many entertainment-oriented motion pictures and television programs.[17] Indeed, the post–World War II atmosphere of nuclear threat and Cold War sparked public fascination with invisible enemies and murky intrigue in which the ordinary people could often seem as the unwitting victims.

Against this backdrop, the shocking assassination of the president in 1963 unleashed a torrent of conspiracy theories in American culture, particularly on screen.[18] Since that time, the conspiracy theory phenomenon has achieved iconic status, calling to mind a cluster of related ideas. It is invoked in such far-flung topics of modern life as Washington political intrigues, UFOs, assassinations, and a host of other circumstances.

By the beginning of the twenty-first century, the conspiracy theory theme was fully woven into contemporary American culture. It reverberated widely, from escapist material in popular movies, television, and novels to solemn declarations in political discussions.

The relationship between representation of events and issues in the entertainment media and political realm is a complex, two-way affair. As a political culture emerged that yielded to the allure of conspiracy theory, the theme was increasingly adopted as a subject for movies and television. Then, in turn, political culture was influenced by the very visions of conspiracy in film and television that it had helped produce in the first place.

On one hand, mass media entertainments, especially film and television productions, often employ recognizable events and issues as subject matter or as backdrops to the stories that they present. To some extent, such portrayals of events and issues are reflections of popular conceptions of them, mirrors of attitudes and interpretations that are widely accepted. (Although not all such productions reflect mass opinion, the use of widely accepted frames of reference assumedly helps assure acceptance by a large audience.)

On the other hand, it is also the case that popular movie and television treatments of certain topics, even when contained in overtly fictionalized accounts, influence public perceptions about the events and issues they contain. As media scholars Dan Nimmo and James E. Combs suggest, such "mediated realties . . . shape what people think about the past by reminding them of what they already think and by perpetuating, and sometimes revising, what people of new generations will believe about history."[19]

The process by which conspiracy theory moved from the periphery to the center stage on screen and in political culture was lengthy. As it progressed to mainstream status in American life, a sense of cynicism enveloped much of American politics. The process started immediately after World War II and grew during the 1950s and the Cold War. It became even more pronounced in the period following the assassination of John F. Kennedy. Throughout these times, a tide of motion pictures and television productions—some based on historical fact and conjecture, others clearly fanciful—has adopted variations on the theme that conspiracies shape many events, hide others, and otherwise dictate much of the course of modern life, all to the disadvantage of the average person.

During this period, the appearance of so many films and television programs with this underlying theme was hardly a spontaneous occurrence. As screen audiences were repeatedly presented with the theme, conspiracy theories were developing into a potent, if sometimes implicit and veiled undercurrent in American politics. By the 1990s and early 2000s, it was not unusual to find conspiracies used as the explanation for a wide range of political events that would otherwise seem to have quite ordinary, if sometimes convoluted, explanations. Thus, a "vast right-wing conspiracy" was suggested as the source of Bill Clinton's troubles, just as conspiracy-like machinations of the "liberal media" were suggested to explain why the picture of world events did not coincide with conservative views. Regardless of a person's opinion about such claims, what these and many other examples clearly show is that conspiracy theory has penetrated mainstream American culture and politics as a powerful way of framing modern experience, which was sometimes ambiguous and confusing.

The Cold War and the Rise of Conspiracy Culture

The evolution of conspiracy theory in the cultural climate in the United States can be traced using screen productions and Washington politics as touchstones. Followed chronologically, one sees how screen media have both reflected and shaped the cultural milieu in which often traumatic events and political controversies have been interpreted with increasing cynicism.

Themes similar to conspiracy theory occasionally, though not frequently, appeared in movies before the mid-twentieth century. In the years just before the late 1940s, conspiracy theory had not been a sustained theme in American movies. Depression-era filmmaking of the 1930s sometimes addressed the subject of organized crime, which has conspiratorial undertones, but movies of that era often dealt with genre themes. Popular moviemaking frequently aimed to give audiences an escape from the realities of the grim economy and its effects. These films seldom revealed the paranoiac sense that fueled conspiracy theory films in the following years.

The coming of World War II changed Hollywood's focus to some extent, prompting more pictures that would either directly or indirectly bolster the war effort. But there was little demand for stories about conspiracy, except perhaps in the narrow sense of espionage, since the world was engaged in a battle with dark forces that were out in the open. Indeed, after the attack on Pearl Harbor in 1941, Hollywood mobilized with the rest of society. It often produced movies to bolster the mood of Americans as they faced the grueling hardships of global war. When not pursuing this path, Hollywood continued to make movies that were extensions of prewar themes. For the most part, movies at this time aimed simply to entertain with light, escapist tales. At times, movies did look at less attractive aspects of American life, as in *film noir* pictures such as *Double Indemnity* (1944). Such works, however, aimed their attention more at corrupted individuals than at large-scale, malicious scheming. When cabals and plots appeared on screen, it was usually as part of a straightforward portrayal of good and evil. The fear and paranoia that were central elements of conspiracy theory narratives after World War II were seldom seen.

In the years after World War II, a more modern version of conspiracy theory emerged as a forceful presence in American screen culture. The postwar rise of the conspiracy theory theme reflected not only changes in popular culture, but also the new political realities of the era.

At the war's end, the world changed abruptly, and film studios looked for ways to keep audiences interested in the movies. The Great Depression was a memory, and there was no longer a need to support a war effort. Hollywood looked for new themes amid the many new distractions that competed for audience attention. Although previous genres did not vanish, Hollywood searched for new subjects. It was a task that would become increasingly more important as television, still in its infancy in the late 1940s, emerged as a powerful new medium in the following decade.

After the war, the United States looked different, and the American people had a new outlook. At the end of the war, the nation was, indeed, jubilant. As a new world dawned across the United States, the future looked bright. It was hardly the kind of world in which conspiracy would seem a worry. The right side had won the war, and it had done so convincingly. And unlike the case in many of the countries in Europe and much of Asia, which were burdened with the enormously costly task of rebuilding nations that had been savaged by the war, economic life in the United States seemed good.

As returning servicemen rejoined civilian society, they flooded the workplace and the marketplace. This helped recreate postwar America in a new image. The baby boom was one signal of a new prosperity. In its wake, suburbs, superhighways, and consumerism came to dominate much of American life. The seeds of many social and economic changes were sown in this era, but the most tumultuous of these changes would take many years to reach maturity. The immediate mood seemed positive and hopeful. The war was over; life could return to normalcy. Or so it seemed.

In fact, somber changes in international politics had been set into motion, and the effects of these were about to manifest themselves throughout American life. By the time the new international situation came to be fully appreciated by the American public under the new rubric of the "Cold War," the stage was already set for the emergence of a new climate of fear and paranoia that would undercut the veneer of exuberance that clad the burgeoning consumer society. A modern age of conspiracy theory was about to begin. Soon, Hollywood responded to this undercurrent of paranoia, sometimes explicitly and sometimes appearing in the guise of genre films. Within a few years, movies with conspiracy theory themes began to appear in American theaters with remarkable frequency.

The forces that caused a sudden surge in conspiracy theory movies took shape in the late 1940s, in the midst of new political contexts that emerged in postwar America. Although a detailed examination is beyond the scope of this book, it is useful to recall some of the highlights from that era—events that so profoundly influenced American culture of the time and had an especially pronounced effect on Hollywood.

During the Cold War years in the United States, the fear of conspiracy sometimes overshadowed many of the more positive aspects of contemporary life.[20] The Cold War environment had not created the growing fear of conspiracy. But the new bipolar world—in which the democracy-oriented nations gathered around the United States were pitted against the communist world led by the Soviet Union—brought it to new heights. The Cold War was a new global type of conflict in which the two poles struggled to assert their dominance in international affairs.

Competing for empire was hardly a new phenomenon, but the postwar context was powerfully shaped by a new and fearsome reality. Humans now possessed the technology of nuclear weapons and soon would have the capability not only of destroying their enemies, but also of extinguishing all human life on the planet. In the United States, this new reality generated enormous anxiety. It was a world in which fear was not irrational, but instead seemed a form of realism. The ways in which American culture processed those fears and anxieties, however, were sometimes extreme.

Thus, in some ways the exhilaration that the Americans felt after World War II was short-lived. Almost immediately, Americans exhibited a new apprehension about the Soviet Union, which tempered their elation at winning the war that had just ended. Although the United States had maintained an uneasy alliance with the Soviets during World War II, the communist behemoth now presented a major new threat that almost erased this memory. The growing rivalry between the United States and USSR, which would last for the next half-century, produced a long series of unsettling events and crises, assuring that tensions remained high. The mood of fear and anxiety started to have a profound effect on the American consciousness.

The first alarm bells rang for many Americans when the Soviets essentially annexed much of Eastern Europe just after the war. (Soviet-sphere states nominally maintained their national identities, but it was clear they were under the control of the behemoth Soviet empire.) Behind the Iron Curtain, Josef Stalin presided over a regime so brutal that even the Soviet leaders who came after him would distance themselves from its excesses.

Although the USSR paid a heavy price in death and destruction during the war, Stalin was determined to rebuild his nation and bring it to the center of the world stage. Accordingly, he engaged in a massive restrengthening of the USSR's military-industrial machine. A central part of this project focused on the Soviet quest for nuclear-weapon technology, which they reasoned would place the USSR on par with the United States, wiping out the American military advantage.

It did not take long for the Soviets to achieve this goal. On August 29, 1949, the USSR shocked the world when it detonated its first atomic bomb. The dynamics of international politics changed overnight.

The significance of this development can hardly be overestimated. The confidence and sense of security that Americans felt so long as their country was the only nuclear power vanished with the realization that a seemingly unfriendly force had now learned the atom bomb's secrets. Soon, citizens throughout the Western world realized how dangerous the world had become. They feared a frightening, potentially apocalyptic future.

The revelation that the Soviet Union had acquired an atomic bomb reverberated throughout Washington and around the world. This startling new reality was hard for Americans to accept. Almost immediately, espionage and conspiracy were suspected. How else, it was reasoned, could the Soviets have so quickly developed the nuclear technology that only the United States had possessed?

In fact, this new development had been years in the making. Although it was not widely known at the time, the Nazi war effort had made substantial progress toward the creation of its own nuclear weaponry. By the end of the war, German scientists who worked in this and other advanced military technology programs were highly prized by the United States and the USSR. In the final days of World War II, both the Soviets and the Americans engaged in frantic efforts to round up these Nazi scientists and technologists so that they could be put to work in their own military research programs, especially those focusing on rocketry and nuclear weapons.[21] Once identified and placed in the service of the war's victors, both the U.S. and Soviet military programs benefited from the knowledge that the one-time Nazi scientists brought.

This was only part of the story of the Soviet atomic bomb, however, and even this much was not well known to the American public. Instead, as Americans sought to understand how their nation's new archrival had acquired nightmarish weapons, attention quickly focused on the possibility that traitors had passed secret atomic knowledge to the Soviets. The suspicion that communist sympathizers had compromised American nuclear security led to a vigorous investigation.

Although some details are still disputed, formerly classified Soviet documents make clear that in fact the USSR did make concerted efforts to steal American nuclear secrets. A refugee German scientist named Karl Fuchs, who had contributed to the Manhattan Project while working for the British, passed some American nuclear secrets to the Soviets. When discovered and confronted, Fuchs implicated others who had been involved in delivering the classified information to Soviet hands. A so-called "courier" named Harry Gold was identified. Through that connection, American intelligence agents identified other coconspirators, the most infamous of whom were the married couple, Ethel and Julius Rosenberg. They were soon arrested and tried under the glare of the national news media. The court proceedings were a sensation, riveting public attention.

Swiftly convicted, Ethel and Julius Rosenberg were sentenced to death in 1951. (Both died in the electric chair two years later.) Public fears were partially calmed, but the convictions suggested to the public that there were, in fact, conspirators in their midst. Fear and anxiety did not seem to be unreasonable paranoia, but the legitimate response to a threat that was all-too real.

This type of event set off widespread fears of Soviet infiltration into American life. Congress became caught up in the mood of the day. Congress had already begun to investigate "un-American activities," and now such investigations were taken up with renewed vigor. In highly publicized hearings, both the House of Representatives and Senate zealously aimed to flush out potential traitors in America's midst. It was the beginning of an anti-communist campaign that later became the hallmark of much of the 1950s.

The most well-known and zealous individual involved was Joseph McCarthy, a Republican senator from Wisconsin.[22] McCarthy, who is so closely associated with this pervasive political and cultural phenomenon that it is often called McCarthyism, began a spirited fight against the Red Menace, as the communist threat was sometimes called. (Although McCarthy is remembered as the most visible figure in the anticommunist fervor, many other members of Congress shared his obsession with a perceived communist enemy.) The search for the unseen enemy was to become so vigorous, however, by the mid-1950s, some people started to think it was a witch hunt.

McCarthy had been honing his anticommunist public stance for several years.[23] In a 1950 speech, for example, he revealed how seriously he feared what he saw as the communist threat. He suggested the steps he would soon undertake in his efforts to stop it. Speaking to a group in West Virginia in February of that year, he held up a piece of paper, saying "I have here in my hand a list of 205 people that were known to the Secretary of State as being members of the Communist Party, and who, nevertheless, are still working and shaping the policy of the State Department."

McCarthy's later televised appearances in Congressional hearings made a fascinating spectacle. The immediacy of the still-young broadcast media made the proceedings more sensational than ever before. Called to testify before Congress, witnesses sat helplessly as McCarthy railed against all those who he thought had communist sympathies. Using threats and public condemnation, he browbeat those testifying, demanding that they reveal the names of others who had ever been associated with communism or socialism in any way. At first, the public applauded these efforts.

Since socialist political groups had been fairly common in the Depression era, there were many people who had some previous association with socialism or communism, however faint, in their pasts. Once revealed, however, the accused were ostracized by society, sometimes losing their jobs, their reputations in their communities, and even the affection of their families.

Hollywood had already been a target of those looking to flush out communists. The movie business had been regarded as a potential threat to the American way of life by some people even before the anticommunist fervor of the Cold War. Not surprisingly, then, the film industry came under the glare of the House Un-American Activities Committee as early as 1947. It is widely remembered that actors, directors, screenwriters, and others who stood accused of communist leanings were subjected to the notorious "blacklist" practices that essentially cut them off from their livelihoods.[24] Less remembered is the fact that some Hollywood insiders cooperated with the search for communists and sympathizers. Those cooperating included Ronald Reagan and Robert Taylor.

A fear of conspiracy at this time was not, then, a product of Hollywood's imagination. Like much of the rest of the country, Hollywood was caught up in the complicated web of fear and paranoia that fueled the conspiracy theory inclinations of that time.

Elsewhere in the world, the end of World War II set the stage for several nationalist struggles that had a major impact on the United States. These sometimes ignited into full-fledged warfare, often pitting communist revolutionaries against governments that had been more sympathetic to American interests. Events in Asia fueled Cold War fears. For many Americans and their allies, these developments seemed to suggest that the communist threat was a global phenomenon.

In China, Mao Zedong's communist forces successfully overran the national government led by Chiang Kai-shek, driving his government into exile on the island of Taiwan. The two leaders remained bitter enemies for the remaining decades of their lives, both claiming that their administrations represented the legitimate government of China. Neither the communist People's Republic of China nor the more democratic Republic of China consented to recognize the other entity. Although the dispute did not evolve into open warfare, the tense situation continued into the following century.

Soon after the rise of the communist regime in China, it seemed as though much of this region could fall to the communists. In neighboring Korea, the situation was just as volatile. As World War II ended, Korea found itself split into halves. With the expulsion of the Japanese invaders who had traumatized the country during the war, the northern half of Korea came under the influence of the Soviet Union and China, while the southern region came under the influence of the United States and its allies. The dividing line between the two regions was the thirty-eighth parallel.

In the mid-1950s, just months after the communist victory in mainland China, the leaders of North Korea felt emboldened enough to launch an armed assault against the south. Although the North Koreans regarded this as a war of liberation, the regime in the south saw it as nothing less than a hostile invasion. Soon, the country was embroiled in a bitter war, in which North Korea was aided by China and USSR, which had newly acquired the status of a nuclear power. Aiding South Korea was the United States, which mustered a contingent of forces from the fledgling United Nations to fend off the attack.

The Korean War (sometimes called the Korean Conflict in the United States, since it was not an officially declared war) was the first major international struggle in which the new international nuclear dynamics came into play. It was only five years earlier that the United States had dropped atomic bombs on Japan. That memory was as fresh as it was horrifying. Some Americans felt that "the bomb" was a weapon that could also be used to thwart the communist advances in Korea.

Yet, in a world in which two superpowers, not just one, possessed the capability to inflict nuclear destruction, the situation was far from clear. Could the United States and its allies use nuclear force without triggering a deadly counterstrike by the Soviets? Would escalation of the conflict into the nuclear realm lead to another world war, this time more terrifying than any war ever undertaken in human history? Questions such as these, nearly apocalyptic in tone and implication, were rampant in the United States. In the end, the nuclear option was not taken, and the war, ugly and bitter as is was, seemed to arrive at a stalemate by 1952.

That same year, General Dwight D. Eisenhower, the heralded Supreme Commander of Allied forces during World War II, was elected to the presidency of the United States, and he assumed leadership of the war effort. The conflict had been costly, both in the number of casualties and in monetary terms. Yet, after grueling months of fighting, the two sides ended up just about where they had started, on opposing sides of the thirty-eighth parallel.

With little enthusiasm for other options, it was finally India that offered a proposal in the United Nations to establish an armistice, with the thirty-eighth parallel as the dividing line. This was subsequently accepted, and a cease-fire was declared in mid-1953. Although the cease-fire was successfully implemented, a lasting settlement was never signed. The situation between North Korea and South Korea and its American ally was to simmer unresolved into the next century.

Elsewhere in Asia, the area that French colonizers called Indochina—a hammered together overseas Department of the French Republic consisting of Cambodia, Laos, and Vietnam—was a source of significant strife. The area was occupied by the Japanese during the World War II, after which it was returned to French control. Of the three regions, Vietnam was the area in which troubles first emerged most forcefully. Communist and nationalist impulses came together there under the leadership of the charismatic Ho Chi Minh, a Vietnamese national who had studied in France before the war and was a member of the French communist party. By the early 1950s, it was clear that the communists had a significant following. Resentful of French rule and their treatment under that regime, opposition to the French-backed local government grew.

The developments in China, Korea, and Vietnam, which the U.S. government viewed with alarm, provided evidence enough for many Americans that the communist threat was not confined to the Soviet Union and its environs, but was instead worldwide. Such anxieties were instrumental in the articulation of what was called the Domino Theory. This was the fear that if more nations succumbed to communist rule, in the not-too-distant future the United States would be surrounded by an angry sea of malicious communist countries, bent on destroying the last few bastions of democracy. The picture that this evoked was truly frightening to Americans. It was a vision of the world that fueled suspicion and anxiety.

Whether or not such fears appear justified in retrospect, there is no doubt that for the most part, American society was swept away with such imagery. The fear and its attendant consequences were very real.

This snapshot of American politics at mid-twentieth century is obviously incomplete and selective, but it serves to demonstrate how conditions developed that were conducive to increased public identification with conspiracy theory thinking. That impulse did not take long to emerge in the most potent and vivid forms of popular culture of the day—movies and the emerging medium of television.

The Red Menace and Its Discontents

In the anxious age of the new Cold War, conspiracy theory gained a new prominence in American popular culture, first in movies and later in the still-fledging medium of television. Hollywood responded to the fears and anxieties of the era in several ways.[1] Sometimes the theme appeared straightforwardly in political dramas. At other times, it was cloaked in different guises. It surfaced in science fiction films regularly, but it sometimes appeared in such popular genres as Westerns and suspense movies.

In the earliest years of the Cold War, the film treatment of the conspiracy theory theme came in the forms of dramas, melodramas, and political thrillers. They typically told stories that were set in the present and dealt with ordinary people, government agents, and malicious conspirators. Directly mirroring society's fears and obsessions of that era, these films featured plots in which communists conspired to dupe Americans and overthrow the U.S. government. Such movies played to anxieties that audiences brought with them to the movie house or drive-in theater. The message was clear: be vigilant, be wary, or you will end up a victim of the wily, scheming communists.

Among the earliest of such films were *The Red Menace* and *Conspirator*, both released in 1949. The very titles of such movies left little to the imagination of prospective viewers about what they would see. *Conspirator*, an MGM film produced in Britain, is now remembered primarily because it starred a young Elizabeth Taylor. It is an unexceptional film with a simple story in which communist conspirators are part of a narrative that is mostly about star-crossed lovers.[2] A young man, who is secretly a communist rev-olutionary, marries an unsuspecting young woman against the wishes of his communist superiors. Unexpectedly, the woman discovers his secret. The communist boss, angered that the group's activities could become known, demands that the young man eliminate his wife. He is unable to carry out that order, however, and instead commits suicide.

The element of communist subterfuge adds some currency to the plot of *Conspirator*, but it could just as easily have been some other secret. Indeed, the story may be closer to *Romeo and Juliet* than to a genuine investigation of the perceived communist menace. Still, the narrative of *Conspirator* sug-gests the idea that hidden in the world of seemingly ordinary people and events, an evil danger may lurk. It's a theme that would be repeated often in the coming years.

The earnest summer film *Red Menace* approaches the communist threat more directly. The film's story follows a young woman and her boyfriend as they flee a communist group with which they have become disillusioned. Over the course of the film, the inner workings of the communist con-spirators are revealed. It is, not surprisingly, an unflattering portrait. But this is not only because of the evil intent demonstrated by the group's leaders, but also because of the wide array of inept, brutish, and self-defeating actions undertaken by the communists. Although the narrative indicates that the conspirators are clearly fearful that their identities will be exposed to federal authorities, they are portrayed as their own worst enemies. The communists turn on their compatriots and engage in outra-geous acts that surely would draw the attention they are supposedly trying to avoid.

Red Menace has many melodramatic elements and the behavior of the central characters is highly exaggerated. At the end of the film, the young woman and her boyfriend encounter a local law enforcement officer and abruptly turn themselves in. The officer listens to their story, and believing that they have seen the error of their ways, decides to let them go. In a remarkable turnaround, the young lovers apparently are completely freed from the influence of communism. They predictably head off for presumed marriage and the pursuit of the American dream.

Despite its flaws, *Red Menace* was nonetheless one of the first Hollywood films that attempted to describe an underground communist conspiracy in the United States. Critically, it met with tepid reaction. *Time* magazine, for exam-ple, pointed out that the film showed American communists possessing "sheer indiscretion and moral decay [that] would surprise even the FBI. . . . The pic-ture might get by if it were either good entertainment or good propaganda, but it is inept on both counts."[3] Indeed, *Red Menace* presented a picture of communists as dangerous and malevolent, but hardly as having the stuff of a serious rival to the moral righteousness and strength of the American way of life.

Films with similar themes continued to appear throughout this period, though many of these movies were not considered major releases. One example from 1951 was the *The Whip Hand*, starring Raymond Burr. It showed how communists took control of an unsuspecting American town.

Another example was the more substantial *I Was a Communist Spy for the FBI*, which was released the same year. Unlike most movies with this theme, the story was based on real events. Its mood was deeply suspicious. The narrative implied that civil rights and union activities were suspect in a world filled with communist sympathizers.

I Was a Communist Spy for the FBI told the story of Matt Cevic, who had been an FBI informer throughout much of the 1940s and later wrote a book about his experiences. The movie version follows Cevic's mission to expose the inner workings of a communist group. Since he is deep undercover, however, even Cevic's family is not aware his membership in the Communist Party is only a ruse. Friends and relatives, therefore, shun him for disloyalty to his country.

Frustrated that even his son feels alienated from him, Cevic writes a secret letter to him, which he hopes will repair the damaged relationship. Before the letter can be delivered to his son, however, it is intercepted by Eve, a schoolteacher who is also a member of the communist group. Her communist superiors order her to investigate Cevic's loyalty to the Party. Eve has started to doubt the communism ideology that previously attracted her, however, and she decides not to tell her superiors of Cevic's deception.

A major section of the film deals with a strike by steel workers, which the communists seek to aggravate by bringing in hired hooligans. Not surprisingly, a riot erupts. Following this development, Eve's reservations about communism are confirmed, and she decides to cooperate with federal authorities. She reveals the names of those who are members of the communist group. Cevic, who the communist leaders still do not suspect, helps her escape to safety. Then, before the communists discover his deception, Cevic is rescued by the FBI. As the film ends, Cevic is a government witness before the House Un-American Activities Committee.

Like other films in this vein, *I Was a Communist Spy for the FBI* was heavy-handed, even given the context of the times. Succumbing to the Hollywood stereotype of "good guys" versus "bad guys," the characters are depicted more as types than as real people. The audience gets little understanding of what motivated people to join the communist group, although it is implied that greed and a generally criminal demeanor are the primary reasons. Others, like the schoolteacher Eve, appear to have been duped. The government agents, on the other hand, are manifestly intelligent, supremely moral, and very brave. In fact, the outcome of the film seldom seems in doubt, since the communists are not portrayed as serious rivals to the far-superior FBI.[4]

I Was a Communist Spy for the FBI tried to tell the story of a conniving communist group by going inside with an undercover government agent.

Another way to approach the theme was to look inside by way of an actual member of such a group. This was obvious enough, but it presented a basic difficulty that the script would need to overcome: how to structure a narrative in which a seeming traitor was the centerpiece.

In these years, Hollywood's production code—the system of self-censorship that the industry had adopted years earlier—strictly regulated what would be permissible on screen in terms of misdeeds and morality. It still dictated how perceived amoral, unpatriotic, and unsavory persons, groups, and situations were to be shown. The code limited what transgressions could be depicted, and it mandated that punishment of the guilty would be clearly apparent. For some stories, therefore, it presented a number of special hurdles to film-makers. Making a film that treated would-be communists as real people, without drawing too much sympathy to the character, would be especially difficult. A character shown to be too stupid to know better—or too evil to want to know better—would not necessarily be a very compelling central character in the climate of those times. Not surprisingly, then, in productions from this period that attempt to tell such a story, modern audiences see the results as lacking depth or realism, though other more positive characteristics may be evident.

One film that faced this situation was the Paramount production of *My Son John*, which was released the following year. The film's narrative affirmed some of society's deepest fears. Its story showed that the communist threat had infiltrated deep into American life. *My Son John* followed the story of a seemingly ordinary man who actually was a communist conspirator.

My Son John was a film with solid Hollywood credentials, and despite its politically lurid story line earned public notice. It was a more prominent production, receiving sufficient notice to earn an Academy Award nomination. The screenplay was written by Leo McCarey, who also directed the film. McCarey was an experienced director with many films to his credit, including the Marx Brothers' zany political send-up *Duck Soup* in 1933. The notable cast included Van Heflin, Dean Jagger, and Helen Hayes, who returned to the screen with much fanfare after a seventeen-year absence.

The story involves John, a Washington bureaucrat with secret ties to the Communist Party. When John returns to his small hometown, his parents are shocked at his behavior. John is disrespectful of his parents, speaks critically of American ideals, and is even rude to the local clergy. John's mother is mortified by her son's words and actions.

John's life turns for the worse when both the FBI and John's mother (a combination that surely ranks near the top of traditional American archetypes) begin to unravel the secret that he is a communist. Overwhelmed by guilt, he subsequently renounces this ideology and decides to turn himself in.

As part of this transformation, John is determined to make amends. Wanting to set the record straight, he records a speech about the evils of communism and a scheming "foreign power," which he intends to have played at his alma mater's upcoming graduation ceremony. But it is too late for John. The communists learn of his betrayal and murder him in an effort to keep their group and its activities secret.[5]

My Son John took an essentially melodramatic approach to the material. Subtlety was hardly its selling point. An article in *Time* magazine, for example, complained, "Dean Jagger, as the small-town schoolteacher father 'who thinks with his heart' is required at one point to hit his son over the head with a Bible."[6] Lest its morality still be unclear, John literally falls dead on the steps of the Lincoln Memorial at the end of the film. Indeed, a more heavy-handed approach is difficult to imagine.

Still, the film did have an impact. In the context of its era, its message was frightening. Instead of an external enemy, *My Son John* captured the heart of conspiracy fears—that the reach of conspiracy extended so far that it could penetrate even an upstanding family from an idyllic village in rural America.

Movies such as these attempted to place the conspiracy theory theme in familiar cinematic forms. These were often variations of the dramas and melodramas that Hollywood was accustomed to making. At the height of Joseph McCarthy's highly visible search for communists in America, however, some films dropped such pretexts altogether. The results sometimes looked more overtly like propaganda exercises.

The most blatant example of this impulse was the 1952 melodrama-fantasy *Invasion U.S.A.* Another film that was rushed to the market in response to the political hysteria of the time, its story starts at a New York bar, where several people are being interviewed by a reporter. During the interview, the dramatic announcement comes that enemy aircraft are headed for Alaska. The scene shifts to a series of devastating events. Invading forces capture Alaska, California is struck with a nuclear bomb, and the cities of Washington, DC, and New York fall to the invaders.

The story then returns to the people who had been interviewed in the New York bar. Some time has passed, and each of these people has returned home to help with the defense. Unfortunately, the struggle does not go well for them or their American compatriots. One by one, each member of the group dies, by gunfire, by flood, or by some other calamity. It is clear that the nation cannot repel the invasion.

But all is not as it seems. Abruptly, viewers learn that the invasion was an illusion. One member of the original group had placed the others in a hypnotic state to make the invasion story seem real. The hypnotist's purpose, it is revealed, was to show how ill-prepared the country was and how susceptible it was be to a foreign—assumedly communist—threat.

Invasion U.S.A. was not a major film. The *Monthly Film Bulletin* called it a "shoddy little production" featuring "a number of incoherent and sensational happenings."[7] But its sensational interpretation of the communist menace crystallized the more paranoid aspects of 1950s anticommunist fervor. It showed external threat and suggested that the country was vulnerable. The anxious climate it represented was one in which the fear of conspiracy could continue to grow.

Hollywood continued to search for ways to explore, perhaps exploit, the conspiracy theme that had so penetrated American culture of the era. Another approach, taken in the 1953 movie *Big Jim McLain*, combined the conspiracy theme with the tried and true detective story. The film featured Hollywood star John Wayne as Jim McLain, a government agent in pursuit of communists in Honolulu.

Wayne, who had been a major star since his leading role in the 1939 film *Stagecoach*, was well suited for the lead role. At the time, he was the president of Motion Picture Association for the Preservation of American Ideals, which had worked with the House Un-American Activities Committee. He had a strong business interest in seeing the movie succeed, as well. He was a principal of Wayne-Fellows, the company that produced the film.

In the role of Jim McLain, Wayne brought the swagger he had used effectively in the Westerns that made him a star. The narrative combines elements of a detective story, a political message, and even a romantic subplot. McLain methodically goes about the business of fighting communists while taking a romantic interest in a young secretary working in the suspect's office. Throughout McLain investigations, the detective element of the story has the obvious political angle of promoting a strongly anticommunist message. As the story unfolds, few opportunities are missed to make this point, which makes for a very arduous viewing experience at times.

This is a very earnest film. It begins with a somber voice asking, "Neighbor, how stands the Union?" These words, quoted from Stephen Vincent Benet's *The Devil and Daniel Webster*, are spoken as the screen fills with iconic American images, including the dome of the U.S. Capitol. Remarkably—especially for a work of fiction—there then appears a testament to the members of Congress, who are extolled for efforts to expose communists in America's midst. Members of Congress are commended for continuing this work "undaunted by the vicious campaign of slander launched against them."

Even in 1952, this was a very unorthodox way to begin a movie. It did not escape the notice of some film writers. Indeed, a review in *The New York Times* offhandedly noted, "That sounds pretty serious, we would say."[8]

In the main part of the film, Jim McLain, the ardent anticommunist, is sent on a new mission with his partner, Max Baxter (played by James Arness, later the popular star of CBS television's long-running *Gunsmoke* series). Their assignment, code-named "Operation Pineapple," is to track down and destroy a communist conspiracy that is trying to undermine America's participation in the Korean War.

The unscrupulous leader of Honolulu's secret communist organization is a man named Sturak (played by Alan Napier). He is a one-dimensionally evil person. Although he has managed to assemble a group of co-conspirators, it's hard to imagine that he could effectively recruit for the communist cause. In fact, one of his most prominent characteristics is an eagerness to terminate members of his own group, which he does whenever he doubts an associate's loyalty. The other members of Sturak's communist group, meanwhile, are shown to be incompetent tough guys and misfits. They are also prone to focusing their violent tendencies on each other. For the modern viewer, there is an unintended irony that can seem almost laughable: the film creates the impression that communists are more a danger to themselves than to anyone else.

Nonetheless, the agents zealously carry out their mission. Even the slight romantic subplot touches on the movie's political agenda. At one point, McLain explains to the secretary he is wooing that there was no use in trying to figure out the communist enemy or why people would succumb to it. "I've heard all the jive," McLain explains. "This one's a commie because mama wouldn't tuck him in at night; that one, because girls wouldn't welcome him with open arms." It all added up to a picture of the communist threat as an inscrutable evil. The film suggests that efforts to understand communists were essentially pointless.

The heroes are mostly successful, of course. But the hero complains that the freedoms guaranteed by the Bill of Rights (here in the specific form of the Fifth Amendment) continue to be exploited by communists. McLain makes it clear that in his view, such rights should not be afforded to anyone other than "honest, decent citizens."

Thanks to the star power of John Wayne and the currency of its plot, *Big Jim McLain* attracted much public attention. Some critics found it heavy-handed. Some found its production values lacking. The trade newspaper *Variety*, for example, concluded that it was "rushed to market and bears evidence of that haste" and as a result was "lacking in clarity" due to "choppy" continuity and a "sketchy" script.[9] Other critics disagreed, however, and were satisfied. In the end, the public supported *Big Jim McLain* sufficiently to make it a financial success. It commanded $3 million at the box office, a sizeable sum for a movie in the early 1950s.

EVOLUTION OF POLITICAL CLIMATE

Even as works such as *Big Jim McLain* were attracting movie audiences, the Cold War political landscape was changing. The end of the Korean War in 1953, ambiguous though it was, gave some relief to a nation that was still adjusting to the new nuclear world. Also that year, the fearsome Soviet leader Josef Stalin died under somewhat cloudy circumstances. Nikita Khrushchev (who some suspected had conspired to eliminate Stalin) then assumed leadership of the world's second superpower.

The following year, Senator Joseph McCarthy's fortunes suddenly changed. Television, still a fledgling medium at that time, played a significant role in this development. The leading anticommunist crusader came under the watchful gaze of CBS news' Edward R. Murrow. In a fateful decision, Murrow and his associates at CBS aimed their spotlight directly on McCarthy. In March 1954, Murrow's popular *See It Now* program presented viewers with a picture of McCarthy that was far from flattering. It seemed to imply that McCarthy had gone over the edge in his zealous pursuit of communists wherever he thought they might be hiding. Already, McCarthy had alienated Army brass with accusations that did not pan out. Now, under the gaze of television cameras, viewers across America saw a picture of an angry man who seemed out of control. Many people were shocked.

The *See It Now* exposé, a milestone in Murrow's career, was a turning point for McCarthy.[10] Although the senator had only recently won reelection to the Senate in 1952, his public support quickly weakened. With this sudden decline in public stature, moreover, his political rivals sensed he was vulnerable. Earlier actions that McCarthy had taken against several members of Congress now came back to haunt him. He was formally censured by the Senate later in 1954, and his prominence diminished. He died only three years later in 1957.

Throughout the 1950s, the fear of communism remained strong, however. After McCarthy's fall from grace, Americans were perhaps less likely to gaze so suspiciously at their neighbors, but they still were anxious about the groundswell of communism that had sprung up across the globe. Eastern Europe, for example, seemed increasingly frightful. And much of Asia seemed beyond the control of American interests. China had already fallen to communism. The Korean War ended as a virtual stalemate, leaving a hostile regime ensconced in the north. In 1954, France was driven from Vietnam after a humiliating defeat in the battle at Dien Bien Phu.

By this time in Hollywood, the climate of fear and paranoia commanded the attention of film-makers and studios. Already an established theme in postwar American culture, films with conspiracy theory motifs continued to appear frequently in American theaters.

SUDDENLY

A neglected film, which deserves more recognition than it usually receives, was released at this time. This was director Lewis Allen's 1954 film *Suddenly*. The film is notable not only for its theme, but also because it starred Frank Sinatra as a man intending to assassinate the president of the United States. Sinatra's appearance in this movie, coupled with his later appearance in the much better known *The Manchurian Candidate* a few years later, gives him the distinction of appearing in two separate films that prefigure the real assassination of John F. Kennedy in 1963. (Indeed, that traumatic event led films of this type to quickly disappear from public view, a development that was easy to manage in the days before cable television and home video recorders made it difficult to hide a movie from public attention.)

The plot of *Suddenly* revolves around an attempt to assassinate the president of the United States during a layover in the small town of Suddenly, California. As the film begins, viewers are introduced to life in the slow-paced village and the local sheriff, Tod Shaw (played by Sterling Hayden), and his love interest, Ellen Benson (Nancy Gates). Also introduced are Ellen's young son and father-in-law, a retired Secret Service agent.

Ellen's husband had died during combat in World War II, and she is still reeling from his death. She's not ready to make emotional commitments to the sheriff. Her life is instead focused on raising her young son. Eager to shield the boy from the world's ills, she is very protective. In one scene, for example, the sheriff buys Ellen's son a toy gun that the boy had admired. Ellen disapproves, however, and voices her displeasure.

The quiet of the town, and of this apparently domestic drama, is broken when the sheriff receives word that the president is about to stop in Suddenly en route to another destination. The nation's leader soon will arrive by train and then transfer to a motorcade for the final leg of his journey. For security reasons, the stop is being kept secret. Only the sheriff and his assistant realize that Suddenly is about to receive this important visitor and that Secret Service agents will arrive in advance to prepare final security arrangements.

At about this time, a car with three men pulls into town. The group is led by John Baron (Frank Sinatra) and it soon becomes clear that he and his shady-looking accomplices know the president's route. What is more, they have come to assassinate him.

Surveying the area, the three conspirators notice a house on a hill that overlooks the train station. They realize it would be an ideal place from which to take aim at the president. They then make their way to the house, which, by coincidence, belongs to none other than Ellen Benson.

Posing as FBI agents, the three would-be assassins convince Ellen to allow them to inspect the property. When Ellen's father-in-law becomes suspicious, however, the three men drop their guises and take the family hostage. They plan to wait at the house until the train carrying the president arrives.

Soon, Sheriff Shaw and the head Secret Service agent unexpectedly arrive to secure the house themselves. They are also taken hostage. Now the three conspirators must manage their hostages as they prepare to carry out their crime.

The film's most tense section, which follows, focuses on the interaction between the would-be assassins, who are busy making their last-minute arrangements, and the hostages, who try desperately to thwart the plot. Along the way, Baron's accomplices are eliminated, but Baron survives. Just as the train's arrival is imminent, however, Ellen—who was previously depicted as gun-shy—seizes the unexpected opportunity to grab a loose revolver. As Baron is about to shoot the president, Ellen shoots and kills the would-be assassin, ending the crisis with a dramatic flair.

Although not considered a major picture, Sinatra's casting was enough to attract the attention of the public and the press. A popular singer with an enthusiastic following, Sinatra had recently gained Hollywood's notice with his performance in the award-winning film *From Here to Eternity* (1953). The decision to cast him as the villain was against type, but it gave him the opportunity to demonstrate ample acting abilities in the unflattering role of Baron. A review in *The New York Times* commended Sinatra "for playing the leading gunman with an easy, cold, vicious sort of gleam . . . .in a melodramatic tour de force."[11]

The conspiracy element of the film is most thoroughly outlined in the dialogue that occurs as the hostages attempt to thwart the plot. The discussion among the characters explains its details. The conspirators, and John Baron, in particular, are guns for hire, according to the narrative. Baron specifically claims that he doesn't have a political agenda. In fact, he says he has no idea why the people who hired him wanted to have the president assassinated. Money is clearly part of Baron's motive for participating in the plot, but there is more. When he was in the service, it is revealed, Baron took unusual pleasure in killing. He derived an exaggerated sense of importance and self-esteem only when handling a gun. Baron is thus presented as little more than a very dangerous deviant.

The fact that the motivations of the would-be assassins' backers are left unstated was reason enough for *New York Times* reviewer Bosley Crowther to temper his assessment of the movie. Although he favorably noted some parts of the film, he judged that despite the positive aspects, "there is not much substance to the picture—no reason is given for the attempt to elim-inate the president."[12] Crowther added that "making a film on the sub-ject of shooting the President took a certain amount of audacity." A some-what similar review in *Variety*, though generally positive, concluded that the film was "slick exploitation" with a "fantastic plot."[13] Interestingly, despite the intense anxieties of the period, to these writers—and probably to most American viewers—the murder of the president seemed unthinkable. They could not know, of course, that a decade later the idea would seem all too possible.

Some of the most telling aspects of *Suddenly* are its traditional sense of morality and its strong affirmation of the potency of America and its institu-tions. Government agents and local law enforcement officials epitomize the basic decency and goodness of the American people. The audience is given no reason to suspect that the story will not have a good outcome. The villains, by contrast, are very deficient. They are portrayed as basically malicious and greedy cowards. More than that, Baron is shown to be a deranged, amoral misfit.

Whether intended as realistic dramas or more contrived thrillers and melo-dramas, films such as these shared a common response to the palpable fear that was rampant at the height of the McCarthy years. Just as McCarthy and his allies suspected seemingly everyone, movies such as these mirrored those paranoid anxieties. Conniving enemies, it was shown, could be anywhere, from the metropolis of New York to quaint villages in America's heartland. The enemy could also be anyone, not only the stranger, the trade unionist, the intellectual, but also the seemingly dutiful civil servant, a young schoolteacher, a seemingly kindly neighbor, even your own son or daughter. No one was safe, it was implied. In fact, people were not safe even from themselves.

Yet, the films rationalized that there was an easy set of answers to the seeming terror: faith, patriotism, vigilance, and, sometimes by implication, the eschewing of all things foreign or intellectual. It was not an unfamiliar recipe, playing as it did upon years of stereotypes and folk wisdom that had already made serious inroads in American motion pictures. In retrospect it is clear that much of the Hollywood establishment, still in the grip of the production code's rigorous self-censorship, was eager to demonstrate its patriotism. Having already been a target of Congressional investigations and suspicions, the industry was anxious to distance itself from those of its members who had been linked to communism or socialism.

A NEW GUISE FOR CONSPIRACY—UFOS AND SCIENCE FICTION MOVIES OF THE 1950S

At the dawn of the Cold War in the late 1940s, several sensational news stories of a very different type had made an impact on American culture. Although at first these seemed unrelated to the communist threat, it was later realized that public reaction to these reports was deeply connected to the climate of fear and anxiety that the tense nuclear age heralded. These stories, which tapped into earlier strands of American popular culture, involved reported sightings of unidentified flying objects, which were sometimes called "flying saucers."

Stories with fantastic, science fiction themes were already established in fictional lore and American popular culture. Nineteenth-century writers helped create a public appetite for the stories of this type. Jules Verne, for example, had success with books such as *Twenty-Thousand Leagues under the Sea* (1870), *Journey to the Center of the Earth* (1864), and *From Earth to the Moon* (1865). Somewhat later, H. G. Wells generated much interest with *The Time Machine* (1895), *Invisible Man* (1897), and *War of the Worlds* (1898). Such works sometimes provided a basis for screen productions beginning in the earliest days of narrative filmmaking. As early as 1902, for example, Georges Méliès's short film *A Trip to the Moon* (*Le voyage dans la lune*), loosely based on the writing of Jules Verne, created a stir among audiences of the still-new moving picture medium.

Science fiction themes continued to appear in movies off and on in the following decades. On radio, meanwhile, *War of the Worlds* provided the basis for the famous 1938 radio play of the same name audaciously produced by

Orson Welles and his Mercury Theater on the Air. That broadcast, dealing with an invasion from Mars, caused a panic among many listeners who failed to realize that the well-crafted radio play was a fictional story, rather than a legitimate news account. On screen, Saturday matinees, popular with younger audiences, featured the serialized exploits of such heroes as space adventurer Flash Gordon, the futurist hero Buck Rogers, and Superman. Such entertainments were not produced for serious, adult audiences in those years, but the science fiction and space travel themes became a familiar part of popular culture.

News Accounts of UFOs

In the late 1940s, the UFO phenomenon dramatically entered the mainstream culture. There had long been isolated accounts of strange lights in the air and unrecognized aircraft, but seldom had such reports made much of an impact on the general public. In 1947, however, two accounts would change that. One had an immediate impact; the influence of the other would not be fully felt for many years.

The widely reported sighting of an unidentified flying object on June 24, 1947, is often regarded as the starting point of the modern UFO phenomenon. It was reported by Kenneth Arnold, an Idaho businessman and private pilot. While flying near Mount Ranier in Washington, Arnold spotted a group of unrecognizable aircraft flying in a strange pattern at a high speed. The objects, he said, were intensely bright. They were unlike the normal aircraft, which, as a pilot, he thought he would have recognized. Arnold was puzzled by what he saw.

After his flight, he filed a routine report with the Civil Aeronautics Administration. He remained intrigued by his experience, however, and during a subsequent stop in Oregon, he mentioned his sighting to several people. By chance, one of the people Arnold encountered happened to be a newspaper reporter. He thought that Arnold's account of strange aircraft would make an interesting news story. The reporter was right. His article about Arnold and flying saucers was picked up by the Associated Press and widely distributed across the country.

Kenneth Arnold's experience was only the first of a series of widely reported UFO sightings.[14] A wave of similar reports closely followed. A few weeks later, for example, members of a United Airlines crew also reported a strange object in the sky. Then, on July 8, 1947, came the famous—or infamous, to some—report of a UFO that had crash landed in Roswell, New Mexico. That story initially received wide notice.

More sensational than sightings by Kenneth Arnold or the United Airlines crew, the Roswell case suggested that not only had a strange flying object been seen, its crashed wreckage had been discovered. Stories circulated immediately, but within days, officials explained that object of speculation was simply a weather balloon made of shiny metallic material. There was nothing unidentified, according to the government; the whole matter was simply a case of mistaken identity.

Although UFO sightings continued to be reported, the Roswell incident was soon forgotten. Largely dismissed as a sighting that had been explained after all, the segment of the public interested in extraterrestrial visitors shifted their attention to reports for which there was less official explanation. Several decades passed before public attention returned to the incident at Roswell, and it was not until a later time that it more fully entered the mainstream of popular culture.

CONSPIRACY THEORY IN SCIENCE FICTION MOVIES

Although science fiction films occasionally appeared from the earliest days of that medium, the post–World War II cultural climate was ripe for a reinvigoration of that theme. The technological advances that materialized during the war—especially nuclear weaponry and rocket-powered missile systems—seemed ample evidence that the march of progress was proceeding at a brisk pace. Although some military technologies also lent themselves to peaceful applications after the war, the nuclear world had frightening possibilities. Weapons could obliterate whole cities, rendering them ruins unfit for habitation due to the lingering radioactive contamination. The advances in rocketry and jet power made it possible to deliver such weapons to their targets as never before. Indeed, as the Cold War progressed, it increasingly seemed that nowhere was safe.

After the war, anxieties about the incredible destructive possibilities of new technology and fears of the communist menace came together in a wave of new science fiction movies. Often fantastic—even for science fiction films—in terms of narrative and plot, they nonetheless provided a form in which some of the extreme articulations of paranoia could be played out. They were frequently dismissed as mindless entertainments fit more for teenagers and children rather than serious viewing fit for adults. A look back at some of these films, however, suggests that they were only superficially masking the very real fears and anxieties that ran throughout American society of that era. The conspiracy theory motif was at the core of many such productions.

The conspiracy impulse took a while to crystallize as explicit elements of these films, though it is implicit in many more of them than may at first seem apparent. Some films—such as *Destination Moon* (1950), an early version of the race to the moon between the United States and the USSR, and *The Flying Saucer* (1950), in which Soviets steal a futuristic aircraft developed by the Americans—hinted at the subterfuge underneath the American and Soviet rivalry.

The much more famous and better crafted movie *The Day the Earth Stood Still* (1951) approaches the conspiracy theme somewhat indirectly. In that film, Michael Rennie portrays an extraterrestrial alien who has landed a large spacecraft in the middle of Washington, DC, amid much hysteria. The unearthly visitor has a remarkably human appearance and even speaks with an elegant English accent. Yet, when the visitor emerges from the craft, military authorities do not know what to make of him. Soldiers surrounding the strange craft panic, and the visitor is shot.

Authorities take the wounded alien to the hospital. As the strange visitor recovers, he receives high-ranking American officials, who are trying to discover who or what he is and what he wants. During his brief stay in the hospital, the visitor tries to persuade officials to organize a meeting of representatives from the world's governments so that he can deliver a message. Suspicious and fearful of the alien, however, officials do not grant the request.

Perplexed by the course of events, the visitor seizes an opportunity to escape from the hospital, with the goal of trying to understand more about humans. Blending in with the local population, he secretly takes up residence in a nearby rooming house where he becomes acquainted with a young widow (played by Patricia Neal) and her son. Initially, no one suspects that their new acquaintance is the being from the spacecraft. Indeed, the visitor's interactions with the mother and son are kind, and at times tender, in stark contrast to the assumptions that have been made about him. (Radio reports are overheard in which he is accused of being a Soviet agent, for example.) Only one man, a seemingly jealous suitor of the woman, becomes suspicious of the visitor.

In the meantime, the visitor has secretly maintained contact with some of the officials who met him in the hospital. The visitor warns them that humans must give up their destructive ways or else they will be destroyed to preserve interplanetary peace. When officials say that the sparring nations of earth would not consent to this, the visitor arranges for a short demonstration in which human technology is rendered unworkable for a short period of time. This creates short-term havoc.

He has made his point, but his true identity is soon discovered. The visitor is once more pursued by authorities and is again shot. This time, the wound appears mortal. The young widow, who is by his side, is convinced that the visitor is good, however. She secretly consents to what seems to be the visitor's final request and delivers a cryptic message to a huge robot standing guard over the spacecraft. This message, which is now a well-known linguistic artifact in popular culture, consists of the words, "Klaatu barada nikto." The strange words send the robot into action. It retrieves the body of the visitor and returns him to the spacecraft. Miraculously, the robot resuscitates the visitor.

Later emerging from the spacecraft under the protection of the giant robot, the visitor delivers his stern warning to all of the earth: Humans must reform their ways and learn not to threaten the peace with their newly found technology of destruction, or earth will be destroyed. It is left for viewers to ponder whether the people of earth will be able to achieve peaceful coexistence and thereby avoid destruction.

In one sense, *The Day the Earth Stood Still* can be viewed as a religious metaphor (the visitor assumes the name of Carpenter—a seeming reference to Jesus of Nazareth—and near the end he is risen from the dead). But it also contains the elements of conspiracy narrative, presented here in a novel way. The story features a shadowy nemesis with perceived ill intent. He hides among the population as he makes preparations to issue an ultimatum. The ease with which the visitor mingles in society and gains the trust of average Americans is alarming. And though the visitor was not a Soviet spy or communist agent, his message is menacing.

In a way, the film used conspiracy theory themes of subterfuge and paranoia to deliver the message that irrational hate and paranoia would lead humans to self-destruction. Although the conspiracy theme is not fully fleshed out, the portrayal of hidden identity and the threat of destruction by unknown forces are highly consistent with conspiracy fears of the times. Its answers are more than stock responses, however, and the movie openly questions the "shoot-first, ask questions later" mentality at a time when Americans had been asked to report their suspicions and root out foreign, or alien, thought.

More explicit expressions of the conspiracy theory theme in science fiction films of the era can be found in such movies as *Invaders from Mars* (1953) and the well-known *Invasion of the Body Snatchers* (1956).

Director William Cameron Menzies's *Invaders from Mars* brought the marriage of conspiracy and extraterrestrial alien invasion into full view. Its story begins with a boy observing the crash landing of a mysterious object on the outskirts of a small town. He reports the sighting to his father, who, in one of the story's many coincidences, happens to be a scientist working at a nearby government installation. The boy's father races off to investigate, but reports that he found nothing unusual. The father's behavior is strange and out of character, however, and he quite uncharacteristically hits his young son. The boy is frightened. He becomes even more alarmed when he notices a strange wound on back of his father's neck.

In the narrative that follows, the young boy, David, watches as not only his parents, but more and more of the townspeople exhibit unusual behavior. It slowly becomes evident that there is something sinister going on, something resembling a conspiracy in which the previously normal townsfolk are engaged in something evil. Because the town is home to institutions conducting advanced rocket and nuclear research, David eventually enlists the aid of local experts. They try to discover the reason for the mysterious behavior. The helpful scientists trace the problem to the crashed object, which turns out not to be a meteor but an alien spacecraft. (Amazingly, the scientists have a fully developed theory about Martian life and seem to know very specific details of the threat it poses. This is even more unlikely than the previous plot elements, but it is useful in moving the narrative along at a brisk pace.) They sneak on board the strange craft to investigate.

Within the spacecraft lurks a strange, monstrous alien—a small, fantastical creature encased in a crystal sphere, with a bulging head and waving tentacles. As the story unfolds, viewers learn that the creature is served by a number of threatening mutants, who have placed implants in unsuspecting townsfolk in order to bring them under the alien's control. These unfortunate citizens are directed to undertake various destructive acts, and when they outlive their usefulness in the scheme, they are eliminated. The motive for this malicious conspiracy, it is revealed, is the alien's desire to thwart further aerospace research by humanity.

In the final section of the film, the plot is exposed and the military springs into action. David, the scientists, and the soldiers manage to escape from the strange spacecraft just before it is destroyed by explosives.

The movie ends with a plot twist that is now relatively familiar in motion pictures. The explosion transitions to a scene of young David awakening in his bed. Racing to tell his parents of his strange fears, his parents tell him that the whole story was just a bad dream. In a final film cliché, however, the last frames of the *Invaders from Mars* show a strange craft landing not far from his home, just as had happened in his supposed dream.

This movie was conceived and presented as a straight science fiction, space-alien picture. Yet, until the last third of the film—when the mutants, the bizarre alien master, and interior of the alien craft are finally shown—most of what the audience sees could be an earthly plot. Although the sophisticated implants that control the townsfolk are the stuff of science fiction, especially in the early 1950s, the supposedly superior Martian invaders use their amazing mind-control abilities by directing earthlings to use conventional explosives and guns to carry out their interplanetary plot. Of course, no one in the story questions why such advanced beings would travel to earth and then resort to such apparently primitive means to accomplish their mission.

There is no specific reason to believe that those involved in the production of *Invaders from Mars* intended it to be a parable about Cold War conspiracy fears. Regardless of intent, that was the context in which the film was released, however. Intentional or not, the movie's underlying motif of ordinary people brought under sinister control squared with the society's general anxieties and Cold War fears about threats thought to be less imaginary. In retrospect, *Invaders from Mars* fits congruently with the political climate, which surely played an implicit part in its success despite its now-dated special effects and naïve plot elements.

Three years later, the general theme of *Invaders from Mars* received a much more sophisticated and chilling treatment in the now-classic *Invasion of the Body Snatchers*, which was directed by Don Siegel. In this movie, there were no bizarre-looking extraterrestrial aliens and no weird mutants to do their bidding. The movie, did, however, retain the idea that seemingly ordinary-looking humans could be far more menacing than they seemed on the surface.

In *Invaders from Mars*, unsuspecting humans were transformed into the un-witting slaves of the aliens. In *Invasion of the Body Snatchers*, this basic idea is reworked in a story showing how replica humans, devoid of emotion and with malicious intent, gradually replace almost every resident of a small California town.

The opening sequence of the film shows a panic-stricken man creating a disturbance in a hospital. A psychiatrist arrives on the scene and convinces the man to explain the source of his fear and anxiety. Calmed by the knowledge that someone will listen to him, the man relates his story. He says he is a doctor named Miles Binnell (played by Kevin McCarthy) and has fled from Santa Mira, a small town nearby. The film then transitions to a long flashback (which lasts until the final moments of the film) in which Binnell recounts the events leading up to the present.

The flashback begins with the doctor's return from a medical conference a few days earlier. Upon his return, he finds that something strange is going on. Numerous residents believe that their loved ones are not really the people they seem to be. Although having the same appearance of the loved ones, these apparent imposters seem to be sinister, emotionless strangers. Many town residents have quickly succumbed to this belief, which Binnell believes may be psychological in nature. He consults with the town's only psychiatrist, who agrees that it is an "epidemic of mass hysteria," a "strange neurosis" most likely caused by "worry about what's going on in the world."

A frantic phone call from a writer friend yields a startling and frightening discovery, however. This causes the doctor to have second thoughts about this initial explanation. The friend and his wife have discovered a seemingly dead body. Later, as Binnell examines the corpse, he notices that it has no fingerprints and that its features have little definition. It is as if the dead body was not a fully formed human. The fact that the body seems to have the same general build and look as the writer is noted, a realization leading to further worries.

Alarmed by the discovery, especially in light of the strange behavior ex-hibited by the townspeople, the friends decide to wait until the following morning to make a report. They want to see if anything changes that would help them better understand what they had discovered.

In a series of scenes that follow, an increasing number of townsfolk suc-cumb to the strange behavior. Eventually, the doctor, his romantic interest (a woman named Becky), the writer, and the writer's wife discover that the reason for the supposed mass hysteria was something far more malevolent than they suspected. Residents of the town have been replaced by duplicates, and the situation seemed to be worsening.

The full importance of this realization occurs when Binnell discovers large pods. These pods, later revealed to have drifted through space for thousands of years, are the source of the replica humans. They slowly absorb the form, mind, and memory of their victims, usurping their human victims' identities when the replicas reach full development. When the replicas fully mature, the humans die the next time they fall asleep. The nearly exact copies then take their place.

By the time of this discovery, however, it is almost too late for the central characters. Already, nearly everyone in the town has been replaced. Now on the run, the doctor and Becky hide as they try to find a way to warn the world outside Santa Mira of the impending danger. They desperately try to stay awake, using medications to forestall the inevitable sleep. (The pharmacological defense against alien invasion is one of the more understated themes suggested by the narrative.)

One by one, however, everyone around Binnell succumbs. In the midst of an attempt to escape the town, even Becky falls victim to the space pod threat. Finally, Binnell just barely makes his way to a neighboring town, but that town is already facing the same threat. Binnell makes hysterical attempts to warn the citizens of the grave danger, but the citizens think he's mad and take him to the hospital, back to the point at which the story began.

As the flashback concludes, a coincidence leads the hospital psychiatrist and resident physician to conclude that Binnell's story is real, after all. They believe that there is a major threat. The film ends with an urgent phone call to alert authorities that the entire nation faces a deadly foe.

Two elements of conspiracy, highly consistent with the political landscape of the times, are evident throughout the film. First, there is the idea that dark forces are at work across the society, but that it is hard to recognize that fact. An imminent threat is masked, but in a way, paradoxically, that is mostly in plain view. What is more, even when the film's hero recognizes this peril, it proves exceedingly difficult to convince others that the danger exists, and that it is not the figment of either an overactive imagination or even of a clinical psychological condition. (That a psychiatrist is a central character in the film is surely no chance element of the script.)

Second, and following from the first point, is the idea that when facing a hard-to-detect enemy acting within society, no one can really be trusted. More than that, in fact, the film suggests that everyone should be suspected. In addition, there is a major problem facing anyone clever enough to figure out the identity of a surrogate. Once a fake human is identified, to whom can a person safely confide? There is no assurance that another replica is not lurking nearby in the form of a seemingly safe, familiar face.

A political reading of the film is hard to avoid, at least as one of several possible interpretations. In the general idea of unsuspecting innocents falling one-by-one into enemy hands, for example, *Invasion of the Body Snatchers* in some ways resembles a depiction of the Domino Theory, the political idea that unprepared nations could fall one by one under communist rule, eventually leaving the United States as the lone free country. This idea was one of the dominating themes articulated by American political leaders at the time. Here, the theme is driven home by making it intimate and personal.

It is cloaked in a dark and disturbing parable of paranoia at the individual, rather than the international, level. Indeed, the film suggests a scenario that is very consonant with the fear of communism that had swept through the nation: hyper-vigilance is the only defense against becoming the last person, or last nation, standing among a throng of foes who are determined to bring about your destruction.[15]

It was not long before yet another movie incarnation of this theme was undertaken in Hollywood. By the time *I Married a Monster from Outer Space* (1958) was released, however, the Soviets had successfully launched the Sputnik space capsule. This advance in rocketry jolted the United States, which suddenly seemed to have fallen behind its arch nemesis in this area of technology. Within months, the United States launched the Explorer space capsule in response. With these developments, the idea of space travel seemed more realistic than ever before. In a *New York Times* column about the movie business, A. H. Weiler reported news of the production this way: "What with Sputniks, Vanguard and Explorer orbiting swiftly in what used to be the lonely blue yonder, the news that Paramount is sponsoring a feature titled "I Married a Monster from Outer Space" is not so startling as it once might have been."[16]

I Married a Monster from Outer Space, along with another science fiction movie, *Invisible Invaders* the next year, were indications that while the theme of malicious imposters remained attractive to Hollywood, the sense of genuine fear and paranoia that was evident in some of the earlier films was now diminishing. What had once been allegorical responses to genuine fears of society had now been reduced to the level of formula, at least for the moment.

CHANGES IN THE 1950S

Science fiction movies such as *Invasion of the Body Snatchers* and *War of the Worlds* (1953) reflected the anxious state of Americans as they adjusted to the grim reality of a Cold War in which both sides possessed the capabilities for nuclear destruction. The Cold War continued for many more years, dramatically escalating just a few years later in crises such as the Bay of Pigs and the Cuban missile crisis. The threat of global war remained well beyond the 1950s, but for most people it was not an all-encompassing obsession. Everyday life continued, and society devised strategies to cope with the fear and paranoia of the nuclear age.

Americans worried about keeping up with the Soviets in an ever-escalating arms race, but they also worried about keeping up with the Joneses. They continued to keep an eye on their neighbors, though now the motive was less likely to be an apprehensive lookout for communism than to see how to best keep up with their neighbor's acquisition of new cars, appliances, and other conspicuous examples of middle-class comfort. Many Americans settled into their suburban homes. They worried about geopolitics, but they also fretted about more mundane things, such as their teenaged children listening to Elvis Presley and rock and roll music.

THE COLD WAR, AMERICAN INSTITUTIONS, AND CONSPIRACY CULTURE

Writing about *Invasion of the Body Snatchers*, Ray Pratt cautions against taking the political paranoia theme as the only way to interpret that film.[17] He suggests that the film also reflects more generalized apprehensions. Principally, these concern the loss of individuality and identity, coming about as big business and consumerism came to dominate everyday life, and also the stifling effects that restrictive assumptions about race and gender had on many Americans of that era. These observations undoubtedly are important. It would be a mistake to see only the highly volatile world of mid-century geopolitics as the forces driving American society along a path that embraced conspiratorial fears. Thus, although the postwar emergence of the Cold War and the fear it created seem to have played the largest part in pushing screen projects with conspiracy themes to the foreground, these other factors were also important.

In the United States, the early years of the Cold War were deeply influenced by the major institutions of society, which were overwhelmingly trusted and often taken at face value. Government, the news media, and industry provided the venues in which the communist threat was interpreted and played out, but they also shaped individual lives in numerous other ways. Many people, for example, assumed that the government solved problems. They also believed the picture of events that appeared in print and broadcast news and that what was good for industry was also good for America. Just as many people had been content to take their cue about dealing with the communist menace from leading figures in government, therefore, many assumed that society's other institutions were looking out for them.

As the postwar world generated material wealth at scales unimaginable before the war, much of the population did not yet see that fissures were developing. These would grow and deeply undercut confidence in these institutions only a few years later. In the early postwar years, however, trust in American institutions still ran high. This is evident across most of the movies Hollywood produced with conspiracy theory themes in which it is the institutions of society that save individuals from conspiratorial threats.

Throughout the 1950s, many incarnations of the conspiracy theory theme appeared on screen. Overall, an important similarity that these films shared is found in marriage of conspiracy theory to a deep fear of unknown externalities. Sometimes the enemy came completely from the outside, and at other times it made its way surreptitiously into the heart of America, but the threat was always external in origin. Along with this was the stance the films took regarding the central American institutions, such as government, and central

American values such as patriotism, faith, and a sense of duty. The conspiracy theory movies of the era affirmed those institutions and those values, holding them up as the best defense against the often faceless external enemy.

By the mid- to late 1950s, evidence of a less literal response to the era's anxieties began to appear. The director Alfred Hitchcock had completed a remake of his own *The Man Who Knew Too Much* (remake 1956; original 1934) casting everyman actor Jimmy Stewart as a man whose family is unwittingly caught up in an international assassination plot. A few years later, Hitchcock's *North by Northwest* cast a decidedly different light on the anxieties of the era. Like Stewart's character in *The Man Who Knew Too Much*, Roger O. Thornhill, the lead character of *North by Northwest*, was an innocent man, here mistaken by international conspirators for someone else and framed for a brazen murder at the United Nations headquarters in New York.

Compared to *The Man Who Knew Too Much*, Hitchcock's approach to international intrigue in *North by Northwest* is infused with far less foreboding and fear and much more wit and ambivalence.[18] To be sure, the film evokes thrills and excitement by placing its main characters in harm's way, even as it suggests an espionage plot that has swept up an innocent man. Yet, the debonair Thornhill (played by Cary Grant) never seems genuinely in peril, and the audience gets the sense that the convoluted case of mistaken identity will be dispatched before the film's end and that the leading man will come away unharmed. Even Thornhill's mother seems to react to the supposedly dire mix-up with a twinkle in her eye and a series of off-handed quips.

Additionally, *North by Northwest* is a film in which U.S. government agents behave ambiguously—sometimes in a heroic manner but other times decidedly not. American agents realize that Thornhill is the victim of mistaken identity. But at first it seems that the government spymaster (simply called "the Professor" throughout the film) does not intend to do anything about helping the innocent man out of his predicament. (The spymaster is played by Leo G. Carroll, a Hitchcock regular who later became more famous in the 1960s television series, *The Man from U.N.C.L.E.*) As the film progresses, Thornhill becomes romantically involved with a young woman named Eve Kendall (played by Eva Marie Saint) whose loyalties are unclear. It later turns out that she is a double-agent loyal to the Americans, but that the American spymaster is willing to jeopardize her life in order to infiltrate the conspiracy abroad. The spymaster explains this away as Eve is sent off. Speaking to Thornhill, the Professor says, "War is hell, Mr. Thornhill, even when it's a cold one."

Two things are significant about Hitchcock's take on the Cold War world in *North by Northwest*. First, in this movie audiences do encounter a world in which there is an implied communist threat involving convoluted plots undertaken by both sides of the struggle. All of these plots, however, seem to cancel each other out. The whole situation is presented as a confusing and ambiguous game. The players take it seriously, but they are not above making jokes and quips. It is a world in which ordinary, everyday people do not seem very important. Once involved, Thornhill also adopts this attitude. Even when he is in grave danger, he seldom drops his witty demeanor. Although Thornhill was undoubtedly intended to be an example of a solid American citizen, he seems to have little or no interest in ideology, instead reserving his energies for the romantic pursuit of Eve.

Second, agents of the U.S. government are not really heroes in the film, but instead are relatively innocuous players in a larger story over which they do not seem to have much control. From one perspective they, too, seem to exhibit conspiratorial behaviors that cause them to make questionable judgments. Their first impulse when Thornhill becomes ensnared in the scheme, for example, is not to save him because he is an innocent bystander, but rather to protect their larger purposes by leaving him to fend for himself. In the last section of the film, the Professor does come to Thornhill's aid and somewhat rehabilitates the image of the noncaring bureaucrat that is given earlier in the story. But by then the film has already cast a skeptical eye on U.S. espionage activities.

Of course, above all Hitchcock was interested in telling a story with thrills, wit, and romance that audiences would embrace. The Cold War backdrop is in some ways arbitrary, and the ideological struggle of the era is not central to the picture's narrative. But Hitchcock's treatment of this context is telling. The situation is serious and even threatening, but it is more or less taken for granted and not an all-consuming factor. Thornhill, an "advertising man," remains glib and unflappable throughout, spending little, if any, time thinking about his unintended part in the Cold War. In addition, Hitchcock slyly suggests that the "good" side in the struggle—as exemplified by the American agents—may sometimes have their own agendas and may not always be thinking primarily about the welfare of innocent Americans. In ways such as these, *North by Northwest* is an important herald of impending changes in the public's thinking about conspiracies, which would be far more skeptical about American institutions than was common in the 1950s. Such changes, however, would be gradual and would not firmly take hold until the following decades.

LATE 1950S POLITICAL DEVELOPMENTS

The tensions of the Cold War never disappeared in the late 1950s, but Americans adjusted to the underlying anxieties of the nuclear age. Daily life provided many distractions. The greatly expanding middle class, rising prosperity, and consumerism took up much of the public's attention.

The Cold War came closer to the doorstep of the United States on January 1, 1959. Although at first this development was not recognized, a new communist threat was emerging only 90 miles from Florida. It was the first day of the new year when, after a short campaign, a group led by Fidel Castro overthrew the regime of Batista y Zaldívar, the Cuban leader whose corrupt regime had led Cuba into turmoil. For a time, Castro was hailed as a reformer who would rechart Cuba's course in a new direction. The United States was initially pleased, taking comfort in the thought that an increasingly noncompliant strongman had been eliminated and replaced with a man who would be more sympathetic to U.S. interests.

This illusion was soon shattered, however. A short while later, it became clear that Castro was a communist, a man far different from the person American officials thought he was. Before long, the charismatic Castro emerged as a leader who was willing to take harsh measures in order to bring about the changes he envisioned for the island nation. Enemies were often eliminated and deviation from Marxist-Leninist doctrine was zealously rooted out and punished. Thus, Castro, who initially was favorably regarded by U.S. officials, soon came to be regarded as an embarrassing pariah, a man who had sneaked communism into America's backyard. The magnitude of the threat to the United States would become apparent in jolting events early in the next decade.

In 1960, Cold War realities asserted themselves more pointedly in the months leading up to the presidential campaign. One major incident was precipitated by the crash landing of an American U-2 plane, a high-altitude aircraft capable of carrying out surveillance missions over hostile territory. One of the planes, piloted by United States Air Force officer Francis Gary Powers, took off from Turkey on a secret mission to photograph sensitive installations in the Soviet Union. The U-2 was detected, however, and after an air skirmish was eventually downed.

Although U.S. military authorities knew the plane was missing, at first they were uncertain about its fate. Realizing that revelation of the spy mission would be embarrassing and would complicate relations with the Soviets, American officials therefore released statements that a plane on a meteorological mission had gone missing, perhaps having veered unintentionally off course because of a malfunction.

Within a short time, however, the American cover story was blown open. The Soviets announced that not only had the plane crashed in its territory, but that it was mostly intact. They recovered significant evidence about the true nature of the plane's mission. More than that, however, Powers had been captured alive. Premier Nikita Khrushchev made the most of the situation, embarrassing the United States with the trial and conviction of the pilot. Powers was imprisoned for espionage. (He gained his freedom in 1962 after being exchanged for a Soviet agent held by the United States.)

The timing of the U-2 incident was unfortunate. With the tensions it produced, a summit meeting that had been planned between the American and Soviet leaders was cancelled.

As the 1950s drew to a close, Americans could not have known of the series of crises and catastrophes that would soon fuel further changes in the social and political landscape. But American society emerged from the 1950s more confident and, in many respects, less fearful than it had entered the decade. Hollywood had often reflected these changing circumstances in productions with conspiracy theory themes. Public attitudes and perceptions about the dangers the nation and its citizens faced would change in the coming decade. The place of conspiracy theory on screen and in popular culture would evolve with these changes.

Conspiracy in the New Frontier

The arrival of the new decade seemed the harbinger of a welcome change. The 1960s, which would later be characterized by tumult and upheaval, largely began with a sense of optimism. In July 1960, the charismatic John F. Kennedy accepted the nomination of the Democratic Party in a Los Angeles convention hall. He voiced a new spirit that was in the air when he told the audience, "We stand today on the edge of a new frontier—the frontier of the 1960s, a frontier of unknown opportunities and perils, a frontier of unfulfilled hopes and threats. . . . The new frontier of which I speak is not a set of promises—it is a set of challenges."

The November electoral contest cast Eisenhower's vice president, Richard M. Nixon, against Kennedy, the dashing young Senator from Massachusetts. Both had anticommunist credentials. Nixon had been an enthusiastic anticommunist when serving in the Senate early in the Cold War. He had maintained that stance and gained visibility—and in some people's eyes, notoriety—during his two terms as vice president. Kennedy, the Democrat, had also been careful to create a strong anticommunist resume during his time in the Senate. Like others of his party, he took pains to make sure that he would not be perceived as "soft" on communism.

The campaign was fiercely fought on both sides. In the fall, presidential candidates debated on live television for the first time.[1] Kennedy, with his Hollywood good looks and a natural ease in front of the cameras, came across to many viewers as a polished and confident man. He seemed the picture of vitality and youth in government. Nixon, by contrast, looked uncomfortable and made a less appealing television figure. (This appearance was amplified by Nixon's determination that he, unlike Kennedy, would not use television make-up under the hot studio lights.)

The fact that Kennedy was Catholic was an issue for many voters. Some people feared that the candidate would have conflicting loyalties and his detractors suggested that Rome might exercise an influence—perhaps hidden—on his actions. Mindful of public perceptions about this and other perceived liabilities, however, the Democratic Party shored up its candidate. The selection of Lyndon Johnson, the masterful Texan politician, as Kennedy's running mate neutralized some of the opposition. The Texan's appearance on the ticket with Kennedy seemed to make a difference and in a close election the Kennedy-Johnson campaign was victorious.

The brief presidency of John F. Kennedy exuded an aura of youthful vitality. This feeling was made more pronounced by Kennedy's appointment of many Washington outsiders. They were heralded as a new crop of America's best and brightest. In the course of Kennedy's presidency, the spirit of what was called a New Frontier could be found in many progressive programs. (These included innovations such as the Peace Corps, a partial treaty to limit nuclear testing, the race to the moon, among others.) Although the perils of the Cold War remained, Americans sensed possibilities for a brighter future, aided by technology and the new generation that was beginning to step to the foreground.

Such feelings may have been premature, however. In many ways, it was a time of contradictions. Kennedy was in office for only a few months when the Cuban situation boiled over. The story of this new crisis began before the new president had taken office. Under Eisenhower's watch, the CIA had secretly planned an operation to overthrow the Castro regime, which by then was recognized as an unfriendly neighbor with intentions harmful to the United States. The plans were not ready until after Eisenhower left office.

Although he had not initiated it, Kennedy gave approval for the plan to be implemented. That mission, which involved sending a contingent of armed Cuban expatriates back to the island, was the Bay of Pigs operation. It was put into action in April 1961. Despite CIA planning, however, things went badly. It presented the United States with another embarrassing situation and, in many ways, one that was deeply humiliating. With this debacle, it seemed that the interests of the powerful U.S. government had been thwarted by the tiny Caribbean nation. At the same time, it clarified for the Cuban leadership that the United States might be willing to take extraordinary steps to bring down the Castro regime.

Despite such crises, Kennedy was largely successful in promoting an optimistic vision for the future. His administration, and the energetic people around it, quickly captured the American imagination.

But new perils continued to appear. Perhaps the most dangerous confrontation of the Cold War occurred in October 1962 in the incident known as the Cuban missile crisis. Of all the international situations of the early 1960s, few rivaled this incident in terms of the inherent danger for catastrophe.[2] The well-known episode involved the deployment of Soviet nuclear missiles in Cuba, bringing the nuclear threat ominously close to home for Americans. The missiles had been transported to the island nation on a Soviet cargo vessel and taken to a Cuban military base. Inexplicably, the missiles were unloaded from their transports and left lying on the ground in plain view, with their unmistakable shape and large identifying marks. American military officials could scarcely believe their eyes when photographs taken during a surveillance flight over the island clearly showed the grave new peril.

Kennedy immediately demanded the removal of the weapons. Khrushchev refused, after which Kennedy ordered a naval blockade of the island. The standoff lasted for eleven days. Americans, and people around the world, feared for the worst. They steeled themselves for the nuclear conflict they had dreaded for more than a decade.

The crisis was complex and there were many points at which it seemed that full-scale armed conflict was imminent.[3] Yet, ultimately an arrangement was made that led the Soviets to withdraw the missiles. (Although not publicized at the time, the United States also removed some missiles from Turkey.) Already facing a power struggle within his regime, the incident dealt a political blow to Khrushchev, who was ousted from power shortly thereafter.

HOLLYWOOD'S VISIONS OF CONSPIRACY IN THE EARLY 1960s

In this complicated political milieu, the American movie industry continued to work the conspiracy theme that had emerged with great force in the previous fifteen years. Two noteworthy films released in 1962, one before and one during the Cuban Missile Crisis, captured some of this mood.

ADVISE AND CONSENT

The first of these films was *Advise and Consent*. It was directed by the well-known auteur Otto Preminger, who had been making movies since the 1930s and had recently achieved new heights of fame with such wide-ranging films such as *The Man with the Golden Arm* (1955), *Anatomy of a Murder* (1959), and *Exodus* (1960). For his new project, Preminger had chosen to adapt Allen Drury's bestselling novel for the screen. The movie debuted in American theaters in June 1962, taking up the themes of a "red menace" and McCarthyism and reworking them for a 1960s audience.

The film follows the inner machinations of the U.S. Senate in a story that centers on the nomination of a controversial nominee for the office of secretary of state. In the narrative, a man named Robert Leffingwell (played by Henry Fonda) is nominated by an increasingly unpopular and, unbeknownst to the public, gravely ill president. The president's candidate preached a political doctrine that emphasized negotiation and possible compromise with the communist world, all in an effort to maintain peaceful coexistence in a dangerous nuclear world.

The story thus reflected an actual dichotomy of public opinion at the time. In the film treatment, the nominee's pragmatic view of the world seemed sensible to some senators, but others found it offensive and a sell-out of American ideals and morality. The president knew that chief among the critics of the nominee would be the aging senator from South Carolina, the crafty Seabright Cooley (Charles Laughton, in his final screen role). The story then follows efforts by the president's allies to secure Senate approval and efforts of opponents to defeat the nomination.

The majority leader of the Senate (played by Walter Pidgeon) knows that Senator Cooley is capable of mounting a ferocious campaign against the nominee. (The fictional Cooley may have reminded viewers of Joseph McCarthy in many respects.[4]) Realizing that the nomination will require careful attention, the Senate leader assigns an earnest and energetic young senator, Brigham Anderson, the job of shepherding the nominee through committee hearings.

Though a member of the majority party, Anderson has some doubts about the nominee he is supposed to guide through the confirmation process. His concerns become amplified when Cooley calls a witness who claims Leffingwell was a member in a communist cell some years earlier. After making these shocking allegations, the committee adjourns and the story turns to backroom politicking.

The president had been unaware of anything dark in Leffingwell's past, but the seriousness of the accusations leads to a private confrontation with the nominee at a White House meeting. Eventually, Leffingwell privately admits that the charges were mostly accurate and that he briefly had been part of a socialist group as a young student. He assures the president and some close advisors that this was far in the past and says that he has long since rebuked that philosophy.

Still, Leffingwell realizes how damaging the charges are. He suggests that the president withdraw his nomination. The president is undeterred, however, and his longtime friend the majority leader feels obligated to do what he can to save the nomination. Knowing that it would be difficult to prove the allegations, the president and his trusted allies in the Senate push forward. When the committee reconvenes, Leffingwell addresses the charges by lying.

Although this appears to save the nomination, the dishonesty disgusts Anderson. Finding it hard to drop the matter, he decides to find the truth. The curmudgeonly Cooley provides Anderson with some clues, and Anderson slowly starts to unravel the true story.

Several upstart senators have other ideas, however. They believe that the charges against Leffingwell are patently false and that the nominee has been smeared for political purposes. (The situation appears ironic since the film portrays these young men as zealous careerists who will stop at almost nothing to advance their standing.) In response, they begin harassing Anderson to stop him from further compromising the nomination.

In the long section of the film that follows, a secondary theme emerges when Anderson's wife receives a series of anonymous phone calls. The voice on the line threatens Anderson, his career, and the well-being of his family if he does not stop his investigation into Leffingwell's background. It is soon revealed that Anderson, too, has a secret: he had a brief homosexual encounter during his military service. Now, knowledge of that encounter is being used to blackmail him.

In a climactic scene, Anderson goes to a gay bar in order to confront his former male lover about the extortion campaign. A crowd of men—all of whom are portrayed as gay stereotypes—greets Anderson as he enters the club. His response is one of shame and disgust.

In line with the widespread social stigma that was associated with homosexuality in the early 1960s, the story continues as Anderson returns not to his home, but to his Senate office. He feels humiliated and compromised. Despondent and seeing no hope of recovering from his plight, he commits suicide.

The final section of *Advise and Consent* deals with the nomination on the floor of the full Senate after Anderson's death. Although viewers have been led to expect more backhanded politics and machinations, something else happens. In noble speeches from both the majority leader and his nemesis, Senator Cooley, senators are urged to vote on the nomination according to their conscience, not according to any promises or for fear of political retribution. Released from prior party obligations, the result is a tie.

It is assumed that the vice president, a mild and thoughtful man who was largely kept in the dark by the president, would cast the deciding vote in favor of his party's nominee. Abruptly, however, the vice president receives a message that the president has died from his illness. The vice president dramatically declines to vote for the candidate, instead saying he will choose his own nominee now that he will become president.

In the end, *Advise and Consent* affirms that the government works, at least on the surface. Despite frequent soap opera-like backroom maneuvers, Congress eventually does the right thing. On a more individual level, the story also shows how the cool-headed and politically sophisticated majority leader, along with the feisty Senator Cooley, can come to recognize their similar aims and work together for the good of the country. Overall, then, it turns out to be a story that does not challenge orthodox assumptions about American government. This was not lost on viewers of the time. In its review of the film, *Time* magazine took note of the "blandly inconclusive ending."[5]

Indeed, *Advise and Consent* is largely political melodrama, especially in its treatment of secrecy and power. The production also has soap opera overtones. The underlying conspiracy theme, however, is powerfully represented in two ways. First, the film depicts a world in which secrets, and conspiracies to withhold and to reveal them, are layered one on top of another. Both the opponents and the supporters of the president's nominee conspire to alternately use and to withhold information in order to manipulate events and tilt the outcome in their favor. Importantly, both sides defend their scheming and deception by arguing that the greater good can be achieved by bending, or even breaking, the rules of government.

Moreover, in piling so many layers of conspiratorial action on one another, the perceived indiscretions of the people involved become cloudy and ambiguous. Preminger apparently meant to suggest that the stigmatizing of homosexuals was as unfair and overly zealous as persecutions of leftists during the height of the McCarthy years. It is by no means certain, however, that he succeeds in leading viewers—especially more recent viewers—to this conclusion. Instead, the highly melodramatic treatment of the themes of secret political pasts and closet homosexuality illuminate little of the controversies associated with either situation. In fact, almost any secret would do for the dramatic purposes of the film, and there does not appear to be anything special about either Leffingwell's leftist past or Anderson's homosexual past. A viewer gets the sense that if it were not for these secrets that were used against the men, then it would just be something, perhaps anything, else.

And this leads to a second important effect of *Advise and Consent*: its vision of the cynical underside of the Washington establishment. Preminger is hardly subtle in this depiction. The film shows a governmental bureaucracy largely populated with people who exhibit petty jealousies and arrogance and are given to selfish maneuvering for power and influence. In representing both the supporters and the opponents of the nominee in this fashion, Preminger conveys a cynical impression of American life. For its time in the early 1960s, this was a somewhat atypical view.

As the director of a popular entertainment, Preminger was not necessarily interested in exploring these themes beyond their immediate dramatic purposes. In some ways, *Advise and Consent* is in the tradition of melodramas such as *Peyton Place* (1957), a big-screen soap opera about the secret, steamy underside of a quaint New England village.[6]

Still, it is ironic that at the same time the film conveys this latent cynicism, it continues to affirm the nobility of the government and its institutions. Preminger is able to accomplish this by keeping his focus on the film's characters. At this moment, then, it is the people, rather than the institutions, that seem dubious to the audience. In the following years, of course, this cynicism would come to be directed at the institutions themselves.

THE MANCHURIAN CANDIDATE

Another film from 1962 also employed the conspiracy theme, but with an international focus and with a much more menacing story line. This is director John Frankenheimer's *The Manchurian Candidate*, the well-known film dealing with a former American P.O.W. who is "brainwashed" and sent back the United States as a sleeper assassin. The film stars Frank Sinatra, who had already appeared in the assassination-themed melodrama *Suddenly*, and also features Laurence Harvey, Janet Leigh, Angela Lansbury, and James Gregory.

Based on a successful novel by Richard Condon, *The Manchurian Candidate* was not necessarily an obvious choice for a mainstream motion picture. Its main premise seemed to stretch credulity. The story suggests that a combination of sophisticated techniques (presumably including torture, hypnotism, and drugs) could turn otherwise all-American soldiers into traitorous, unwitting killing machines. In some ways this seemed closer to far-fetched science fiction than to a tale of political intrigue.

Although the book version of *The Manchurian Candidate* was popular, executives at the United Artists studio were not convinced that it would be a good idea to go ahead with a movie treatment. According to the screenwriter, George Axelrod, "They didn't want to make it because they thought that it was un-American."[7]

The project had an important advocate, however. Frank Sinatra, by then a major entertainment star and slated to appear in the leading role, was committed to the film as an actor and as an investor. He had friends in high places and soon the project received influential endorsements, which put the film executives' fears to rest. Indeed, Sinatra arranged for both the Democratic Party national finance chair and no less than President Kennedy himself (who Sinatra had known for some time) to call United Artists' officers in support of the picture.[8] The project was soon underway.

The finished picture closely followed Condon's original story line. The plot offers a murky and, in many ways, equally far-fetched critique of both the overzealous anticommunists of the previous decade and those who opposed them.

The narrative begins during the Korean War, as a squad of American soldiers, two of whom are Raymond Shaw (played by Laurence Harvey) and Bennett Marco (played by Frank Sinatra), are on patrol in hostile territory. Somehow the men lose their way and are attacked by North Korean troops. After a brief battle, the Americans are captured. What follows is a bizarre sequence that combines elements of the thriller, fantasy, science fiction, and political satire into an extravagant conspiracy-laden tale.

An indefinite period of time passes, and now the soldiers appear to be sitting in a very American-looking parlor, where they are guests of honor at a meeting of the local flower club. The meeting is presided over by a matronly American woman, who enthusiastically talks about hydrangeas. Something is clearly amiss, however. This becomes very apparent when the woman, in a matter-of-fact tone, asks one soldier, Raymond, if he has ever murdered anyone.

"No, sir," Raymond replies. This odd manner of addressing a woman leads to events even more confusing. The picture cuts back to where the woman had been standing, only to reveal that instead of the woman, there is a communist scientist. And instead of a garden club meeting in a parlor, the man is standing in the front of a sterile lecture hall, filled with military and scientific types who are apparently Soviet, Chinese, and North Korean communists.

In this way, director Frankenheimer begins to suggest how thoroughly the American captives have been brainwashed. As the scene unfolds, the communist scientist—still appearing to be the Garden Club lady to the captives—instructs Raymond to kill one fellow soldier by strangulation. He does so in a zombie-like fashion. Then he is ordered to kill another American soldier by gunshot, which he also does without hesitation. It is shocking enough that Raymond has killed his compatriots without hesitation or self-awareness; it is just as telling that the other soldiers sit by as the spectacle unfolds, offering no resistance and revealing no awareness of what has happened.

This prologue to the movie is followed by the homecoming of Raymond after the war. None of the men in the unit, it turns out, have any recollection of their captivity. Instead, they remember being lost for a short while and then finding their way back to the command center. They have recollections of how two of their comrades died in combat and how Raymond heroically saved the surviving members of the unit. Based on these memories, Raymond has been awarded a medal of valor for his supposed heroism. He is now returned stateside as a war hero.

Raymond's mother (Angela Lansbury) has big plans. She parlays Raymond's homecoming into an opportunity to bolster support for her husband's political ambitions, or rather, her lofty ambitions for him. Her husband is the most strident anticommunist character in the movie, a United States senator named John Iselin (played by James Gregory). Although he is not considered the leading candidate and is regarded as a long-shot, Iselin is a contender for his party's nomination in the upcoming presidential campaign. Despite his wife's enthusiasm, however, Iselin is a somewhat unlikely presidential aspirant. He is portrayed as little more than a buffoon with a weakness for alcohol. It soon becomes apparent to the movie's audience that Iselin's patriotic, anticommunist declarations are not based on his own thinking. Behind the scenes, his entire public persona has been orchestrated by his scheming wife, Raymond's mother.

Raymond, who detests his stepfather and who appears to loathe his mother's interference in his life, has his own ideas, however. Rejecting his mother's suggestions, he accepts an offer to go to New York. There he plans to begin a newspaper career.

In the time that follows, Raymond's career develops. One day, he receives a phone call that triggers a subliminal command, prompting Raymond to report to a New York apartment. Apparently in a trance the whole time, he is then examined by communist agents. Surprisingly, during the examination the communist scientist from earlier in the film reappears. The sinister character is content when he confirms that his subject remains unaware of what really happened. He also determines that Raymond remains under their influence and that he still does not realize that anything is out of the ordinary.

In the central part of the film, viewers see cracks develop in communist deception. The scene shifts to the story of Bennett Marco, who served in Korea with Raymond and remained in the service after the war, attaining the rank of major. Marco is troubled by repeated nightmares, however. The dreams seem bizarre and sinister. They always focus on hazy and jumbled memories of the Garden Club hallucination, an incident that Marco does not consciously remember. Slowly, however, his amnesia about the incident begins to fade. He begins to regain a cloudy memory of what really had happened to the two members of his unit who had died at Raymond's hands.

Marco dutifully reports his vague suspicions to his superiors, unsure if he is experiencing a psychological condition or if the vaguely returning memories are real. It is only when another member of his unit independently reports similar nightmares that American military officials take the matter seriously. They assign Marco to investigate what has happened and what, if anything, these strange dreams mean.

Raymond's mother, meanwhile, takes on an ever-increasing role as the film heads toward a climax. Already, viewers realize that she is cold and calculating and that she is angling in every way possible to assure that her husband receives the nomination.

As Marco begins to figure out what is happening, however, the situation becomes more chaotic. Viewers discover that Raymond's mother is his communist controller and that she is willing to sacrifice her son to the cause. Now under her spell, Raymond commits several murders to advance this plan.

Finally, the main point of the plot is revealed. Raymond has been selected to assassinate the front-running presidential nominee on national television. According to the scheme, this is supposed to cause the party to clamor for the tough-minded Senator Iselin to accept the nomination, just as Raymond's mother planned.

The appointed time draws near, but it is unclear whether Marco will be able to thwart the plan in time. Raymond has his intended victim in his gun sights from a hidden location above the convention hall. Just when it appears Marco is an instant too late, Raymond redirects his focus to a new target. In an abrupt plot twist, Raymond shoots the senator and his mother instead of his assigned target. At the same moment, Marco and a police officer burst into the room, and the officer shoots Raymond dead. Then, following a brief denouement, the improbable tale draws to a close.

The Manchurian Candidate brought together conspiracy themes as it reframed 1950s-style anticommunist fears into a complicated package.[9] Its fantastic portrayal of brainwashing brings a science fiction element to the film to explain how seeming innocents could turn against their homeland. This portrayal was more subtle than the mind-control elements of 1950s science fiction movies such as *Invaders from Mars*, but in terms of dramatic effect, it worked in the same way. Communism was again seen as a thief of free will. Almost no amount of caution, the film seems to suggest on one level, is too much when confronted with an enemy that can deceive and control the people. The story implies that defeat can come without people even being aware that the fight has started.

Frankenheimer's skillful direction glosses over several inconsistencies within the story that extend beyond the dubious possibility of mind control in the way the movie suggests. As the film nears the end, the pace quickens, and viewers have little time to think about the many leaps in logic and the many strokes of luck that would be required for the assassination plot to achieve the outcome the conspirators envision.

The absurdity of some plot elements is nonetheless difficult to miss, and since Frankenheimer toys with traditional symbols of the all-American life, a satirical reading of the film is suggested. Certainly, there are few dramas in American filmmaking that take the seeming delight that this film does in portraying the dark side of motherhood as construed in mid-twentieth century America. Raymond, robbed of his free will, turns out to be the victim of his mother's misguided scheming, having no choice in the matter. A throwaway line early in the film turns out to be prophetic and portending monstrous consequences: "It's a terrible thing to hate your mother," he says. Indeed, Raymond's mother is not merely controlling in the way that assumedly bad mothers are; she is literally his "controller" in an elaborate plot that destroys both of them.

On a broader level, there can hardly have been more dramatic circumstances to accompany the debut of this film. Hitting American theaters on October 24, 1962, its release coincided with the height of the Cuban missile crisis, a time when many Americans feared—quite correctly according to previously secret documents that have since been released—that a nuclear nightmare could occur at any moment. Although the public remained relatively calm during the crisis, a quiet sense of panic was nonetheless evident. Many Americans flocked to supermarkets in order to stock up with provisions in the event that war broke out, even if most citizens tried to go about their business and carry on normal life during those tense days. In such a context, *The Manchurian Candidate* was surely not much respite for a fearful public, but the currency of the subject matter could not be seriously debated. Fortunately, the Cuban missile crisis ended a few days later with the Soviet agreement to remove its missiles from the island, and life returned to normalcy in most ways. But a portentous context had been established for a film that was to remain a fascinating cultural artifact in future years.

Of course, the aspect of the film that has proven to be most intriguing over time is not the brainwashing theme, but rather the assassination subject matter. In this, *The Manchurian Candidate* was unintentionally prescient. When John F. Kennedy was assassinated only a year after the film's initial release, its plot seemed more troubling than entertaining. And the idea—even if it had been lost on many viewers at the time—that a film dealing with assassination could have satirical undertones no longer seemed fitting.

Indeed, the conspiratorial nature of the movie's assassination plot, in which foreign enemies have "conditioned" ordinary Americans to do their violent bidding, was inflammatory. This was all the more true since it was not then clear—and for many people even today, not ever clear—that the real assassination of the president was not the product of a sinister, convoluted international conspiracy. The upshot of this was that national trauma and unease prompted by Kennedy's death radically changed the context in which audiences could be expected to interpret Frankenheimer's film of the previous year.

The fate of *The Manchurian Candidate* in the years after its debut deserves mention. The film was released before widespread cable and satellite television, with their dozens and then hundreds of channels, and before the advent of home-viewing technologies such as video tapes, DVDs, and computer downloads. In the early 1960s, once movies left the theaters, there were limited options to see them again. They might be re-released or continue making the rounds of second- and third-tier movie houses, or they might be licensed for television broadcast on one of the few networks or perhaps directly to a local television station. After its initial run, however, it was not unusual for a movie to largely fade from view, only occasionally resurfacing.

Yet, it was unusual for a popular movie that had received considerable press coverage and many good reviews to disappear completely from the scene. But although *The Manchurian Candidate* had received good notices and was reasonably popular, it did disappear from public view at some point after the assassination of the president. Screenwriter Axelrod claimed it was shelved very shortly after the tragedy in Dallas because "having an assassination picture floating around seemed to be in grotesque bad taste. Particularly since Frank [Sinatra] had been friends with the president."[10] Other accounts differ about when the film was pulled from circulation, however, and some put the date years after the original release.[11] The exact details about *The Manchurian Candidate*'s disappearance from public view are still not clear, but many accounts do concur that there was a specific decision to remove the movie from circulation. Such accounts imply that the explosive subject matter was the primary reason, although it is sometimes suggested that business reasons also came into play. (Sinatra, who at one time owned rights to the film, had an accounting dispute with United Artists, which, some people suggest, may be part of the explanation.[12])

Still, the story of *The Manchurian Candidate*'s disappearance from public view has since taken on nearly urban-legend characteristics. This is indicative of how the movie's reputation became entwined in the public fascination with intrigue and conspiracy that grew more prominent after 1963. Frank Sinatra's links to the president, which have been well documented, undoubtedly caused some uneasiness about the film. Some reports suggest that Sinatra learned that Kennedy's named assassin, Lee Harvey Oswald, had watched *Suddenly* (the earlier assassination film in which Sinatra starred) shortly before the assassination, and that this caused the actor to have both films pulled from circulation.[13] In other versions of the story, the decision appears to be a more measured one, in which the studio, as much as or more than the star, deemed the film had run its course anyway.

Regardless, the film largely drifted from public consciousness, although it was not completely forgotten. Over time, popular culture in the United States embraced Kennedy's memory and revealed a fascination with his assassination. At the same time, Sinatra grew from star to living legend. These topics seemed naturally to converge in Frankenheimer's movie, which though not seen over the years was still occasionally discussed. By the late 1980s, Sinatra seems to have dropped whatever objections he may have had and studio executives decided that the time was ripe to rerelease the film. (By then, not only was public fascination with the JFK assassination conspiracy theories the subject of mainstream conversation, but there was a huge new market for older films created by the success of home video technology.) With much fanfare and press attention, then, *The Manchurian Candidate* resurfaced in American theaters in a rerelease in 1988, along with mass distribution of the movie on videocassette. Its years away from public view had only enhanced its reputation, and its long inaccessibility had created a curiosity factor that gave the movie a newfound impact in the popular culture's embrace of conspiracies, assassination stories, and star power. But that was in the future.

At the beginning of 1963, however, the future again looked brighter. Having stared down the Soviets in the Cuban missile crisis several months earlier, it seemed that the world had stepped back from the brink of calamity and that cooler heads could prevail. On the international front, there was a sense of relief.

Domestically, however, the seeds of social unrest were already planted. American society was headed to a period of unrest and massive change. The burgeoning Civil Rights movement was coming to a head, and the Women's Movement, the Vietnam War, and other sources of social tension lay on the horizon. Indeed, in the coming months and years, the internal dynamics of American society began to respond to the fissures that had been developing for some time. Cultural clashes based on generation, race, gender, politics, and ideology, all of which had been festering for years, would dramatically alter the national climate by decade's end. In January of 1963, however, most of those changes remained in the future.

DR. NO

Shortly after *The Manchurian Candidate* opened in American theaters, a new movie premiered in Great Britain that marked a major change in the way that conspiracy was portrayed on screen. It would not be until the following spring, in May 1963 that this film appeared in American theaters. The film was the durable *Dr. No*, and it was the introduction of novelist Ian Fleming's character James Bond to the big screen. It was soon apparent that *Dr. No* was a sensation, which in some ways coincided neatly with a similar aura that John F. Kennedy had succeeded in projecting from the White House.

The well-known character of James Bond, which is now fully ensconced in popular culture, is a charismatic British secret agent. He has been given the numerical designation of 007 by his superiors, indicating he is one of a select few agents that has been given the oft-mentioned "license to kill." In his capacity as a superspy, Bond is thrust into the most extreme and dangerous situations. His superiors do not necessarily expect him to survive.

Facing danger and circumstances of life and death on a global as well as personal level, James Bond (played by Sean Connery) can be counted on to act with aplomb. What is more, he reeks with traditional (in today's terms, perhaps more accurately, reactionary) male swagger and machismo. Indeed, throughout this picture (as well as later entries in the Bond series), clear and present dangers scarcely interrupt the lead character's pursuit of fleeting sexual encounters with the attractive young women he meets along the way. (In ways that are perhaps unflattering, the hyper-sexual Bond of motion pictures mirrors the more sensational aspects of John F. Kennedy's later public persona, especially in the cynical incarnations of it that appeared long after the 1960s.) Indeed, the many women characters primarily serve as romantic foils for Bond.

Dr. No and its sequels were immediate sensations that captured the interest of American movie-goers. Such films presented an exciting and glamorous take on the dreary fears of the Cold War. They suggested that the forces of evil could be overcome without even the need to give up sarcastic witticisms or to abstain from an exotic nightlife.[14] No matter that Bond was British, since for American audiences he was clearly a surrogate for the American position in the ongoing Cold War. True, American secret agents, when they appear at all in the stories, are placed in subsidiary roles and clearly come across to viewers as secondary characters. This didn't diminish enthusiasm for the Bond character among American audiences, however. So fully did the character enter the popular imagination that by the mid-1960s American children could play with small plastic James Bond toys or collect James Bond trading cards.

Despite the many surface distractions, the plot of *Dr. No* is squarely concerned with international conspiracy and intrigue. The movie follows Bond as he tries to thwart a plan formulated by an immensely powerful group that calls itself SPECTRE, an acronym for the exceedingly plodding name of Special Executor for Counter-Intelligence, Terrorism, Revenge, and Extortion. This group has only one goal in mind, as the Bond character notes: "world domination."

Because of their deep penetration into American popular culture, the Bond films played an important part in transmitting a now-changing version of conspiracy theory into the American mainstream. The theme is omnipresent in the narrative of *Dr. No* and most of the other Bond films. Yet, despite the fact that it lies in plain view, it is sometimes overlooked, perhaps because of the distractions presented by the picturesque locales, colorful action sequences, science fiction-like story lines, and the lead character's libido.

A look at the plot of *Dr. No* reveals how the conspiracy theme of the film is woven into other plot elements. The story begins with the disappearance of an intelligence operative who had been working undercover in Jamaica. Fearing the worst, Bond is summoned from an upper class London casino. He is told that the missing operative had been gathering intelligence, which was to be shared with the CIA and which may have something to do with efforts to disrupt NASA's planned space flights. To solve the mystery, Bond is dispatched to the Caribbean, where he is to meet a CIA agent with more information.

Action, more than intrigue, soon takes center stage in the story. No sooner does Bond arrive in Jamaica than the driver of a car allegedly sent to bring Bond to the embassy diverts his route to a remote area, where he and Bond struggle. Before Bond can find out who was behind this attempt on his life, the driver commits suicide by swallowing a cyanide capsule that was concealed in a cigarette.

After this encounter, Bond eventually arrives at the embassy to begin his investigation. He quickly establishes that the man and his secretary have probably been killed.

The next sections of the film deal with Bond's efforts to establish why the operative would have been killed. It comes to light that the man had recently taken up fishing, or so it was said, and that he had frequently chartered a boat to take him near a small offshore island called Crab Key. Bond then learns that the missing man was not fishing at all, but gathering mineral specimens. Some of the rocks recovered from Crab Key were radioactive, a fact that seemed to suggest that Crab Key was not what it seemed.

The CIA agent assigned to help Bond initially dismisses Bond's interest in Crab Key. The island is the private property of a Chinese man named Dr. No, who forbids visitors. It does not otherwise seem threatening despite local lore warning of a fire-breathing monster guarding the island, a story the CIA agent thinks was created by Dr. No to frighten intruders away. Crab Key seems compelling to Bond, however, and he makes arrangements to travel there under cover of darkness.

Shortly after putting ashore, Bond encounters an attractive young woman (played by Ursula Andress) who is collecting shells on the beach. The intruders are soon discovered, however, and a billowing voice orders them to surrender. They successfully elude their pursuers temporarily, but later a clanging, clumsily disguised vehicle armed with flamethrowers returns for them. Having little choice, Bond and the woman surrender.

The final third of the movie takes a futuristic turn. After Bond and the woman are taken to a hidden complex, details of the plot and of Dr. No's identity are revealed. Implying that Bond will not live to use the information against him, Dr. No informs Bond that he is working for the sinister SPECTRE organization and that they aim to take over the world. Bond is not impressed, dismissing the complicated, technologically advanced scheme as little more than a tired old story. An angered Dr. No then sends Bond off with the guards, apparently to be killed.

Bond escapes, however, and makes his way to a huge control room. From there, a powerful, nuclear-powered weapon is being prepared for an imminent launch. Its goal is to disrupt a NASA mission.

After learning of the evil scheme, Bond springs into action in typical action-film fashion. The British agent creates general chaos in the control room and then overloads the nuclear reactor. In the climactic scenes, Dr. No is killed, the plot foiled, and Bond escapes with the woman.

It is hard to imagine a more sinister conspiracy than one designed to conquer the whole world, but the film exudes little feeling of menace or threat. The cool, sophisticated hero aloofly dismisses even potentially lethal confrontations with sarcastic comments. In *Dr. No*, global conspiracy is presented as little more than a bar room brawl. And in the context of the film, the audience is not surprised to see the film's hero often taking shocking plot developments lightly.

It is this stance, seemingly laden with irony, that makes *Dr. No* a major turning point in screen portrayals of the conspiracy theory theme. Rather than the anxiety-filled drama or melodrama of earlier Cold War-era conspiracy themed films, the mood is lighter, the danger more entertaining than threatening, and the villainy of conspirators so wrapped up in blinding egotism that it is not difficult to defeat. Yet, the tone is not cynical at its core. The film possesses a modernist outlook, showing an abiding confidence that the problems can and will be solved and that potentially destructive technologies can be harnessed for the greater good.

Overall, the movie suggests that what is progressive and modern can defeat what is conspiratorial and evil. It demonstrates a point of view in which the open societies of the West will overcome the secretive, scheming enemies in the East or anywhere else. This may seem an ironic stance for a supposed "spy" movie, but this outlook is apparent even in the espionage plot. Recall that the spies in *Dr. No* and its successor movies are spies more in name than anything else. In the narrative, an astonishing number of characters seem to know all about the supposedly secret agents. It may prompt a viewer to wonder why the pretense of secrecy is maintained at all. But the darkness of evil conspirators is easily defeated by the film's hero, who officially has a secret status but who does not seem to have any special attachment to it.

In the end, *Dr. No,* like the follow-up Bond films *Goldfinger, Thunderball,* and many later sequels, showed a picture of conspiracy that was not so much the stuff of fear as an entertaining diversion. It was a fictional world that was more fun than threatening. Real life, however, didn't follow this lead.

UPHEAVAL

The assassination of John F. Kennedy in November of 1963 sent shock-waves across the nation and around the world. But there were other important events that November. One of these events, occurring just days before John F. Kennedy's death, had the makings of a conspiracy myth of its own. Earlier in the month, a military *coup d'etat* toppled an American ally, South Vietnam's leader Ngo Dinh Diem. The conflict in Vietnam had not yet boiled over into the divisive spectacle that it later became, but already the United States was deeply involved monetarily and, for several years, militarily in the form of American "advisors." The Domino Theory that had come to prominence in the 1950s was still a major influence on U.S. policy, and when it seemed that the increasing unpopularity of Diem's regime was contributing to poor progress in combating the communists, U.S. support for him wavered.

In fact, South Vietnam's American-backed struggle against the communist insurgency was faltering, a development made worse by the increasing disillusionment that many South Vietnamese citizens felt toward Diem's government and its policies that were sometimes seen as harsh and unfair. A group of South Vietnamese military officials plotted to overthrow Diem, but they were reluctant to proceed without some indication that South Vietnam would continue to have U.S. support if they were successful in their bid to oust Diem. The coup's leaders received word that Diem no longer had American support and that the U.S. would not stand in the way. (Support had been waning for some time. The American ambassador, Henry Cabot Lodge, had sent a memorandum to Washington in August in which he reported: "We are launched on a course from which there is no respectable turning back: the overthrow of the Diem government."[15]) Accordingly, they put their plan into action on the first day of November. Diem and his brother, who was the despised head of the secret police, escaped, but they were soon apprehended. The following day, November 2, 1963, the bodies of both men were found; they had been stabbed and shot.

Only weeks before his own death, Kennedy seemed surprised and saddened by this grisly fate of America's ally in South Vietnam. Speaking of Diem and his government, he explained to a friend, "They were in a difficult position. They did the best they could for their country."[16]

The details of Diem's downfall remain murky, even though there seems little doubt that the conspirators believed they had the backing of at least some officials in the U.S. government. The story of Diem's overthrow and death, and the role of American officials in it, might have generated much more attention from conspiracy theory–minded observers than it did, but Kennedy's assassination only weeks later assured that this episode in South Vietnam would be overshadowed in the United States for a very long time. Today, few Americans remember Diem or that he met his death in a violent coup. The death of the American president, however, remains a focal point in American memory.

Indeed, November 1963 is mostly recalled for the assassination of the American president just days after the murder of South Vietnam's Diem. The president's death in the context of an ongoing Cold War with the communist world prompted many questions. Who was involved? Was there a conspiracy? Not unlike the speculations of conspiracy theorists in later years, in the immediate aftermath of the assassination such questions were front and center for the nation's most powerful people as well as ordinary citizens.

The story of John F. Kennedy's death is widely known and has spawned a mountain of articles, television and film documentaries, and books. Indeed, no other event in the traumatic years of the Cold War has inspired as much speculation and intrigue. This event, far more than any other, is the linchpin in the modern ascent of conspiracy theory in American consciousness. And though it took some time to fully materialize, it was Kennedy's assassination, and the questions that many people felt remained unanswered after it, that eventually propelled conspiracy theory into the full daylight of mainstream American thought.

The trauma of November 22, 1963, monopolized public attention for the next days. Soon, the world came to know of a man named Lee Harvey Oswald, a seeming misfit who was also an ex-Marine. Oswald, an employee at the Book Depository building from which the fatal shots were said to have fired, had drawn suspicion when seen leaving the building, and he was later identified as having left work early that day. Before his capture several hours later, he murdered a Dallas police officer in front of witnesses. He was quickly apprehended after a brief struggle in a Dallas movie theater.

News crews from television, radio, and the print media swarmed to the Dallas police station, where Oswald was held for interrogation. Two days later, on November 24, he was escorted by Dallas police in preparation for transfer to the Dallas County jail. As television crews looked on, a man named Jack Ruby lunged forward. Then, in front of television cameras that were broadcasting live from the basement of the Dallas police headquarters, Ruby shot Oswald. He was rushed to the hospital, but he did not survive. Only two days after the president's death, Oswald, the one-time soldier who later seemed to have turned on his country and had mysterious connections to the Soviet Union and Cuba, was dead. Although his death may not have been an unwelcome development for the grieving American public, he died before trial, before loose ends could be resolved. There seemed to be many unanswered questions.

Ruby, Oswald's murderer, was a somewhat shadowy figure, and this later proved to have a powerful effect in fueling conspiracy-minded speculations. The owner of a Dallas nightclub, he was known to, and seemed to sometimes associate with, members of the Dallas police department. More suspiciously to some, he also seemed to have hazy underworld connections.

Oswald's death led to more questions and more mysteries. In the span of two days, then, the youthful president of a nation had died, and the seeds for full-blown conspiracy theorizing had been sown.

However these events may strike the modern observer, in their day they signaled profound fear, in addition to the more obvious shock and grief. The anxieties of the Cold War had conditioned the American public to fear the worst: invasion, betrayal, nuclear disaster. Yet, such dire fates had largely been avoided. With the assassination of the president, however, reality presented a starkly different face: tragedy and calamity that were not avoided. The abstract fear of previous years had materialized. Now it was left for the nation's leaders to sort out the truth, to put those rumors that were judged to be unfounded to rest, and to try to restore some confidence and sense of normalcy to a seriously rattled public.

The official version of events was presented to the American public only ten months after the assassination. It came in a formidable document entitled *Report of the President's Commission on the Assassination of President Kennedy*, more commonly known as the Warren Commission report.

Carrying the imprimatur of the federal government, the report was the result of an investigation launched only days after the assassination. The process began on November 29, 1963, the date on which newly sworn-in President Lyndon Johnson issued Executive Order 11130, which authorized a high-profile government investigation into Kennedy's murder. The bipartisan effort brought together many stalwart members of the political establishment, lending an air of authority and impartiality to the proceedings. Chaired by Earl Warren, then Chief Justice of the Supreme Court, the commission also included two members of the United States Senate (Richard B. Russell and John Sherman Cooper), two members of the House of Representatives (Hale Boggs and future-president Gerald R. Ford), and other leading Washington figures.

Two aspects of the assassination would prove to be points of contention in future thinking. First, there were the details of the shooting itself. The time, direction, and number of shots fired would later be disputed and form one of the most basic elements of skepticism about the official account. Along these same lines came questions about the trajectory of bullets, the position of the president's body during and after the moment when shots were fired, the follow-up actions of security and medical personnel, as well as many others.

The importance of the Warren Report can hardly be overestimated. It was later a wellspring of conspiracy theory thinking and is worth considering. The following sections, which are here edited to focus on the main narrative, are instructive:

> The motorcade ... proceeded through residential neighborhoods, stopping twice at the President's request to greet well-wishers among the friendly crowds. . . .

> At a speed of about 11 miles per hour . . . [the president's car] started down the gradual descent toward a railroad overpass under which the motorcade would proceed before reaching the Stemmons Freeway. The front of the Texas School Book Depository was now on the President's right, and he waved to the crowd assembled there as he passed the building. Dealey Plaza—an open, landscaped area marking the western end of downtown Dallas stretched out to the President's left . . .

> Seconds later shots resounded in rapid succession. The President's hands moved to his neck. He appeared to stiffen momentarily and lurch slightly forward in his seat. A bullet had entered the base of the back of his neck slightly to the right of the spine. It traveled downward and exited from the front of the neck, causing a nick in the left lower portion of the knot in the President's necktie. [Governor Connally, also riding in the car, was also shot.] . . . Another bullet then struck President Kennedy in the rear portion of his head, causing a massive and fatal wound. The President fell to the left into Mrs. Kennedy's lap. . . .

> At Parkland [hospital], the President was immediately treated by a team of physicians. . . . The doctors noted irregular breathing movements and a possible heartbeat, although they could not detect a pulsebeat. They observed the extensive wound in the President's head and a small wound approximately one-fourth inch in diameter in the lower third of his neck. . . . At 1 p.m., after all heart activity ceased and the Last Rites were administered by a priest, President Kennedy was pronounced dead.[17]

In addition to addressing questions about how the president was shot and what the follow-up actions had been, the Warren Commission also sought to answer an even bigger question: Did Oswald act alone? In answering this question, the Warren Commission confirmed the so-called "lone gunman" version of events, refuting suspicions that some sort of conspiracy had been at work. The report summarized the commission's findings about the question this way:

> Based upon the investigation . . . the Commission concluded that there is no credible evidence that Lee Harvey Oswald was part of a conspiracy to assassinate President Kennedy. . . . Review of Oswald's life and activities since 1959, although productive in illuminating the character of Lee Harvey Oswald . . . did not produce any meaningful evidence of a conspiracy. The Commission discovered no evidence that the Soviet Union or Cuba were involved in the assassination of President Kennedy. Nor did the Commission's investigation of Jack Ruby produce any grounds for believing that Ruby's killing of Oswald was part

of a conspiracy. The conclusion that there is no evidence of a conspiracy was also reached independently by Dean Rusk, the Secretary of State; Robert S. McNamara, the Secretary of Defense; C. Douglas Dillon, the Secretary of the Treasury; Robert F. Kennedy, the Attorney General; J. Edgar Hoover, the Director of the FBI; John A. McCone, the Director of the CIA; and James J. Rowley, the Chief of the Secret Service. . . . [18]

Thus, according to the official version of events, the case, traumatic though it was, was closed. The lone perpetrator was dead, and while not every detail was fully illuminated, the story was plainly discernible: Oswald had acted alone.

In the aftermath of the assassination, memory of November 1963 came to be dominated by the death of John Kennedy, whose reputation soon rose to stratospheric heights. He had won the presidency by only a slight margin, but his passing was interpreted as martyrdom, and his presidency of "1,000 days" passed into popular legend. He would, for more than a generation, be revered by much of the public. The days of his presidency, which often had been perilous, were remembered in a glowing, idealized manner, sometimes as the modern incarnation of King Arthur's mythic Camelot, which had been the subject of a popular Broadway play a few years earlier.

The release of the Warren Report reassured much of the American public, which had not yet become as wary and cynical about government as would be the case in later years. It could not change the traumatic outcome, of course, but the Report did seem to indicate that America could carry on with its business, secure in the knowledge that it was only one criminal mind, rather than a shadowy array of dark forces, that had carried out the evil deed. As it had done before, the nation would pick up the pieces and move forward.

Yet, many people were not completely satisfied with the official version of events. Some people were perhaps only mildly skeptical of its investigations, wondering if in haste the commission had left out details that would add further clarity to the event. Others came to be much more skeptical. To those people, both soon after the Report's first release and far into the future, the official findings were much more problematic. At best, the conclusions seemed inept; at worst, they were evidence of far darker and more dangerous forces. Indeed, the assassination of John F. Kennedy was not only a pivotal point in American history, it became the fountainhead of modern conspiracy theorizing in American culture. The ambiguities, unresolved details, and missing information in the Warren Report, while never appearing to significantly cast doubt on its findings to many people, became for others the Holy Grail of conspiracy.

THE ABRUPT END OF A BRIEF ERA

During Kennedy's brief presidency, American society had negotiated highs and lows, and fears of conspiracy that seemed so prevalent a decade earlier subsided to a noticeable degree. There were dangerous crises, but before the president's assassination shocked the nation, it stared down these crises. For some people, the spirit of the New Frontier seemed to suggest that America's moral dignity and technological resourcefulness could handle any problem.

Looking back at conspiracy theory in films of the early 1960s, the progression of the theme is noticeable. Movies such as *Advise and Consent* and *The Manchurian Candidate* significantly updated the conspiracy theme's treatment on film. The aura of anxiety and fear that was so prevalent in 1950s conspiracy films was lessened. These movies were evidence that popular culture was processing the raw emotion, which had been evident in many earlier works. Such films remade conspiracy story lines with wit and urbanity, adding a filmic self-consciousness. They suggested a reduction of generalized, overarching Cold War fears into a more manageable and human scale. Even as real-world events such as the Bay of Pigs invasion and the Cuban missile crisis added frightening dimensions to international politics, these movies lacked hysteria. They did not fuel panic. Sometimes, they even seemed to wink knowingly, even as they told tales of murderous plots.

Meanwhile, the introduction of secret agent films, such as the James Bond movies, sometimes added a light touch and spirit of adventure to the conspiracy theme. Indeed, though in the Bond films the villains inhabit a dark, claustrophobic world, the hero certainly does not. Although some other spy films had a more sinister feel, the Bond movies had none of this. They suggested a world in which the response to conspiracy need not be one of dread and anxiety. In fact, other than some heroics and modern gadgetry, defeating a conspiratorial enemy seemed to require little deviation from life's pleasure at all. Such movies were undoubtedly popular partly because they drained the fear and anxiety out of tense and dangerous situations. In telling their stories in the ways they did, these movies reinforced the idea that conspiracy was not necessarily something to be feared as much as it was a decade earlier.

The death of the president reverberated throughout the American society, of course, including its popular culture. Soon, new anxieties and fears would turn up on screen.

Shock and Upheaval

The assassination of the president shook America to its core, but life went on, and with it, politics. Unexpectedly assuming the presidency under tragic circumstances, Lyndon Johnson brought a strong interest in promoting a progressive social agenda that in some ways harkened back to the spirit of the New Deal.

Yet, international affairs soon intruded. In August of 1964, two U.S. destroyers sailing off the coast of North Vietnam in the Gulf of Tonkin were attacked by vessels of the communist North Vietnam, creating an international crisis. Johnson immediately sought Congressional approval for retaliatory military action. Congress complied swiftly by passing the Tonkin Gulf Resolution, which granted the president sweeping powers to conduct military operations, essentially giving Johnson the power to make war without a formal declaration of war. American soldiers had been stationed in South Vietnam for some time for the purposes of advising and supporting the pro-U.S. regime in South Vietnam in its struggle against North Vietnam. In the months after the Tonkin Gulf Resolution, however, American participation in the conflict began to dramatically escalate. This eventually led to a major American combat role and the full-blown war that was to become so divisive in America.

Even though he had only assumed the presidency a few months earlier, by mid-1964 Johnson looked ahead to the presidential election that was fast approaching in November. Republican Barry Goldwater mounted a strong challenge to unseat Johnson, but to no avail. When Election Day came only twelve months after the assassination, the American people were still grappling with the sudden death of the previous president. They were not yet ready to make a significant break with the past. Accordingly, after a hotly contested and sometimes hyperbolic campaign season, voters selected Johnson by an overwhelming margin.

Despite the tragic circumstances under which he originally inherited the Oval Office, Johnson now believed he had a strong mandate of his own. Always a shrewd politician, he set out to capitalize on his victory quickly. He knew that his mandate could diminish, and so he aimed to obtain approval for his ambitious social agenda before the traditional "honeymoon" with Congress (also under firm Democratic control) or the citizenry wore off. Although the newly elected chief executive may have realized that the glow surrounding his presidency would inevitably diminish over time, he probably did not yet realize how far he would fall in the coming months.

POST-ASSASSINATION TREATMENT OF CONSPIRACY THEME ON SCREEN

Eighteen months earlier, in spring of 1963, the first James Bond movie adventure, *Dr. No*, had premiered in American theaters. Featuring the fantastic exploits of a superspy, it was an entertaining but essentially diversionary tale. In many ways, the image of fictional secret agent James Bond was thoroughly consistent with the cool and sophisticated aura surrounding the Kennedy White House and the New Frontier spirit of the times.[1] Using high technology and an acerbic wit to outsmart international villains, James Bond plainly confronted evil and dispatched villains, all without losing his sense of humor and seldom breaking into a sweat. Still, at its heart, the story line of *Dr. No* was a modern incarnation of conspiracy, now stripped of paranoia and instead wrapped in an urbane aesthetic.

Dr. No was quickly followed by sequels. *From Russia with Love*, which was released in the United States in 1964, follows Bond's efforts to steal a Soviet decoding machine before it can be snatched by the sinister SPECTRE organization. *Goldfinger* involved a plot to steal America's gold reserves from Fort Knox. It had its American release later the same year. *Thunderball*, which involved a scheme to steal nuclear bombs, was issued a year later in 1965.

All the early James Bond films presented essentially the same theme. The villains in these movies aimed their sights high, usually leading a conspiracy that sets out to achieve global domination. The scheming is on a grand scale, but the colossal plans generate only a mild fear and apprehension for some of the characters, and none for the hero. Instead, the world that the James Bond movies present is for the most part a parody of geopolitical realities of the 1960s. There are dangerous enemies with cold, calculating plots involving death and destruction. Bond is always a cool and sophisticated hero, however, and he takes even the most outlandishly dangerous situations in stride.

Indeed, Bond never seems very worried, even when repeatedly facing death. By extension, it seems that if Bond doesn't worry, why should the audience? For viewers, it was far more pleasant to bask in the scenery, the handsome and beautiful people, and the good-natured banter, which Bond seems to muster even when it appears he was about to die. In short, this fictional movie-world was an escape from reality for viewers of the era. The Bond movies did feature conspiracy, but it was conspiracy of a special type: cold, calculating, but ultimately doomed to failure. It was not a picture of conspiracy that was rooted in fear and paranoia. If anything, the ridiculous extremes in which the conspiracies are shown suggests that global conspiracy was somewhat silly.

The Bond films continued to be popular after the death of the president, but the context had changed. Indeed, the groundwork for more serious in-carnations of the conspiracy theory theme in American culture became firmer after 1963, even though more fanciful versions of the conspiracy continued to appear on screen. Since the end of World War II, the anxieties of the Cold War had been a wellspring for the imaginations of Hollywood writers and directors. This resulted in conspiracy-themed productions across several genres of moviemaking, ranging from relatively realistic dramas to thrillers to science fiction. By the early 1960s, the fictional world of movies was coming to terms, at least in part, with the often fantastical visions of conspiracy and paranoia that had erupted in the 1950s.

Now, however, history had intervened. The assassination in November 1963 confronted the public with questions and anxieties. For some, it seemed to be an increasingly plausible possibility that the dark dreams of the past had played a part in John Kennedy's murder. Although that reading of the assassination was downplayed by the Warren Commission, the context of the times proved more powerful than denials from a presidential commission. Uneasiness remained in the air, even though on the surface life had seemingly returned to normal. The national trauma was a fertile breeding ground, rich in suspicions and anxieties. It played a large part in fueling a long series of conspiracy theories about that tragic event. Already by 1964, theories about conspiracy and assassination set out on a trajectory of their own, on a path that would prove to be unstoppable for decades to come. In the mid-1960s, however, how the film industry would respond to the theme was not yet known.

The stark contrast between the newer, almost flippant treatment of conspir-acy theory in such movies as the James Bond series, and the real-world suspi-cions prompted by the Kennedy assassination could not have been more strik-ing. For example, as the saga continued in the second Bond film, *Goldfinger*, the hero becomes involved in another far-fetched scheme by powerful, but colorful, criminal conspirators. The escapist theme again provided audiences with a glimpse into a dangerous world that did not really offer much real dan-ger. In the meantime, however, a darker, more jarring picture of conspiracy was being readied for release.

SEVEN DAYS IN MAY

Director John Frankenheimer had popularized the idea of an American assassin controlled by sinister foreign powers in his thriller *The Manchurian Candidate*. Those themes remained available for cultural consumption and transformation, and, indeed, the real-life assassination prompted fears along those lines. The Warren Commission had taken special care to address the question of foreign influences on Lee Harvey Oswald, the man they identified as the lone killer.

In 1964, Frankenheimer issued another film with a conspiratorial theme, *Seven Days in May*.[2] This new movie possessed underlying premises that were even more disturbing than the nightmarish brainwashing scheme in *The Manchurian Candidate*. The new film located the enemy conspirators not in the capital of some enemy nation, but rather, from within the heart of the United States.

The story revolves around a plot by American military leaders to overthrow the president and seize control of the United States government. To audiences of 1964, the idea may have seemed very far-fetched. Importantly, then, Frankenheimer's film helped introduce the theme of betrayal and conspiracy at the very highest levels of government into the mainstream. Indeed, ideas that once may have seemed patently absurd are today not far from the commonplace in conspiracy theory thinking. But in 1964 the basic premise seemed unthinkable. Few Americans seriously believed that the American way of life could face a greater threat from its own leaders than from real or imagined external enemies.

In *Seven Days in May*, the American people are bitterly divided over an agreement that the president of the United States, Jordan Lyman (played by veteran actor Fredric March), has made with the Soviets with respect to disarmament. Disapproval of the president's intentions is widespread. One opposition group secretly wants to take drastic action. It is led by Air Force General James Scott (played by Burt Lancaster) and includes members of Congress, powerful figures in the media, and senior Pentagon military leaders.

The general's assistant is Col. "Jiggs" Casey (played by Kirk Douglas). A straight-laced career officer steeped in tradition, he is unaware of the secret group. A consummate professional, he believes that it is his job—and indeed, the job of all the military—to strictly adhere to the policies set forth by the civilian government. Accordingly, he separates his privately held views on the disarmament treaty, which are basically in agreement with Scott, from what he sees as his constitutional duty to carry out the orders of the civilian leadership, even if he does not agree with them politically.

As he goes about his routine duties, Jiggs slowly learns of several odd Pentagon communications. At first, these seem harmless, but there seems to be an air of secrecy among top officers and their aides. Jiggs becomes mildly suspicious. He eventually learns about a new unit called ECOMCON (Emergency Communications Control). Jiggs is perplexed when by chance he encounters an officer from the unit, who offhandedly remarks how curious he thinks it is that ECOMCON seems to be preparing to seize control of the government.

Gradually, as these and other odd facts come to his attention, Jiggs senses something ominous. Finally, he concludes that dissatisfaction with the disarmament policy has become so severe among key leaders in Washington that a secret group is plotting to depose the president and take control of the government. Jiggs believes the coup is quickly approaching and that there is little time to mull over the evidence. Hoping he is wrong but feeling duty-bound to report his suspicions, he makes a late-night visit to the White House to personally inform the president.

At first, the president and his advisors find Jiggs' claim unbelievable, but Jiggs has recovered a note—left behind at a closed-door meeting among the top military conspirators—that mentions the ECOMCON unit. Since the president and his advisors have no knowledge of this unit, a quiet investigation is launched. The president assigns two close associates to find the truth. One is sent to find out if the ECOMCON base exists. The other is dispatched overseas to meet with an admiral, who seems to know something about what is planned even though he does not appear to be directly involved.

At the Pentagon, General Scott has become suspicious and orders Jiggs to take a short leave so that he does not discover anything about the plot. Unable to follow up with what is happening in Scott's office, Jiggs instead tracks down a woman with whom the married general has previously had a secret affair. Jiggs soon acquires compromising letters, which Scott had previously written to the woman.

Meanwhile, the senator discovers the location of the base in an isolated desert area. When he finally enters the compound, however, he is taken into protective custody and held incommunicado. After escaping, however, the senator returns to Washington with an eyewitness report of a base that is so secret that even the president had been unaware of its existence.

With details of the conspiracy confirmed, the president determines that General Scott, as the ringleader, must be confronted. Although some key evidence is subsequently lost, the president believes that the love letters Jiggs has uncovered can be used to force the general's resignation. (In a bow to the morality of the day, the characters show great regret at the prospect of resorting to such measures.)

As an unsuspecting Scott prepares to carry out the coup, he is abruptly summoned to the White House where he learns that the president has discovered the truth. In a tense confrontation, the president demands that Scott and all involved immediately resign from their positions. Scott scoffs at this suggestion, figuring that the president must not have much evidence, since nothing concrete has yet been presented.

In the midst of this confrontation, however, the president receives dramatic news: the missing evidence has been located. The arrogant Scott refuses to back down, however. Now overcome with what appears to be advanced mega-lomania, he announces to the president that the population would greatly prefer him anyway and that it is only a matter of time before he will lead the nation to stronger, better days. But it is too late for the general. His allies have abandoned him and the general is left lacking the means to fulfill his plan. He leaves in defeat.

The president is happy to have broken up the conspiracy, of course, but he takes little pleasure in his victory. In one of the film's most interesting twists, he concludes that the public should never know how close the U.S. government had come to being overthrown by a military plot. In these dangerous times, he reasoned, it would be unwise to give the public any reason to doubt the strength and vigor of the U.S. Constitution, lest their confidence be hopelessly undermined.

Seven Days in May shows how a fiendish conspiracy to depose the elected American president is thwarted. What is more, this is followed with a new conspiracy of sorts—admittedly more benign—to implement a massive cover-up, making sure that the true events never became known. According to the president's reasoning in the film, knowledge of the conspiracy and its near-success would so rattle the nation that awareness of it could damage public confidence and, in a way, pose a new peril to society. It was better, he claimed, to keep the entire matter secret.

The secrecy-cloaked ending to the story is an odd facet to a story that extols constitutional values. In retrospect, it is all the more remarkable since it provides early evidence in American popular culture for an impulse that would, within a matter of a few years, take firm hold in American society. This is the suggestion that leaders cannot be counted upon to be forthcoming with information and that the unsuspecting public can expect to be manipulated through the careful selection of what knowledge is made known by officials.

Though in the story the president's decision to maintain secrecy is presented as a relatively innocuous example of this impulse, *Seven Days in May* is one of the earliest high-profile venues in which the idea is presented to mainstream America at all. And so even though the president and his men are successful in thwarting a plot against the constitutional democracy, even the heroes of the story see nothing inherently objectionable to withholding information that a viewer might reasonably assume was a vital piece of American history. An implicit suggestion seems to be that the known, revealed history of the nation may be only a part of the story and that other significant parts remain hidden.

With this film, Frankenheimer pushed the general theme of conspiracy more prominently into the foreground, continuing with ideas he explored in *The Manchurian Candidate*. As he further explored the theme, it underwent a significant transformation. The fear and paranoia of conspiracy no longer emerges from hostile foreign enemies, but rather from within the nation. By placing the heart of the plot deep within the most central institutions of the United States—in the very institutions with which Americans entrust their security—Frankenheimer suggests that the enemy to be feared may not only be the external enemy, or even others within American society. Instead, the film implies that Americans may be their own enemy. Although the implications of the finale may have been missed by many members of the original audience, in hindsight it is clear that the narrative reveals that even victories may conceal the truth. With secretive villains and with heroes that fear what the truth would do to America, it is clear that trust is a relative concept. The upshot is that *Seven Days in May* slyly introduces a cynical interpretation of an American society that, on the surface, looks to be sound and secure.

Seven Days in May is, in almost all respects, a film equal or superior to the director's more well-known film *The Manchurian Candidate*. In terms of acting, the fine performances of Frank Sinatra, Angela Lansbury, and several other cast members provided a firm foundation for the psychologically thrilling story of the earlier film. Still, the performances in *Seven Days in May*, especially from leads Burt Lancaster and Kirk Douglas, were modulated and nuanced in ways that fleshed out the personalities of the main protagonists. Lancaster was particularly convincing in his portrayal of Gen. Scott, a man overtaken by megalomania.[3] In a part that other actors might have been tempted to overplay, Lancaster's version of Scott was as a man who saw none of his own, sizeable failings and inconsistencies. By playing the scheming general as a man in a disarmingly straightforward manner, Lancaster contributed to the film's success in suggesting that conspiracies are not necessarily far away and deeply hidden. As with Scott, who regularly appeared in the media and was, therefore, in plain sight, *Seven Days in May* shows how a conspiracy can be closer than we might think.

Frankenheimer's fine directing and the cast's strong performances certainly worked in the film's favor. Another person's contributions to its success cannot be overlooked, however—that of the film's scriptwriter, the legendary Rod Serling.

CONSPIRACY IN SCIENCE FICTION AND FANTASY TELEVISION

Like Frankenheimer, Serling had worked in the nascent television industry during the 1950s. He had risen to prominence on the strength of his ample writing abilities. At the same time, he had frequently been frustrated by television's constraints—specifically by the limitations imposed by the networks' censorship practices of the 1950s regarding politics. A smart, insightful writer, Serling was interested in addressing issues of the day within the context of his scripts, but he found that it was quite difficult to get network approval for even mild references to political topics.

Undeterred, Serling eventually adopted an approach that allowed for commentary on such topics; he draped the issues under the cloak of science fiction and fantasy. This indirect strategy allowed him to explore serious contemporary themes without unduly raising the ire of network censors.

The result of Serling's exploration of storytelling within science fiction and fantasy forms was the well-known anthology series, *The Twilight Zone*. It appeared on the CBS schedule in 1959 and continued with first-run episodes until 1964. Appearing on camera as narrator, Serling introduced every episode of the series, which featured modern-day parables with endings that usually included an unexpected narrative turn. The anxieties of the age often played a part in the stories. Viewers can find episodes dealing with themes such as nuclear holocaust, totalitarianism, and censorship, among others. As the trick endings emphasized, things are not always as they seem, situations that appear innocuous can be foreboding, and doom may be around the corner. Although outright conspiracies were not usually the main focus of the story lines, the general tone of the series was fully consistent with the paranoiac undercurrents that had propelled the conspiracy theory throughout the Cold War years.

An episode from 1960 entitled "The Monsters Are Due on Maple Street" captures much of the essence of the series. Penned by Serling, it tells the story of ordinary people who, as the result of misunderstanding, turn against one another.

As the story begins, it seems it is about to rehash a theme that was thoroughly worked in 1950s science fiction movies: invasion from outer space. The story begins when the relative calm of a suburban neighborhood is broken by mysterious events including power interruptions, all of which leads the residents to believe that they are about to be attacked. They soon succumb to fear and suspicion. Tensions escalate, and the residents begin fighting among themselves. Gunfire erupts.

The last scene reveals that extraterrestrial invaders really are plotting an invasion, but their tactics are not direct. The aliens have realized they could easily induce the earthlings to destroy themselves. Driving home this point, Serling's narration of the final scene explained: "The tools of conquest do not necessarily come with bombs and explosions and fallout. There are weapons that are simply thoughts, attitudes, and prejudices to be found only in the minds of men. For the record, prejudices can kill, and suspicion can destroy, and the thoughtless, frightened search for a scapegoat has a fall-out all of its own . . . ."[4]

The paranoid and paranormal underpinnings of *The Twilight Zone* were also found in a program with a similar perspective, *The Outer Limits*. Originally broadcast from 1963 to 1965, it made an endurable impression on American popular culture.

The beginning and ending sequences of each episode captured its paranoiac and conspiratorial essence. To the sounds of eerie music, each episode of the series melodramatically began with a somber voice informing viewers that their television sets had been hijacked and were no longer under their control. Later, after the week's bizarre story had concluded, the same voice returned, ominously announcing, "We now return control of your television set to you."

The cultural impact of *The Twilight Zone* and *The Outer Limits* was far greater than the initial ratings and audience profiles might have predicted. Although successful in certain terms during their first-runs, neither was a breakaway hit. And the science fiction and fantasy themes, in the context of the times, were largely regarded as aiming for younger viewers, not remotely something that could be regarded as serious adult fare. Like more overt examples of conspiracy theory on screen, these shows exhibited a mood of anxiety and apprehension and regularly featured the theme of hidden menace. Both shows became staples in the rerun market, and over the years both developed strong fan bases that only increased in visibility with the explosive popularity of home video technologies fifteen years after their initial incarnations had ceased production.[5]

As interest in *The Twilight Zone* and *The Outer Limits* may have foreshadowed, the science fiction genre grew in popularity throughout the 1960s. In large measure, however, such programming was still considered to be programming for young people, not something that was of interest to adults.

The CBS series *Lost in Space*, which debuted in 1965, seemed to confirm this attitude. It had a story line that loosely adapted the nineteenth-century novel *The Swiss Family Robinson*. The original was about the adventures of a shipwrecked family; this new television version recreated the story with an outer space theme. Indeed, *Lost in Space*, which contributed the often satirized line "Danger, Will Robinson!" to the cultural lexicon, was clearly aimed at a young audience. Although the continuing plot line involved a traitorous stowaway, a character named Dr. Smith, that character soon became something of a buffoon and hardly signified a real menace. The supposed villain of the series, he soon became notorious for his astonishing cowardice and self-centeredness. Quite obviously, the series was not part of the previous decade's science fiction portrayal of paranoia and fear.

The following year, NBC also ventured into the science fiction genre with *Star Trek*, which was created by producer Gene Roddenberry. Modestly successful at the time, it later became an enormous pop-culture phenomenon. It was clearly more popular after its initial run than when it was in production. The series aimed for an uplifting, if melodramatic, exploration of the human condition.

Star Trek did treat some Cold War themes vicariously. The heroes were representatives of an interplanetary Federation, clearly a stand-in for the U.S. and Western powers. On the other side were villainous beings. The Klingons were a fierce, warrior race and seemed to be a substitute for the Soviets and their sphere of influence in many stories. Another group, the Romulans, seemed to be surrogates for the People's Republic of China. Overall, the series featured adventures in which the heroes wandered about on their mission of exploration, while often engaging in the outer-space equivalent of gunboat diplomacy.

Of course, *Star Trek*, though earning only enough interest to last three seasons on NBC's schedule, later became a phenomenal hit in syndicated reruns. A litany of productions eventually followed, with a successful string of feature-length motion pictures, spin-off television series, animated series, books and paraphernalia, as well as a highly successful cottage industry of *Star Trek*-themed conventions, which attracted ardent fan support.

Star Trek focused on a basically positive message. In many ways, it was the antithesis of the fear-laden science fiction productions of the 1950s, which had largely informed the underlying mood and tone of *The Twilight Zone* and *The Outer Limits*. The darker theme of these other shows, however, was resurrected in another, less remembered television series in 1967.

A clear throwback to the "secret alien invasion" theme that was a hallmark of 1950s science fiction movies, the new show was called *The Invaders*. The series focused on the efforts of its main character, David Vincent (played by Roy Thinnes), to expose a silent invasion by extraterrestrial aliens that, unbeknownst to humanity, was already underway.

By chance, Vincent had witnessed an alien craft and learned that the intruders were masquerading as ordinary-looking humans. The faux earthlings were convincing replications in every respect except one: they could not move the fourth finger on their hands. The quirk of the aliens' unbendable fingers gave both Vincent and viewers a sometimes subtle way of detecting the hidden enemy. Of course, to most people he encountered, Vincent seemed to be a crackpot, and so the series followed his efforts to undermine the invasion efforts as he unsuccessfully tried to warn humanity.

The series was only marginally successful, but it did serve to reintroduce and update a significant theme from the previous decade. Perhaps the currency of the idea of hidden invaders was less obvious in the late 1960s, when other issues had become more prominent in American culture, but it remained a potent theme, if for changing reasons. No longer was it only the external threat of communism that had captured public attention. Instead, this was the era in which the idea that hidden internal enemies—enemies perhaps within the very heart of American institutions themselves—was beginning to percolate with increasing frequency.

RUSH TO JUDGMENT

The Warren Commission's report had placated much of the American public, and by 1967 the new political imperative seemed not to be a direct threat from the Soviet Union, but rather the increasingly complex and problematic war in Vietnam. Yet, as the Vietnam conflict had escalated—as American casualties mounted and as the U.S. military increasingly relied upon conscription to fill it ranks—cracks in American society became deeper and more widespread. As a result, the conditions for skepticism and alienation became more evident.

The war was a major factor in this development, but it was not the only one. As the conflict in Southeast Asia became unpopular, other changes in the social landscape, such as increasing racial tensions, contributed to the erosion of trust between the government and the citizenry. Indeed, with these changes it became more common to question the central institutions of American life. This primed some segments of the American public to embrace a more thoroughly skeptical stance toward officialdom. One place in which this phenomenon surfaced most obviously was in the growing skepticism about the government's account of the Kennedy assassination.

The 1967 documentary film *Rush to Judgment* was evidence of this impulse. In this film, writer Mark Lane and director Emile de Antonio argued that the Warren Commission's work was not only hurried and sloppy, but more importantly, a white-wash. The suggestion that a government investigation was conducted poorly, though not likely to meet with much official praise, would not have been out of bounds in American politics at that time or in many others. The idea that the Warren Commission was not so much inept as covering up the truth, however, was an incendiary accusation.

Lane began following the Kennedy assassination investigation immediately after the tragic event. According to a later statement, as early as November 26, 1963, he doubted official accounts, saying "When I sat down to analyze the charges [against Oswald] to place them alongside what was then known about the case, I quickly found that the weaknesses were blatant."[6] Soon, he began writing about the case with the aim of bringing his concerns to public attention. Major publications expressed little interest in his story, but the left-leaning *National Guardian* agreed to publish his article. It appeared in December 1963.

As time passed, Lane's skepticism grew. He particularly doubted the account of some key witnesses who had supposedly seen Oswald in the book depository building from which the fatal shot was said to have been fired. Lane claimed that reports of the murder weapon having Oswald's palm-print on it were false, and he said laboratory tests were inconclusive. In fact, he found the evidence underwhelming at best. It was not surprising, therefore, that when the Commission's final report was released, he took issue with most of its key findings. His book on the topic, also called *Rush to Judgment*,[7] brought Lane to public attention in 1966.

The biggest mistake of the Warren Commission, according to Lane, was not just its finding that Oswald had acted alone in carrying out the assassination. More than disputing simply whether or not Oswald was the sole killer, Lane insisted that the Commission had not even shown that Oswald was involved at all. He railed against the Commission for what he saw as its refusal to consider evidence that cast doubt on the official line or that contradicted the Commission's findings.

Lane's book, the first of several he would write with similar themes, became a national bestseller, clearly indicating that there was a public appetite for the inflammatory ideas he had suggested. By the time the movie version was released the following year, then, there was a willing and waiting audience.

De Antonio was already known as a gadfly director with a leftist slant. His film *Point of Order* (1964) had documented the McCarthy hearings, casting not only the senator but the American system more generally in a negative light. Playing to audiences a decade after the events had occurred, de Antonio constructed the movie by selecting and reediting footage that was originally filmed by CBS News. (De Antonio reportedly paid CBS for the rights to the footage and gave them a stake in any future profits.[8]) Hardly aiming at a fair portrayal, de Antonio was instead interested in exposing what he saw as the inherent flaws of the capitalist system. Though his views, by any measure of American attitudes of the day, were never those of the majority, *Point of Order* did attract curious and perhaps mildly sympathetic viewers in addition to hard-core leftists. Now, with *Rush to Judgment*, he turned to a more contemporary event.

Like the book, de Antonio's film treatment of the subject cast the government's account of the assassination into doubt. And by the time of its release, what had seemed politically blasphemous months earlier now did not seem so extreme to many people. Far from regarding its material as outlandish speculation, a review in *Variety* said simply that "For many it will seem . . . convincing . . . [raising] severe doubts about the thoroughness and even integrity of the Warren Commission's [Report]."[9] In sum, the reviewer judged that the film was "sober and unexcited, making its points with quiet and controlled definiteness, sans hysterics or frenzied accusations," and that the "point of the film is neatly summed up by one interviewee: 'The Warren Commission, I think, had to report in their book what they wanted the world to believe. . . . It had to read like they wanted it to read. They had to prove that Oswald did it alone.'"

In both its film and book forms, *Rush to Judgment*, though somewhat forgotten among the general public in later years, was a significant milestone in the development of modern conspiracy theory culture in the United States. It set the stage for later and often more convoluted, incarnations of such theorizing and, importantly, it proved that there was a public interest in such fare.

Film—and to a lesser extent, television—had already set the stage for such thinking, of course, even if inadvertently. And although the idea that the corruption from within the system was at the heart of American problems was far from the most widely held view—indeed, it remained at the fringes of American politics—elements of these ideas nonetheless began to penetrate everyday America more prominently than in the past.

The world of espionage and conspiracy that the James Bond films continued to keep in the forefront of public attention was sometimes displayed in televised entertainments of the day. These incarnations of the theme ran the gamut, from the outright silly to the psychologically complex.

Typifying the sillier side of things was the series *Get Smart*, which had been created by comedy writers Mel Brooks and Buck Henry. Debuting on the NBC network in 1965, it followed the misadventures of bumbling secret agent Maxwell Smart (played by Don Adams). The character of Agent 86, as Smart was called, had similarities to Inspector Clouseau, the main character in the 1963 movie *The Pink Panther* from director Blake Edwards. Both heroes were successful almost accidentally, despite colossal ineptness. Blake had created a slapstick parody of detective movies, which were usually dramatic in tone. *Get Smart*, by contrast, parodied a genre that already had taken on parody-like characteristics, spoofing not only the often tongue-in-cheek Bond movies, but also lightweight television dramas such as *The Man from U.N.C.L.E.*, which ran from 1964–1968. (The series generated a spin-off entitled *The Girl from U.N.C.L.E.*, which ran for a single season from fall 1966 to spring 1967.)[10]

The conspiracy element in *Get Smart* was found in a worldwide battle being waged between the heroes and their organization, CONTROL, and their counterparts in the evil organization KAOS. In a typical half-hour episode, some dastardly scheme hatched by KAOS would require Agent 86 and his much more competent female partner, Agent 99, to save the day. The best laid plans of bumbling Agent 86 would go awry, the ultra-secret high-tech gadgets would malfunction in comical ways, the villains would revel in pettiness even as they schemed for world domination. Yet, the heroes triumphed and the villains usually lived to come back another day, though usually neither party would be much wiser in subsequent encounters.

Creators Brooks and Henry had created a vehicle that was just intelligent enough, just tongue-in-cheek enough to entertain mid-1960s audiences who were looking for escapist entertainment. The comic treatment of Cold War themes found a willing audience. Though it may not have been at the forefront in the minds of viewers in that era, it was also one more piece of entertainment that, together with other screen treatments with similar themes, slowly undercut the doom-and-gloom seriousness of earlier productions.

With *Get Smart*, television treatment of the espionage theme stepped beyond the simply unbelievable and aimed off-handedly for the ridiculous. Keeping the hallmarks of genre—secret organization, highly advanced technological gadgets and weaponry, incredibly well-organized secret international enemies—the series played everything for laughs. And in doing so, the series slyly pointed out how preposterous many of the conventions in previous spy-oriented films and television shows had been.

More significantly, although *Get Smart* presented the picture of a "good" organization that was able to come out on top, CONTROL was really quite incompetent. (Of course, in *Get Smart*, both sides of the supposed struggle between good and evil were badly managed.) The upshot was that the secret-maneuvering and conspiracy-laden world of espionage came across as little more than an irrelevant sideshow. Obviously, *Get Smart* was a light and momentary diversion for its audience, which did not take any part of it to resemble reality. Yet, despite its apparent place as a television fluff, its popularity insured that a weekly alternative portrait of reality—one in which secrets and fear and paranoia were harmless—received a thorough airing.

A more standard, noncomic treatment of the spy world appeared in *The Man from U.N.C.L.E.*, which took the essential elements of the Bond series and reworked them for an episodic treatment on television. The series focused on two main characters, Napoleon Solo (played by Robert Vaughn) and the Russian-born Illya Kuryakin (David McCallum), who worked for a secret organization named the United Network Command for Law and Enforcement (UNCLE). The head of this supersecret network of spies and undercover operatives (a part that was played by Leo G. Carroll, who had been cast as the spy-master in Alfred Hitchcock's *North by Northwest*) orchestrated the agency's ongoing battle against the sinister outfit THRUSH.

Another television production, also with a more serious intent, was the drama *Mission: Impossible*. Perhaps the most successful of such series, it aired from 1966 until 1973, withstanding several major cast changes along the way. (Years later, it resurfaced in the popular movie series with actor Tom Cruise in the lead role.) Here again are stories featuring a secret organization— the Impossible Mission Force (IMF) in this case. The IMF was given cases of international intrigue that were too sensitive to be addressed through normal channels. Appearing to possess a quasi-official status, only loosely connected to the federal government, the IMF was freed from the constraints of official government. In fact, as was repeated every week, the faceless voice that gave the IMF its missions reminded the leader that if the IMF agents were discovered, the government would "disavow any knowledge" of the group or its mission.

The IMF leader assembled his team each week for missions that were often behind the Iron Curtain or that had to do with malevolent regimes in the developing world. (Later episodes focused more on domestic criminal organizations.) Their covert actions required an eclectic combination of skills, impersonation and disguise, electronic technologies, brute strength, as well as master planning.

Mission: Impossible did not usually focus on a conspiracy directly, but its overall premises reinforced elements of this theme. The idea that a supersecret agency would go about business with only borderline legal authorization was presented as offhanded derring-do, but it was clearly at odds with the traditional concept of law and order. In fact, as with other espionage screen productions, the underlying premise of *Mission: Impossible* seemed to be that official rules and regulations—the sorts of things that governed international diplomacy, for instance—were too cumbersome and ineffective for the really difficult problems. So when a troublesome dictator in a faraway nation caused a tense situation, or when an unnamed government with allegiance to a hostile superpower threatened to upset the era's balance of power, then other, clandestine operations were the best response.

More conspiratorial still was *The Prisoner*, a British show that was imported for American television in 1967–1968.[11] The story followed the efforts of an unnamed former secret agent (played by Patrick McGoohan) who finds himself held captive in an idyllic town called the Village. Although it seems like a holiday resort, the man learns that he has been stripped of his former identity and given a new one: Number Six. Episodes typically focus on Number Six's attempts to escape and his captors' efforts to extract unspecified, presumably classified information from him. Number Six stays one step ahead of his mysterious captors' schemes, which usually involve trickery, mind control, or psychological manipulation. He often nearly reaches freedom. But except in the psychedelic last episode of the series, he is always recaptured and returned to his Village prison.

Although most viewers probably assumed that Number Six was supposed to be the same character that McGoohan played in his popular *Danger Man* series (it was retitled *Secret Agent* when shown in the United States), this is never explicitly stated. Instead, the audience is unsure of exactly who Number Six is, why and by whom he has been captured, and what, if anything, his captors want him to reveal. The Village is a place where conspiracy is incarnate. But it is never clear how many of the Village's other residents are captives and how many are sided with the apparently wicked people who run the community. It is a murky story with an *Alice in Wonderland* feel. But its novel depiction of the conspiracy theory theme helped the series become a cult classic. Although the entire series consisted of only seventeen episodes, it influenced later productions, such as the movie *The Truman Show*.

A TIME OF TUMULT

For the United States, 1968 was a year of upheaval. The Kennedy assassination, though still an object of speculation, was history. America faced too many current crises to spend much time focusing on that. They also faced a polarizing election season, which had the added surprise of Lyndon Johnson's announcement that he would not seek reelection in November, a development that triggered a wild dash for the Oval Office among many contestants.

Beyond the election, many events that year could be mentioned as having a significant impact on the American psyche, but three will suffice to make the point: two were the assassinations of both Robert Kennedy and Martin Luther King, Jr.; the other was the increasingly dire turn of events in the Vietnam War.

The shocking assassinations of Bobby Kennedy and Martin Luther King, Jr. deepened American anxieties. Many people felt that the United States was veering into unknown territory; to some people it seemed as though the nation was approaching anarchy.

The year of bitter combat in Vietnam, meanwhile, came at a time when Americans were beginning to tire of that war and starting to demand answers as to how and when it would end. Whatever their differences—and these were many—what the new assassinations and the escalating violence in Vietnam had in common was that they presented new, troubling narratives, with emotional elements that made simple explanations hard to accept for many people. After two decades of conspiracy theory thinking in politics and the media, moreover, there was a readily available alternative to official explanation. Perhaps there really was a conspiracy.

By 1968, therefore, a number of elements were lining up in American culture, affecting the mindset of many of those who were becoming increasingly alienated from the cultural mainstream. Paradoxically, the original focus of conspiracy theory had been on the outside, on external enemies—especially communists—who posed a threat sometimes hidden and sometimes underestimated. Now, however, conspiracy theory thinking did not so much look outside as within. It posed troubling questions: What if America's problems were not caused by outsiders or by Americans who had sided with outsiders? What if these seeming threats to the "system" did not originate outside of that system, but rather from within it? What if the enemy is not them, but us?

Fueling such thoughts were the deep divisions that were emerging throughout the nation. These cleavages were both many and varied. Now, it was not simply a united American mainstream standing against threats, real or potential, from the outside. No, it was more often one group of Americans looking with suspicion at other groups of Americans. The young were cast against the old, though in that day what was considered "old" might not seem so today. (Recall the often-repeated slogan: "Don't trust anyone over thirty!") The Women's Liberation movement seemed, to some, to cast women against men; white was cast against black; war hawks against peace-niks; traditionalists against hippies. And so it went.

Such high-relief contrasts were never fully accurate, of course. Things were not that simple, and there were significant variations within, as well as across, the different groups. But by 1968, many Americans felt that the glue holding their society together was starting to come undone.

No one controversy fully captures the complexities of the chasm that was widening between Americans, but developments in the Vietnam War probably played the largest part in shaping the American cultural and political climate of the next few years.

In 1968, North Vietnamese leaders determined to make a grand push to the South in hopes of bringing the war to a swift conclusion with terms favorable to the communist regime in Hanoi. At the same time, Lyndon Johnson was eager to keep American forces from defeat, but he was also increasingly troubled by the increasingly vocal and violent antiwar protesters whose message was seeping into the mainstream. As both sides acted to advance their interests, by the end of the year the outcomes were far different from what either had envisioned.

Briefly stated, the military and political outcomes were diametrically opposed to each other. Militarily, the North Vietnamese plan to flood South Vietnam with units of its regular army failed to bring about any major military advantage. It was a great, decisive victory North Vietnam sought. In fact, when North Vietnamese forces came up against American combat units and their South Vietnamese allies, it was the United States that came out on top time after time.

Yet, 1968 was far from a victory for the United States. Despite its military successes, the intense fighting of that year was a public relations nightmare for the Johnson administration. Victories on the field did come, but they were often hard fought and ugly, generating many deaths and injuries. One by one, it is true, these victories did add up, but they did not combine to produce a broadly visible improvement in the war. Instead, results seemed incremental. In fact, they were often short-lived. American units engaged the enemy, but frequently after a tough win, they moved on to other areas. It did not seem to make much of a difference. Back home, Americans wondered if these apparently meager results were worth the increasingly high cost in young American lives.

An early victim of the increasing American doubts was the presidency of Lyndon Johnson. On the evening of March 31, 1968, a weary president addressed the nation, beginning his speech with these words: "Good evening, my fellow Americans. Tonight I want to speak to you of peace in Vietnam and Southeast Asia. No other question so preoccupies our people. No other dream so absorbs the 250 million human beings who live in that part of the world. No other goal motivates American policy in Southeast Asia."

The president went on to recount the challenges that had been faced and that still were ahead, and he repeated his desire to negotiate an end to the conflict. He detailed the situation and tried to explain to Americans what had happened and what might happen next. As the speech drew to a close, he abruptly changed topics, switching his attention to the upcoming November election. In a slow, deliberate, and clearly demoralized voice, he then made a startling announcement, saying:

> With America's sons in the fields far away, with America's future under challenge right here at home, with our hopes and the world's hopes for peace in the balance every day, I do not believe that I should devote an hour or a day of my time to any personal partisan causes or to any duties other than the awesome duties of this office—the Presidency of your country.

> Accordingly, I shall not seek, and I will not accept, the nomination of my party for another term as your President.

It was news that stunned the nation. Even most of the president's closet advisors had not realized Johnson would take himself out of the race.

Days after Johnson's surprise announcement that he would not run in November, MGM studios released a new film from director Stanley Kubrick, whose 1964 satire *Dr. Strangelove* previously had made an indelible impression with movie audiences and critics. That movie was a dark satire, involving the unintentional start of a nuclear war between the Soviet Union and the United States. Featuring comic actor Peter Sellers, it brazenly spoofed the inner workings of nuclear deterrence policies that relied on the concept of mutually assured destruction, the idea that no one would start a nuclear war because it would lead to catastrophe for everyone. Mocking human arrogance and stupidity, the most famous scene in the movie is probably at its end, with an American bombardier riding a falling nuclear bomb as if it were a bucking bronco from a rodeo show. Paranoia and fear, therefore, were certainly underlying the plot, and the film reinforced conspiracy-related ideas, especially the notion that the secrecy workings of governments—domestic and foreign—could be inept and incompetent.

Kubrick's new film, *2001: A Space Odyssey*, went in a completely different direction. Nominally a science fiction film, it nonetheless relies upon conspiratorial underpinnings within its core narrative. So, while a major part of *2001: A Space Odyssey* is a strange, almost hallucinogenic exploration of the suggested intersection of extraterrestrial life and human evolution, the film also makes a statement about secretive governments and the potentially untrustworthy products of modern industry.

In the story, human explorers stationed on a government moon base discover a large, mysterious black slab that is clearly not a naturally occurring object. The object has unusual properties and it defies the efforts of scientists to understand it. One would think that news of the discovery of this strange, unworldly object would spread quickly, but that it not the case. Claiming that the momentous discovery holds "the potential for cultural shock and social disorientation," the government withholds this startling information from the public. Indeed, the government takes great pains to keep knowledge of the object a secret, going as far as quarantining the moon base with false stories of a medical epidemic. Scientists continue to study the object. While examining it one day, it suddenly emits a powerful radio beam that seemed aimed at Jupiter.

The plot then shifts to a spacecraft bound for Jupiter, a long mission in which some of the human crew has been placed in hibernation while others perform the routine tasks of navigation and spacecraft maintenance. Aiding the crew is a powerful supercomputer, nicknamed HAL. (The name of the computer is often assumed to be a stand-in for the computer-making giant of that era, IBM, since each letter of the fictional name is only one removed from IBM alphabetically.)

At first, the soft-spoken HAL seems a dutiful servant to the human crew, controlling spacecraft functions. Slowly, however, it appears that HAL may not be performing according to plan. Two members of the crew decide to discuss their increasing apprehension about HAL. Because the computer monitors all activity and communications on board, however, the crew members attempt to discuss their reservations secretly. Speaking so that HAL cannot overhear them, they agree that HAL should be disabled if its behavior becomes more erratic and unreliable. Unbeknownst to them, however, HAL has been programmed for lip-reading capabilities, and it therefore becomes aware of the contingency plan for it to be disconnected. The situation between crew and HAL soon deteriorates to an alarming level.

Eventually, the two crew members do conclude that HAL must be shut down. By then, however, the computer has become determined to prevent its disconnection regardless of human cost. HAL resorts to murder in an effort to assure its continued operation. It is only after a harrowing confrontation with the computer that crew-member Dave Bowman disables it. The movie then moves on to its final segment, an abstract, hallucinogenic-like account of Bowman's solitary experience as he reaches the spacecraft's final destination.

Although it is often understated in the story, many central elements of *2001: A Space Odyssey* are steeped in the conspiracy theme. The script, by Kubrick and science fiction writer Arthur C. Clarke, coolly paints a picture of government that feels little obligation to inform its citizens about a potentially history-changing discovery. This secrecy is explained away by the claim that public awareness could lead to panic. To a lesser extent, it is also implied that there might be security reasons for keeping knowledge of the mysterious object's discovery secret.

These were familiar justifications for official secrecy, both in the real world of experience and in the fictional world of films and novels. After all, the Manhattan Project, which had developed nuclear weapons for the United States during World War II, was a very closely guarded secret. (Even a cursory scanning of history would reveal many more.) Yet, by the time *2001: A Space Odyssey* appeared in theaters, the public climate had changed substantially since the early days of the Cold War. Obsessive government secrecy about the mysterious object, especially when it was not at all clear that there was any risk to the nation or humanity, did not seem so easy to justify in the context of the late 1960s. It was at this time, after all, that skepticism about government and societal institutions was growing.

Indeed, by the late 1960s, obsessive government secrecy had started to develop a bad reputation in some quarters of America. These were the days, after all, when George Orwell's book *1984*, with its frightening imagery of an omnipresent "big brother" government, had become a fixture in high school classrooms. This apprehensive attitude would become more pronounced with the coming of the Nixon presidency the following year. Nixon's administration would later exhibit a penchant for secrecy and nondisclosure about the workings of government. This was apparent in its angry reaction to the 1971 revelation of the Pentagon Papers, the secret government report that revealed inconsistencies with official accounts of the Vietnam War. In retrospect, the secretive elements in the *2001: A Space Odyssey* seem somewhat mundanely consistent with the actual political experience in the years immediately following.

The second conspiracy-oriented element of *2001: A Space Odyssey* involving the computer HAL is perhaps more subtle. Often interpreted simply as a human-versus-machine conflict, this part of the narrative shows how crew members, who are presented essentially as innocent bystanders, could become the victims of a cold, ruthless product of American big business. (Indeed, in several early scenes of the movie there are conspicuous, sometimes amusing, references to large corporate enterprises.) In the Vietnam War era, many members of the younger generation viewed big business as part of an ominous "military-industrial complex." In some ways, then, the increasing malevolence of HAL could appear congruent with certain political outlooks of the day.

Although the conspiracy aspects of *2001: A Space Odyssey* are not the elements mostly recalled by viewers or critics, they are nonetheless evident for those wishing to look.[12] In some ways, then, *2001: A Space Odyssey* continues the vein of science fiction filmmaking that became prominent in the 1950s and that included conspiracy-minded political subtexts.

THE NIXON PRESIDENCY

The unpopularity of Johnson's war policies ultimately was too heavy a load for Hubert Humphrey, the vice president who became the Democratic nominee for president. Richard M. Nixon, the Republican, was not saddled with Johnson's war legacy. He announced that he had a plan, which he could not reveal yet, to bring an honorable end to the conflict. He persuaded many people that this new approach would be preferable to a continuation of Democratic policies.

Although Humphrey spoke of making a surprise comeback when the ballots were tallied, such an outcome was not to be. Instead, voters turned to Richard Nixon, whose candidacy was surely bolstered by unease in middle America about society's tensions and also by his promise of a secret plan to end the war in Southeast Asia.

Once in office, Nixon proved to be as polarizing figure as he had sometimes been earlier in his career. Of course, by the time he took office, American society had already undergone significant challenges, and it is hard to imagine that there would be any wholesale turning back on developments that many Americans thought to be improvements, but others saw as evidence of social decay.

The Vietnam War, the Women's Movement, and the Civil Rights Movement altered American life, and a conservative backlash was not surprising. And as a Republican president, Nixon was the voice of that sentiment. (In retrospect, many of his views seem much more moderate than they appeared to many observers in the late 1960s and early 1970s.)

Whatever else he set out to do from the Oval Office, it was the Vietnam War that soon overpowered Nixon's presidency as it had Lyndon Johnson's. It turned out that there really was no secret plan—at least not one that most people would find specific enough to call a plan. Yet, Nixon and his aide Henry Kissinger did have a general idea about what might be possible to accomplish in order to bring an end to American participation in the divisive war.

Nixon often spoke of his desire to end the Vietnam War "with honor," and he frequently declared that he wanted to "win the peace." To many people, perhaps, nothing in these words seemed to overtly indicate that Nixon had anything other than a military victory in mind. Yet, under Kissinger's influence, Nixon had actually established a much more pragmatic view. As became apparent, it was his administration's desire to negotiate a settlement with North Vietnam on one hand, while building up the South Vietnamese government's ability to fight the war on its own, on the other.

Liberal and left-leaning Americans never trusted Nixon, however. There was no honeymoon period for many of them. Instead, from the earliest days of the Nixon presidency, these skeptics were leery of the president and his motives.

Of course, a vivid controversy can be a very attractive proposition politically, and Nixon was not shy about taking on these skeptics in order to further his agenda. The president had a willing assistant in this undertaking. Spiro Agnew, the vice president, gladly assumed the role of pit bull, needling leftists, intellectuals, and the news media along the way. His colorful rhetoric aimed at consolidating the conservatives and moderates behind the president. He constantly cast those who opposed the administration as either witting or unwitting enemies of America.

The administration's penchant for secrecy in war strategy and its engagement in exercises of mutual antagonism with liberals and leftists came together to create some enormous political difficulties, as is well known. One of the most telling examples of this came about when it was decided to put additional pressure on the North Vietnamese communists by following them into Cambodia, a country bordering South Vietnam, through which the communist supply-lines ran. Whether the American people would have supported this as a necessary strategy or been outraged that it was an expansion of the war will never be known with certainty, since there was no public awareness of these activities for a time.

Eventually, Nixon did announce that American forces would cross the Cambodia border. During a televised speech in April 1970, Nixon announced, "In cooperation with the armed forces of South Vietnam, attacks are being launched this week to clean out major enemy sanctuaries on the Cambodian Vietnam border." Previous incursions into Cambodia had been secret. Now the intentions of the president were public, and it did not take long for Americans to react.

The response to these revelations was dramatic, particularly on American college campuses. Large demonstrations were quickly mounted, as many students expressed outrage at what they viewed as Nixon's immoral expansion of a war. Tension and violence followed, setting conditions for one of the most iconic domestic confrontations of the Vietnam War years. This, of course, was the tragic confrontation between student demonstrators and National Guard troops on the campus of Kent State University. The scene erupted into violence, culminating with the deaths of four students and resulting in public uproar.

Taken cumulatively, these events greatly enhanced the development of a conspiracy theory mindset in American society. Secret machinations, mutual alienation of those holding opposing political beliefs, and disruption of the status quo in the American social order all combined to make a fertile breeding ground for a powerful new incarnation of the conspiracy theory worldview. It soon was reflected in screen media.

Yet, despite his controversial style, Nixon was successful in his bid for reelection in 1972. The policy of gradually shifting responsibility for war from American troops to the forces of South Vietnam progressed, and by then the number of Americans serving had dropped dramatically. In addition, peace talks progressed reasonably well, and an agreement between communist North Vietnam and the United States seemed attainable by late 1972, though not without occasional setbacks.

Of course, a real conspiracy of sorts was propagated by the Nixon White House during the campaign season that year. Always wary that real or imagined enemies would undo his success and power, Nixon had covertly authorized a small group of operatives to burglarize Democratic offices located in the Washington, DC, Watergate complex. It seemed to be another one of the "dirty tricks," of which his political opponents constantly complained. But on this occasion the deed could not be immediately traced back to anyone holding high office. In fact, at first, it was not clear that it was anything other than a random, petty crime.

Thus, Richard Nixon, who had incurred the wrath of war opponents and political foes since assuming the presidency, was nonetheless returned to that office in November. Just before his second-term inauguration, the deal to end American participation in the Vietnam War was finalized. The military draft was summarily terminated, and soon American prisoners of war began their long trip home. America, it seemed, was ready to move on from its long, divisive war and begin a new chapter. Nixon looked to put that period behind him.

The good times were not immediately around the corner, however. Only months after beginning his second term, the truth about the Watergate affair started to become known. Soon, it became a national scandal of historic proportions. Conspiracy was to come out of the darkness and into the blinding light and spectacle of the news media's glare.

Scandal and Skepticism

As history records, the Watergate scandal eventually brought down the Nixon presidency. Before that, however, the popular culture already reflected messages of jaded cynicism. These ideas took hold even more firmly after Nixon was driven from office. In the milieu, conspiracy theory again took on new meanings and nuances, just as had been the case in previous decades.

In the years following World War II, the conspiracy theory theme was a reliable barometer of public moods and perceptions. So, the fear and anxieties of the early Cold War years produced one manifestation of the theme, and late 1950s and early 1960s produced another, which was frequently a cooler and more cosmopolitan view. The assassination of John F. Kennedy changed that, though by the end of the 1960s this was not necessarily in the way one would have expected. Indeed, by that time, the focus of conspiracy theorizing had largely shifted away from foreign enemies to domestic ones.

The first months of Nixon's second term were marked by the signing of a peace treaty between the United States and North Vietnam, essentially ending American participation in the divisive conflict. It was not long, however, before the nation descended into the depths of the Watergate scandal. By then, the American people already had grown weary. Many people were highly skeptical of government and its perceived transgressions during the war. With revelations about Watergate slowly coming to light, Americans now confronted a situation in which that skepticism grew.

This skepticism fueled the conspiracy theory phenomenon. It sent that impulse in the American imagination off in new directions and toward new conclusions. As always, ideas about conspiracy focused on an enemy that was often unseen. Increasingly, however, the enemy was not an external force.

A batch of new films drove home this point in 1973 and 1974. In rapid succession, Hollywood released *Executive Action* (late 1973), *The Conversation* (spring 1974), *The Parallax View*, and *Chinatown* (both June 1974). Each presented its own dark take on conspiracy theory, emphasizing various forms of alienation along the way. These films, which had been in production before the national spectacle of Watergate, eerily coincided with that unfolding real-life drama.

The first of these movies was director David Miller's *Executive Action*, which revisits the Kennedy assassination. In many ways, it prefigures Oliver Stone's later and more well-known *JFK*, though it is noteworthy in its own right. If Miller's movie seemed to repeat themes that appeared on screen earlier, however, it was with good reason; it was based on a story by Donald Freed and Mark Lane, the latter of whom had written *Rush to Judgment*, the basis for the Emil de Antonio film of the same name.

The movie sets out to dramatize how a conspiracy could have been behind the murder of the president in 1963, using fiction as a means of suggesting how it could have really happened. According to the narrative, established figures from within American business and government decide that Kennedy must be removed. They set in motion the events that will lead to the president's death, while assuring that their tracks will be hidden by framing Lee Harvey Oswald for the crime. With reliable star Burt Lancaster heading the cast, *Executive Action* also included Hollywood veterans Robert Ryan and Will Geer, as well as lesser known, but veteran television actors John Anderson and Paul Carr.

Lancaster, Ryan, and Geer play the chief villains, concocting the scheme and assuring that it will be carried out. Lancaster, the most famous and probably most versatile and gifted of this group, plays James Farrington, the chief architect of the scheme. (This type of role was not unfamiliar for him; he had played a scheming general in the standout *Seven Days in May*.) Geer, whose career had started in the 1930s and who had since played many roles in film and television—he was later familiar to TV audiences as Grandpa in *The Waltons*—was skilled at playing wise and sincere characters. Ryan, too, sometimes portrayed solid, upstanding characters—one example was his major role as General Grey in the 1965 World War II epic, *Battle of the Bulge*—though he also was often selected for parts that were more malicious and heartless. Casting familiar faces for the instigators of the plot was not a benign decision, of course. It helped reinforce the idea that familiar, rather than unknown, forces could be at the core of such a plot.

The conspirators in *Executive Action* are motivated to act because of their belief that Kennedy's policies have dramatically veered from their own—and therefore the nation's—interests. Farrington (Burt Lancaster) is the first to reach this conclusion, and he convinces a power broker named Foster (played by Robert Ryan) that drastic action is required. After some persuasion, an experienced politician named Ferguson (Will Geer) comes to agree with them. Together, these men arrange for the assassination. With the help of coincidences that are fortuitous for the conspirators, they set up a supposedly innocent Oswald to take the blame.

Executive Action debuted in American theaters in November of 1973, and it is hard to imagine timing that could have been more serendipitous. It not only came at the ten-year anniversary of the president's murder, it also premiered as the national crisis of Watergate was unfolding. That scandal became a colossal spectacle, focusing the spotlight on the inner workings of the Nixon White House in a particularly unflattering way.

Congressional hearings on the Watergate burglary and subsequent cover-up had riveted American television audiences during the summer. Shortly after these ended, a new round of hearings opened in September and would last until February 1974. Over the course of these extensive inquiries, more and more of the White House's maneuvers around the law became evident. One thing that was made crystal clear was the penchant Nixon and his closest associates had for secrecy. Though sometimes this had been in the interests of national security, it was also the cover for politically motivated acts, many of which were of questionable legality. As the full story of Watergate became known, an ugly picture emerged. To many people, it seemed consistent with the phrase "high crimes and misdemeanors."

As this unflattering portrait came into focus with a steady stream of new revelations, many of Nixon's former supporters started to abandon him. Indeed, Watergate had a shattering effect on the American people. It was a Constitutional crisis, to be sure, but even more than that, it was a crisis of faith.

Significantly, it was against the backdrop of these unfolding events that *Executive Action* premiered. Though not about Watergate, or even Nixon, the movie's main theme was nonetheless consistent with attitudes about American institutions that had been developing since the previous decade and that were now reaching a boiling point. This was the idea that the central institutions of American life not only did not work for the American people, but also were sometimes actively working against it. This theme had been seen before, but in the context of the Watergate crisis, it took on a new and more alienating tone.

Consider, for example, the opening words of *Variety*'s review of *Executive Action*, which reveal how the Watergate political climate sometimes influenced perceptions about the movie. The review begins: "The open lesion known as Watergate revealed a form of governmental-industrial syphilis, which in turn had made more plausible to millions the theory of an assassination conspiracy against President John F. Kennedy."[1] Similarly, though couched in less flamboyant language, *Cleveland Press* reviewer Toni Mastroianni judged that although the movie did not fully make its case for conspiracy, it was nonetheless "consistently engrossing."[2] Tellingly, Mastroianni noted that the picture of conspiracy painted in the movie did not involve "noisy speech makers or sinister cloak and dagger types." Rather, it was perpetrated by "ordinary, practical, hard-headed businessmen . . . .The Watergate revelations uncovered the same sort of clean cut, ordinary types and it doesn't take too much imagination to project such types into acts of greater enormity."

Some reviewers, such as Roger Ebert, were less impressed and assessed *Executive Action* as a more mediocre production.[3] In his view, *Executive Action* was simply rehashing conspiracy theories that already were floating around in popular culture. Indeed, there is much to support this view, as the movie introduced little that was new for those paying attention to the rampant theorizing that the assassination had provoked. Yet, in the guise of a fictionalized account, the dramatization of such theories on the big screen brought them to a much larger audience.

The Watergate events created a political environment of suspicion and distrust that assured the messages were heard, possibly making the film's premise seem more plausible than it otherwise may have seemed. After all, taken at face value, the film makes charges of monumental proportions. Though the names and identities of the conspirators are fictional, it seemed clear the film-makers were not merely creating a diversionary entertainment, but were actually aiming to present the story as an essentially truthful account of what happened a decade earlier, albeit with some details missing. *Executive Action* was not a blockbuster, but it was a moderate success that pushed the controversial idea that Americans of considerable stature had somehow been involved in the traumatic death of the president in 1963.

Although not taking things so literally and not necessarily invoking the Kennedy assassination as their touchstones, films released in the following months reiterated the conspiracy theme in various ways.

THE CONVERSATION

In spring of 1974, for example, Francis Ford Coppola showed a less political, but equally conspiratorial worldview in his renowned film, *The Conversation*. Sometimes compared to *Blow-Up*, Italian director Michelangelo Antonioni's 1966 film that has some thematic similarities, *The Conversation* shows the underside of modern culture, in which moral ambiguity abounds and where the line between public and private behavior is very blurry. It is a world in which conspiracy comfortably slips into everyday experience. Less literally articulated but just as suggestively implied as in *Executive Action*, Coppola's fictional world also resonated with the real-life aura created by Watergate.

The plot of *The Conversation* revolves around an unlikely character named Harry Caul, convincingly portrayed by Gene Hackman. Caul is an expert in the field of surveillance, specializing in audio techniques such as eavesdropping with electronic bugging devices. He is a private man, ill at ease in the social world and is generally cautious, if not outright suspicious, of the people he encounters. Caul is adept at his work, however, and makes a decent living selling his high-tech (by 1970s standards) services to corporate and private clients.

The story follows Caul's work for a client known simply as the Director (played by Robert Duvall). Caul thinks that it is just another job and that he is collecting information about the Director's wife and her suspected lover for divorce proceedings. A potentially lurid and secret matter, it is nonetheless typical of the sort of work he performs in documenting the underside of respectable society.

For much of the story, viewers follow the events on screen with this understanding, essentially seeing things as Harry Caul sees them. While trailing the targeted couple, however, the story takes a dramatic turn. As he listens next door, Harry Caul hears what he thinks is the young couple being murdered. Startled by this event, he enters the room to investigate. When he enters, however, the bodies are missing. Unnerved, he cannot help thinking that the couple has been murdered with his unwitting help. He assumes that he has been used by the Director to find the couple in an incriminating situation so that they could be found and eliminated.

Soon, however, Caul discovers that his assumptions were drastically wrong. Instead of being relieved, however, he discovers that the situation is even darker and more sinister than it first appeared. Upon arriving at the Director's office to make his report, he discovers that the Director's wife is alive. Indeed, she is speaking with reporters about the death of her husband, the Director, who had just perished in an automobile accident.

Now, Caul's anxieties are fully realized as it dawns on him that he has been used in a murder plot, not by the Director, but by the Director's wife and her lover. He recognizes that his subjects had known he was recording them and that they had manipulated circumstances to deceive him as they plotted their own murder scheme. From a law enforcement point of view, he realized, he would appear to be an accomplice. He is left feeling used, trapped, and set up.

Then, to make matter worse, Caul receives a mysterious phone call, apparently from the lover of the Director's wife. "We know you know," the voice on the telephone says ominously. "We'll be listening to you." Indeed, it is obvious that the master of audio surveillance has been the victim of his own craft. With no viable options and no place to turn, the film ends as Harry Caul comes to his wits end in a frantic search for bugging devices in his own apartment.

Lurking in the story under layers of deception, the conspiracy element of *The Conversation* is on a small, personal level. It is far from the picture of large-scale conspiracy in movies such as *Executive Action*. Yet, this more intimate portrait of betrayal, secrecy, and double-cross can bring viewers to the emotional core of paranoid-laden conspiracy as much as stories of grander, more global plots. More than a story about schemers in foreign lands or among the institutional elites of our own society, *The Conversation*'s intimate portrayal of conspiracy plays on the growing feeling of alienation that many Americans came to feel in the wake of a divisive and sometimes violent decade. After Vietnam protests, race riots, generational confrontations, and now Watergate, the suspicious, withdrawn character of Harry Caul, while perhaps not an archetypal "everyman," was nonetheless a character that a viewer could understand. His unwitting contact with conspiracy did not necessarily seem so far-fetched. In a way, then, the Harry Caul's character presented a 1970s version of the paranoid person from films of two decades earlier.[4]

In June, Hollywood released two more films with conspiracy-theory angles. One was *The Parallax View*, which centered on conspiracy at the institutional level. The other, which on the surface may seem less conspiratorial, was director Roman Polanski's *Chinatown*, known more widely as an example of late *film noir* American filmmaking.

THE PARALLAX VIEW

A few weeks after the debut of *The Conversation*, the Paramount studio released director Alan J. Pakula's political thriller *The Parallax View*. It was a movie with a conspiracy theme as blatant as any that had yet appeared. A vehicle for Warren Beatty, the popular sex symbol who had risen to fame in the 1967 hit *Bonnie and Clyde*, the new film portrayed an elaborate political conspiracy with eerie similarities to the assassinations of the 1960s.

An atmosphere of skepticism and alienation runs throughout the story, which implies a corrupt system that is permeated by conspirators. Many earlier films had portrayed conspiracy as something evil-doers would undertake to accomplish some other aim, usually to acquire more wealth or to grab political power. *The Parallax View* is much more cynical than that, however. In this film, conspiracy is not a byproduct of a corrupt organization. It is the main purpose of a corrupt organization. It is conspiracy for the sake of conspiracy, a perspective revealing such alienation that it is difficult to imagine as the plot of a mainstream film from an earlier era.

The movie begins with a political rally that leads from a street parade to a reception atop the futuristic Seattle Space Needle. There, a prominent senator is shot and killed in front of scores of witnesses and television cameras. (It is a scene that director Pakula appears to have modeled after the real assassination scene of Robert F. Kennedy in 1968.) The crowd quickly confronts the person they believe was the shooter, but he runs from the scene. Security personnel chase the apparent assassin to the roof of the Space Needle. As they struggle with the presumed killer, the man loses his balance and falls to his death.

In the next scene, a panel of somber men sits behind an imposing bench in a dimly lit room. The men are revealed to be a Warren Commission-like investigatory panel, charged to look into the senator's death. They sternly announce that the assassination was the work of one deranged man, that there was no conspiracy. (Interestingly, the narrative assumes that people would automatically assume that a conspiracy was involved.)

When the scene shifts to three years later, investigative reporter Joseph Frady (Beatty) is introduced. He is an ambitious, but somewhat reckless character prone to acting impulsively. One day, a mysterious woman from Frady's past appears at his door in a distraught, nearly hysterical state. After she calms down somewhat, Frady asks what has upset her so much. She then shows him a photograph that was taken just moments before the senator's assassination. She and several other people appear in the photo with the senator. The people in the picture, she says, have been dying under mysterious circumstances. She suspects foul play and fears she that will be next. Frady doesn't know what to make of the woman's claims. He is intrigued, however, and decides to look into the deaths.

After some research, Frady discovers that although there seem to be quite ordinary reasons for the deaths, something does not seem right. He decides to investigate more, at first thinking that maybe his suspicions were wrong, after all. Just then, however, he learns that his female acquaintance in the photo has died. Believing that this occurrence cannot be a simple coincidence, he takes up the case in earnest.

With his editor's begrudging approval, Frady sets off in search of clues. Like many films of its time, various car chases and foot chases dominate much of the action. Eventually, Frady begins to form a theory about the deaths of the people in the photo. He reasons that it may have to do with something, or someone, that all of the victims saw at the scene of the assassination. Perhaps it was something that seemed innocuous at the time, he thinks. He concludes that the group may have unknowingly witnessed a clue pointing to conspiracy.

As the tension mounts, Frady meets with another person in the photo on a yacht. Despite elaborate attempts to keep this rendezvous secret, they are discovered. The yacht is blown up, killing the other man.

Because of the size of the explosion, people think that Frady was also killed. This allows him to assume a new identity and to go undercover in pursuit of a puzzling lead. He has come across a company called the Parallax Corporation, and he thinks that it is somehow involved in the string of deaths. More than that, however, Frady soon comes to believe that the company is involved in recruiting and training assassins.

After assuming a false identity, Frady contacts the Parallax Corporation, pretending to be looking for a job. Eventually, he is contacted by a sinister company agent who invites him to join the organization for training.

Frady reports to the company's West coast office, which is situated in an ordinary high-rise office building. Within the company offices, however, Frady submits to an extraordinary training session. In a scene reminiscent of the brainwashing segment of *The Manchurian Candidate*, Frady is bombarded with images and sound in rapid succession. The session seems to be aimed at manipulating the trainee for some sinister mission. Yet, the first session ends without incident and Frady leaves the building to await further instructions at a later time.

As he is leaving, however, Frady sees a man he recognizes from the mysterious photograph. In the photo, the man was wearing a waiter's uniform, but his appearance outside the Parallax building causes Frady to think the man was not simply a waiter. Frady immediately suspects that the man is a Parallax operative and follows him. Eventually, Frady figures out that the man has placed a bomb on a plane carrying another senator, but he figures out a way to thwart the new assassination attempt without giving himself away.

Before he can make much more progress with his investigation, however, the Parallax Corporation completes its own investigation of Frady and discovers that he has used a fake identity. Although Frady tries to cover up his deception with another fabricated story, the company's suspicions have been aroused.

Frady slips past Parallax personnel following him and instead follows other Parallax operatives to a huge indoor arena where a rehearsal is underway for a political rally. Preparing to stage the event for television that night, a marching band practices and a sound check is conducted. Finally, the guest of honor—yet another senator—appears for the final rehearsal. Frady, meanwhile, has deduced that another assassination is planned and takes the guise of a security guard in an attempt to thwart it. From a cat walk overlooking the arena, he frantically tries to determine the conspirators' next move.

The last moments of the film show the fruitless efforts of Frady as he tries to prevent the new tragedy. The senator is shot during the rehearsal, but making matters worse, the whole event seems to have been a set up. A person in the crowd at the arena looks up to a cat walk and sees Frady, who is mistaken—perhaps intentionally—for the killer. Unable to explain himself from his high vantage point overlooking the arena, he attempts to run. He does not make it.

The film closes with yet another appearance of the solemn investigatory body that appeared earlier in the film. Now, however, they report that they have completed an examination of the evidence for the new assassination, and they have concluded that a delusional Joseph Frady was the lone assassin. In the end, then, the conspiracy continues and no one is the wiser.

In *The Parallax View*, shocking ideas about assassination in American life are given a mainstream treatment as part of an exciting thriller. Many of the ideas had been in circulation for some time, but they had always seemed to be fringe ideas. Here it is presented as a standard, noncontroversial theme. It was not completely effective, however. As the reviewer for *Time* commented, "Though a touch of paranoid fantasizing can energize an entertainment, too much of it is just plain crazy—neither truthful or useful."[5] Still, *The Parallax*

View brought more public notice to the conspiracy ideas even though it did not necessarily make a very convincing case.

CHINATOWN

Director Roman Polanski's *Chinatown* does not, at first, seem to be part of the conspiracy theory story in American movies. It is well respected, but it is usually recalled as an incarnation of *film noir* moviemaking and as a vehicle for star Jack Nicholson's bravura acting performance. Yet, the story it tells centers around not just one, but two intertwining conspiracies.

Chinatown tells the story of a private detective who investigates what seems to be a relatively routine case involving matrimonial infidelity. Soon, however, he is caught up in a vast criminal conspiracy involving water resources, government corruption, and murder. At one point in the movie, the detective's antagonist says tellingly: "You may think you know what you're dealing with, but believe me, you don't." Indeed, *Chinatown*'s narrative has many layers, and the conspiracy of the film appears in many ways.

In the story, private detective Jake Gittes (Nicholson), formerly an investigator in the Los Angeles police department, takes on a new case in which a well-to-do wife asks for help in getting evidence of her husband's supposedly secret affair. The object of the investigation is a man named Mulwray, a high-ranking engineer with the county who oversees public works such as water projects. Water is, of course, of special importance, since the surrounding area has little of its own and must divert it from elsewhere. A recent proposal from the water commission, it turns out, is highly controversial and highly political. The proposal involved a major project to redirect water to new areas. Mulwray is a high-profile opponent of the project for the water-starved region.

Gittes and his associates have little difficulty collecting incriminating evidence. One day, they discover Mulwray meeting an attractive young woman. This provides an easy opportunity for the detectives to take compromising photographs. Gittes reports his success to his client. How Mrs. Mulwray will use the evidence is between her and her husband, he thinks. He assumes that the case is closed. Gittes is subsequently surprised, then, to find that the scandalous photos have turned up in the newspaper.

This is only Gittes's first surprise, however. He is soon visited by another woman who informs him that she—not the woman who previously hired Gittes—is the real Mrs. Mulwray. The woman is outraged. She accuses Gittes of helping to discredit her husband and threatens to take vigorous legal action against the detective. Confused and slightly embarrassed, Gittes aims to uncover what has happened. He realizes that he was duped as part of someone else's scheme against Mulwray and that now his reputation and financial solvency are on the line.

From there, the story becomes increasingly complex. Viewers follow Gittes as he tries to discover the truth and protect his reputation. Along the way, there are many mysterious occurrences, including unexpected deaths, strange behavior, and seeming blackmail.

The more events unfold, the more the audience discovers that detective Gittes is not a typical movie hero. Although successful with his business, he is prone to impulsive and self-destructive behavior and often jumps to conclusions that turn out to be quite wide of the mark. In this case, though he deftly figures out where the mysteries within the mystery are, he is prone to piecing the real story together incorrectly. This forces him to constantly rework his operating assumptions. Indeed, these are not typical qualities for a movie detective, but they are typical of much human behavior and are therefore quite believable in the context of a case with many twists and turns.

Many of Gittes's difficulties with the case come about because he does not realize at first that he is dealing with not one, but two matters. The investigation of the Mulwray's supposed affair soon turns into a murder investigation when Mulwray is found dead. As Gittes tries to uncover the circumstances of Mulwray's death, however, he stumbles upon evidence that reveals a much larger criminal scheme, involving the water supply for Los Angeles.

All of these leads are confusing. Gittes tries to determine how the unknown woman, Mulwray's murder, and a seemingly large-scale municipal corruption scheme are related, if at all. He is both helped and hindered by the partial co-operation of the real Mrs. Mulwray, who still appears to be hiding something as Gittes continues the investigation.

Director Polanski and screenwriter Robert Towne adroitly blend the two story lines of the affair-turned-murder and the government corruption scheme. The audience gets few hints beyond what Gittes discovers, increasing the sense of confusion, betrayal, and fearful anticipation. It is soon revealed, however, that there is a common thread.

At the center of these mysteries is a character named Noah Cross (played by John Huston, director of the 1941 *film noir* classic, *The Maltese Falcon*). As Gittes learns, Mulwray and Cross had been well-to-do business partners. At one time, they jointly owned the water company that was later sold to the city of Los Angeles. This sale had been Mulwray's idea, and although Cross was reluctant, his partner eventually convinced him to go along with it. It is not clear why he finally agreed.

Since that time, the former business partners became estranged. Mulwray went to work for the city to oversee its water operations in a responsible way, but Cross continued to harbor the belief that water could be the key to an even greater fortune than he had already amassed.

Accordingly, Cross concocted a massive deception. In the elaborate scheme, Cross, his henchmen, and corrupt city workers have secretly begun to divert water away from where it was supposed to go in the farmlands that surrounded the city. In the middle of the night, when they would not be noticed, they took control of waterworks and diverted vast amounts of water into the ocean. The result was an apparent drought in the surrounding area. In fact, it was an artificially created water shortage that was designed to drive the farmers out of business and make their farmlands worthless. Cross and his associates secretly then bought the land under false names.

Meanwhile, the city was about to act on a bond issue for the construction of a new dam, supposedly to address the growing water shortages. Once approval for construction was obtained, however, Cross aimed to extend the city limits to include the surrounding farmlands. This would make the water available to the lands that had been artificially deprived. Then, the land that Cross had acquired, which was supposedly worthless, would suddenly skyrocket in value. It was a convoluted, conspiracy theory-like scheme, but one that had carefully been worked out.

At first, Gittes does not realize that Cross was involved in the case at all. Mulwray's murder seems to be related to the woman with whom he was having an affair, leading Gittes to zealously pursue that woman's identity. After much confusion, in which his investigation is complicated by a romantic involvement with the now-widowed Mrs. Mulwray, new truths become known. Gittes accidentally discovers that Cross is, in fact, Mrs. Mulwray's father. What is more, Mrs. Mulwray seems to know much more about the mysterious blonde woman seen with her late-husband than she is willing to admit. Finally, Gittes learns the truth. The mysterious woman is her own sister and her child; the woman was the result of an incestuous relationship between Mrs. Mulwray and her father, Noah Cross.

In the last section of the movie, Gittes figures out that Mulwray had been murdered by Cross in a violent confrontation. (Mulwray, it seems, had discovered and opposed the water conspiracy, and he had also tried to help shield his wife's daughter from Cross.) The final moments of the movie bring all of the characters together in the Chinatown section of Los Angeles. As Gittes tries to help Mrs. Mulwray and her daughter flee to Mexico, they are discovered by Cross and law enforcement officers. In a dramatic confrontation, Cross interrupts the escape with the police nearby. Rather than let her father have contact with her daughter, however, Mrs. Mulwray opens fire, wounding but not killing Cross. Instantaneously, however, the police respond by firing into her escaping car. One bullet finds its mark.

In the downbeat ending, Cross leaves with his newly found daughter, leaving the audience to wonder if he will abuse her. From what is shown on screen, it appears that the water scheme will go undiscovered and unpunished. For his part, the police tell a dejected Gittes, "Forget it, Jake. It's Chinatown."

The audacious conspiracy to manipulate water and land is central part to the story in *Chinatown*. In the story, unknowing people are manipulated and become involved in conspiratorial schemes that they know nothing about. What is more, the city is tricked into paying for the conspiracy with public funds. Indeed, the scale and scope of the water-and-land conspiracy in *Chinatown* is significant, and the potential victims of the scheme are many.

In telling the story, then, *Chinatown* combines this grand conspiracy with a more typical murder mystery story in the *film noir* tradition of murky deeds and flawed protagonists.[6] In this potent combination, the massive conspiracy is easily taken as just another component. And so *Chinatown* helped further the image of conspiracy as a relatively commonplace type of wrongdoing. Many viewers may not have even regarded the conspiracy element as a much of conspiracy, but rather just another Hollywood portrayal of crime. Yet, by intertwining a deeply intimate and personal story of abuse and betrayal with the larger narrative about wide-ranging corruption in the "system," *Chinatown* brings the larger conspiracy to a more human level.

THREE DAYS OF THE CONDOR

Also released in 1975 was director Sydney Pollack's movie *Three Days of the Condor*.[7] It was a more traditional portrayal of the covert world of espionage and intrigue, but its treatment of a conspiracy that infiltrated the Central Intelligence Agency was certainly evidence of the more cynical attitude that movie-goers brought with them to the theater in the mid-1970s.

Somewhat like *The Conversation*, the story focuses on an ordinary man, in this case a low-level intelligence analyst named Joe Turner (played by Robert Redford), who works in the CIA's New York office. The bookish and office-bound Turner spends his time combing through books, magazines, and other materials looking for information that can be used by the CIA. One day, he comes across a seemingly ordinary novel that seems to have odd and puzzling sections. Suspecting that the novel could be some sort of covertly distributed message or sinister code, he sends a routine report to his superiors. He expects a reply after his bosses wade through the piles of information that they regularly receive.

Before he receives any feedback on his report, however, his ordinary life takes a dramatic turn. While he takes a break, gunmen enter the office and murder everyone there. When Turner sees what has happened, he realizes that he is in danger and immediately goes into hiding. Following standard procedures, he calls a supposedly secure phone number to report the incident and asks what to do. At the other end of the phone line is an agent (played by Cliff Robertson) who advises Turner about what he should do next. The agent, who has given Turner the code name Condor, informs Turner that he is to be brought in for his own safety. Turner complies and meets with another agent who is to bring him to safety.

Turner is double-crossed, however, as the man sent to assure his safety tries to kill him. After a struggle, Turner escapes, still not sure what he has stumbled onto or what he should do. In the next sections of the movie,

Turner tries to determine if his agency contact is or is not in on the plot. Not trusting anyone, he sets out to investigate the office murders on his own.

Tracking clues that he finds while keeping the CIA at bay, events reach a climax as Turner traces the conspiracy to a shadowy man. As he zeroes in on the leader of the conspiracy, he is discovered by a man he recognizes as the lead assassin (played by Max von Sydow) in the office murders. Surprisingly, however, the assassin kills the conspirator, not Turner, adding more confusion to the plot.

In one of many plot twists, it is revealed that the assassin now works for the real CIA, rather than the conspiracy that had infiltrated part of it. Having nothing against Turner, the assassin tries to persuade Turner to leave the country. Turner, however, is determined not to leave.

In the final section of the film, Turner encounters his agency contact. Although this man had once seemed benevolent, Turner recognizes that the agent now cannot be trusted. But Turner has already discovered what the conspirators had hoped to keep hidden—the novel Turner had come across earlier actually outlines a secret plan to invade Middle Eastern countries. Turner plans to use this knowledge to stay alive. He tells Higgins he has already given the secret plans to the press. If what Turner says is true, that would bring much attention to him, thereby drawing enough publicity that it would make it hard for his enemies to terminate him.

As this outline suggests, *Three Days of the Condor* is in many ways a standard espionage thriller. As with many spy movies, it contains overt villains, covert villains, double-crosses, and sudden twists and turns. What is different about it, which is especially obvious given the historical context in which it was produced, is the degree of suspicion and cynicism that the movie portrays. At one point, *Three Days of the Condor* shows that only a small group of corrupt insiders are working for the CIA, but at other times the story seems to suggest that nothing about the CIA can be trusted. In a turn that would have been unlikely in movies from earlier years, the main character is a hero almost because he is peripheral to the agency, not because he epitomizes it. Indeed, though the Turner character is an insider of sorts, he is in many ways more of an outsider, a mostly mild-mannered ordinary man who is almost killed just going about his job. And rather than help him, the trustworthiness of his CIA superiors is thrown seriously into doubt. Overall, *Three Days of the Condor*'s interpretation of the traditional spy story is again not one that reaffirms trust in society or its institutions.[8]

WATERGATE RIPPLES

In 1976, the nation celebrated the two-hundredth anniversary of the United States with a multitude of bicentennial observations. Despite the upheavals of Vietnam and the 1960s and despite the Constitutional crisis precipitated by the Watergate scandal, it had survived.

Gerald Ford, who assumed the presidency upon Nixon's resignation in 1974, had tried to move the nation beyond the traumas of Watergate and the Vietnam War. He faced other crises, however, including a worsening economy. He ran a vigorous campaign in his quest to return to the Oval Office for a full term. By 1976, however, Americans looked for a new beginning, and in November of that year, they elected Jimmy Carter to be the thirty-ninth president of the United States. Despite new leadership, the legacies of America's recent controversies were still felt in American life.

Indeed, even as Americans looked to the future, they were still processing the recent past. In fact, in the next few years, films (and to a lesser extent, television productions) began to examine national traumas from the preceding years more intensely.

In 1976, for example, director Alan J. Pakula brought the true story of the *Washington Post*'s investigative reporting about the Watergate affair to the screen. It was based on the nonfiction bestseller *All the President's Men*, which reporters Bob Woodward and Carl Bernstein had written about their groundbreaking investigation. A film about the inner workings of a newspaper in the midst of an unfolding scandal, it was a compelling story, but not necessarily one that seemed destined for the big screen. Yet, actor Robert Redford had purchased the rights to the book. Responsibility for transforming the book into an A-list movie was turned over to William Goldman, who previously had written the script of Redford's breakout movie, *Butch Cassidy and the Sundance Kid*. With this script, Pakula aimed to breathe cinematic life into the behind-the-scenes account of the investigative reporters.

All the President's Men premiered in April of 1976. Led by a solid cast that included Redford in the role of reporter Woodward and star Dustin Hoffman as Bernstein, it offered a new opportunity for audiences to reflect on the times of crisis that had recently passed. The movie also helped solidify a public understanding of the event as a real-world conspiracy that did present the nation with a grave crisis. Following events that were too recent to really be history, the movie version of *All the President's Men* was one indication on how sense was being made of a confusing and confrontational national experience, from which it had yet to fully heal.

The film mostly focuses on one seemingly simple question: Who was behind the burglary of the Democratic offices in the Watergate office building? Appearing in 1976, the audience for the movie already knew the answer, of course, since that information had slowly and painfully come to light not only in the pages of *The Washington Post* and other news publications that investigated, but by the long series of Congressional hearings, the investigations of the Special Prosecutor, and the following convictions of many implicated figures in a trail that led all the way to the White House. Remarkably, however, Pakula's film revisited this familiar ground and provided a taut insider's account that was largely faithful to the events and slowly revealed an emotional core.

The film begins with the break-in on August 17, 1972. History shows that at first this burglary did not strike many people as a very remarkable event, but as recreated by Pakula, the movie audience immediately notices that this is no ordinary crime. The break-in is undertaken by a group of men who are exceptionally well dressed for burglars and who coordinate the burglary with two-way radios. Despite the apparent planning, however, they are un-expectedly caught in the act. Later, Woodward, a still-new reporter for the *Post*, covers the preliminary court proceedings. His curiosity is immediately aroused.

Unlike many conspiracy movies, there was no need for Pakula to plant the idea of conspiracy in the minds of the audience. The story was too well known for that. Yet, he also could not hope to use revelation of a conspiracy as a dramatic plot element. Instead, the film takes this knowledge as a given. Rather than relying upon building suspense by slowly revealing the plot to the audience, the director emphasizes the painstaking process of uncovering the truth to capture audience attention and build tension.

The film follows Woodward and Bernstein as they follow leads, make phone calls, track down witnesses, and wade through paper records. Often, they reach a dead end. The procedural element of the film, which dominates much of its running time, was well received by film writers and viewers, who saw it as an essentially accurate portrayal of journalistic practice in the 1970s. As a conspiracy theory movie, however, the presentation of conspiracy as a known fact rather than as a secret yet to be discovered sets the film apart from many others with this theme.

Presented as a true story—with the obvious caveat that specific dialogue and other minor elements had been invented—*All the President's Men* largely does maintain a focus on the routine, day-to-day process in which a picture of the truth slowly emerges only with devotion to checking and double-checking sources. Although not inherently cinematic, Goldman's script gives Pakula material with which to build a convincing narrative.[9]

One element in the film, however, relies less on the routines and drudgery of reporting. This is the film's portrayal of Woodward's secret informant from inside government, a man simply called by the nickname Deep Throat. As played by veteran actor Hal Holbrook, the Deep Throat character is one of the most compelling in the film. Though he does not appear very often or for very long, the movie's treatment of the meetings between Woodward and Deep Throat firmly connect *All the President's Men* with the long line of fictionalized conspiracy and espionage thrillers that had become established in American popular culture. These encounters are usually set in a dimly lit parking garage, and Deep Throat, on first appearance in the movie, is literally a man in the shadows. Viewers first notice him partially emerging from the darkness as he lights a cigarette. (In the 1990s, the fictional *X-Files* television show regularly employed this way of filming one of its main villains, the character known as the Cigarette Smoking Man.)

Deep Throat adds an air of intrigue to a well-worn story. Clearly, this man knows much useful—and incriminating—information, but he declines to reveal very much of it. He only occasionally offers real clues, instead wishing simply to confirm information that Woodward has already discovered. At one point, however, Deep Throat seems to think Woodward and his partner have failed to see the obvious. Almost chastising Woodward, he finally instructs Woodward to "follow the money." Indeed, it is the money trail leading from the burglary suspects to those who financially backed them that takes up much of the reporters' time and attention.

As the world already knew by the time the film was released, the money trail was traced directly back to the White House. It led from the bank account of an arrested burglars, to a regional GOP fund-raiser for the Nixon re-election campaign, to the national re-election office, and finally to the White House itself. The path led not only from the beginning to the end of a money trail, it led a nation into deeper cynicism and skepticism than even the preceding Vietnam War years had generated.

Broadly speaking, most of the major conspiracy theory films of the 1970s had overtly political orientations. They focused, in one way or another, on the infiltration or corruption of the American system. Taken together, they presented as unflattering a picture of the American system as had ever been presented by Hollywood. These films presented a world in which ordinary Americans, who still exhibited an innate goodness, were betrayed by the very institutions of society that had made the nation great. Looking back, it is clear how closely the images of conspiracy offered by Hollywood followed the awareness and reaction to real conspiracy that had become the focus of the society at large. A popular slogan in the 1960s counterculture had been "Don't trust anyone over thirty." For many people in the mid-1970s, the level of apprehension extended beyond that.

All the President's Men stands at a crossroad of history, moviemaking, and the evolution of conspiracy theory culture in the United States.[10] A thoroughly mainstream motion picture about a well-known public event, it was a screen incarnation of the idea that a major conspiracy not only could appear in America, it already had. In some ways, this opened the conspiracy theory theme to a new world of possibilities for filmmaking.

NEW INCARNATIONS OF CONSPIRACY THEORY

Indeed, by the late 1970s the conspiracy theory theme began to push further along the new directions that had materialized earlier. The conspiracies depicted were not only large in scale; they frequently involved the central institutions of American life. What had once been the trusted was now potentially suspect. Gradually, everything and everyone was fair game for conspiracy theory. It would take a number of years for this phenomenon to fully mature, but it was obviously underway by the end of the decade.

CAPRICORN ONE

The increasing rise of cynicism in conspiracy theory movies of the 1970s reached its culmination in *Capricorn One*. A standard B-movie in its day, its take on the conspiracy theme adds an original twist that foreshadowed the future path that conspiracy theory would take in the popular culture.

Not concerned with political assassins or a grand scheme to seize the reins of government, the conspiracy outlined in *Capricorn One* is instigated by a seemingly dedicated government scientist. At the center of the conspiracy is NASA scientist James Kelloway (played by Hal Holbrook). He is committed to his work and leads the NASA effort to send astronauts to Mars.

The Mars exploration mission he leads is under pressure, and Congressional leaders have threatened to cut off future funding if the pace of progress does not quicken. Unexpectedly, tests reveal that the space vessel's life support system will not function properly in the upcoming mission. The scheduled launch cannot take place without endangering the lives of the astronauts. Yet, cancellation of the flight would likely result in Congress killing the program. Kelloway cannot live with this possibility, and keeping the test results secret, he decides to take drastic action.

In the scheme, Kelloway plans to deceive the outside world, as well as most of his colleagues. Making elaborate plans, he is determined to make it appear that the mission is proceeding as usual. Using radio, television, and computer trickery, the unsuspecting world will think they see the astronauts take off, land on Mars, and then safely return home. Only Kelloway and his henchmen (who are many) will know the truth—that the entire flight is a charade.

At first, the astronauts scheduled for the flight are unaware of the plan. They prepare for the flight and secure themselves in the space capsule for the final countdown. Moments before lift-off, however, the three astronauts are surprised to find a government agent unsealing their space capsule and asking them to come with him immediately. The astronauts are quickly whisked away, but because the conspirators have tampered with the equipment, everyone else—including the NASA personnel overseeing the mission from the control room—believes the men are still in the capsule and that things are going along as planned. Within minutes, the rocket is launched into space. Only the conspirators and the astronauts know that there are no human passengers on board.

The astronauts, meanwhile, have been taken to a remote location. Not knowing why they have been removed from the spacecraft or what is going on, they are surprised to see the lead scientist, Kelloway. He explains the scheme and solicits their help. He wants the astronauts to fake televised reports, which will be beamed back to the control room and then broadcast to a worldwide television audience. In addition, the highlight of the scheme calls for the astronauts to fake a Mars landing by acting out the event on a huge movie-studio-like set that has been prepared to simulate the appearance of the Martian surface.

If all went well, the return mission would also be faked. Then, to add one final note of credibility to the scheme, the actual Mars spacecraft, which Kelloway was controlling from his secret control center, would be diverted slightly off course just before it parachuted into the ocean. At the last moment, the conspirators would secretly take the astronauts to the capsule so that they would be there when the real rescue team would find them. No one will realize the deception, Kelloway reasoned, unless the astronauts refused to go along with the complicated hoax.

The astronauts express outrage upon learning of the convoluted scheme. They refuse Kelloway's requests. The scientist tries to justify the plan, explaining that he had gone to such lengths because "I just care so goddam much I just think its worth it . . . It'll keep something alive that shouldn't die." Defending the scheme to the skeptical astronauts, he declares, "Nobody gives a crap about anything anymore" and complains that there's "nothing more to believe in."

The astronauts remain unconvinced, however. The commander of the crew, Col. Charles Brubaker (James Brolin) says the plot represents "everything that I hate." Brubaker's crewmates, Lt. Col. Peter Willis (Sam Waterson) and Commander John Walker (O.J. Simpson) express similar reservations.

Realizing that there is no hope of voluntary cooperation, Kelloway reveals the depth of his desperation. Implying that unspecified external "forces" have an interest in seeing the Mars program continue at all costs, Kelloway threatens to have the families of the astronauts killed if they do not go along with the scheme. The astronauts reluctantly go along.

Not surprisingly, however, as the plan is carried out, minor glitches in the scheme eventually are noticed. A low-level NASA technician, for example, notices that the television signals, which are supposedly coming from the spacecraft, seem to originate much closer. His superiors are skeptical of this finding, but he later mentions it to a friend, who, by coincidence, is a reporter.

Later, the suspicious NASA technician mysteriously disappears and the reporter begins an investigation. As the story continues to unfold, the grand plot slowly unravels. The story culminates with the astronauts' attempt to escape from the conspirators.

In the final section of the movie, the story follows the astronauts' attempts to outrun their pursuers, who assumedly plan to kill them in order to keep the plot secret. As the astronauts flee on foot across the desert, they are relentlessly pursued by gun-wielding black helicopters. (Indeed, black helicopters, which in subsequent years became an almost clichéd hallmark of conspiracy theory narratives, make some of their first appearances in *Capricorn One*.)

Taken as a whole, *Capricorn One* is an entertaining, though dated, mix of science fiction and action, tied together with a large-scale conspiracy theme. Within the context of the film, the massive conspiracy is the glue that the director uses to hold the film together. As employed in *Capricorn One*, however, the theme is largely a received notion. The film assumes that viewers will easily accept the idea that vaguely defined interests within the American establishment would resort to a massive conspiracy in order to maintain the status quo. Indeed, though only the immediate conspirators (such as Kelloway) are specifically identified in the film, the logic of the story clearly implies that business, government, and military figures are implicated. The story of *Capricorn One* is one in which the conspirators are centered in the halls of power.

In most respects, *Capricorn One* is not a remarkable film. It is unlikely that audiences or critics would place it among the top films of its era. Yet, in terms of pushing along the thematic development of conspiracy theory in popular culture, the movie does deserve special note. Perhaps the most significant idea in *Capricorn One* is that nothing reported is necessarily the truth. The story is based on the idea that sinister forces can shape society's beliefs, contorting reality for their own purposes. In the movie's world, it is true that some institutions, notably news organizations (which were held in relatively high regard during the Watergate era) do not appear to be part of the amorphous cabal. But these organizations are easily duped and are manipulated by the conspirators to further their secret agenda.

More obviously, although the faked Mars landing in film remains in the realm of fiction, in the years following, an eerily similar suspicion about the veracity of the real NASA moon landing entered conspiratorial culture in the United States.[11] The assumptions that it would not be difficult to fake such large-scale events and that it would be easy for such efforts to avoid detection—both quite dubious propositions—later became a relatively common belief among some conspiracy theory advocates.

Yet from another perspective, *Capricorn One* seems to inadvertently demonstrate that grand conspiracies, such as that of the film's story, are in most respects preposterous. Indeed, even in the fictional world of the movie, the scheme only barely works. Even then, the story is filled with ignored details, leaps of logic, and highly improbable coincidences. In sum, the conspiracy is not very convincing if taken seriously.

It is doubtful, however, that the conspiracy element was intended to be taken so seriously, and it seems even more unlikely that even the writers would imagine anyone would take it literally. Instead, *Capricorn One* is an action thriller enveloped in the paranoia of the times. It functions better as a comment about America's mood than as a textbook for real conspiracy-making.

From a broader perspective, an important theme in *Capricorn One* is that perceived reality is suspect. In a way, the movie, perhaps unwittingly, promoted the type of belief structure that helped pave the way for the assumption, much later, that almost any event could be faked, including the terror attacks of September 11, 2001.

Thus, although the conspiracy theory theme had once been used to tell stories of grabs for power, by the late 1970s the scope of conspiracy in movie fiction had expanded dramatically. The plots to overthrow governments, prevalent in earlier conspiracy theory movies, look somewhat pedestrian when compared to bigger schemes to manipulate society's thoughts and actions as appeared on screen by the late 1970s. Perhaps the reality of Watergate had raised the bar, condemning stories that were simply about juntas and coups to the realm of the ordinary. To get attention now, film-makers interested in the conspiracy theory theme increasingly resorted to stories in which there were ever more complex and comprehensive schemes and deceptions, even if the underlying motivations were still the vices that have always driven characters, fictional or real, to misbehave.

OTHER LATE 1970S FILMS

A group of films from 1978 and 1979 with science fiction themes further demonstrates this point. The evil-doers in director Michael Crichton's 1978 film *Coma*, for example have basic, criminal motivations; they run a corrupt money-making scheme. The conspirators' plans, however, utilize elaborate deceptions that require the complicity of many accessories to the crime.

Simply put, the villains in *Coma* have a grand scheme: For preselected patients undergoing routine surgery, the conspirators induce a comatose state. They cover up their actions so that these events appear to be ordinary, if unfortunate, medical outcomes. These patients are then transferred to a medical center where they supposedly receive appropriate care. That's how it appears to the next of kin and the outside world, anyway.

In reality, the plotters have induced brain death, and the supposed patients are essentially murder victims. Yet, their bodies are kept on minimal life support for a horrific purpose. When clients have orders, the organs from the supposedly comatose patients are harvested and sold.

Like other films from this era, *Coma* suggests that society's central institutions—in this case the health system—have been infiltrated. And like conspiracy theory films from this and earlier eras, *Coma* suggests that people can encounter a deadly peril and not even realize it.

In the context of late-1970s cinema and political culture, it was perhaps fitting that *Invasion of the Body Snatchers* was remade as a Hollywood movie. Although the film was updated for 1970s audiences, the new version retained the theme of paranoia and fear that was central to the original two decades earlier. The first *Invasion of the Body Snatchers*, of course, was often interpreted as a commentary on, or at least a reflection of, fears of international communism of the 1950s. These general anxieties were made concrete in the film through a story in which an entire population was secretly replaced with hostile invaders. In the 1978 version, the fear of communism had largely waned, perhaps replaced with a more generic fear that society's institutions were rotting from the inside, a process of decay aided by forces that were robbing people of individuality and free thought.

Elsewhere, the spectacular success of George Lucas's *Star Wars* movie in 1977 resuscitated Hollywood's interest in outer space-oriented science fiction tales. Two years later, director Ridley Scott's *Alien* was released. It was a darker incarnation of this genre with an unmistakable conspiracy theme. Although mostly remembered for the frightening depiction of an alien life-form, the narrative in this film, as well as its sequel several years later, involved a huge corporation that secretly schemed to capture an alien for the purposes of conducting military tests.

The story is set far in the future. It begins as the small crew aboard the spaceship Nostromo, a commercial transport vessel that is traveling deep in space, receives a strange signal. It seems to have originated on a nearby moon. A team is quickly dispatched to investigate. Arriving on the strange moon's surface, they discover a derelict alien vessel, the crew of which apparently died some time ago. As they examine the wreckage, they also discover a room filled with small egg-like pods. While examining one of the pods, a crew member is attacked and incapacitated. He is taken back to the Nostromo for medical care.

The creature has attached itself to its victim, slowly draining the life from him. Unexpectedly, however, the creature becomes detached and the victim seems to recover. Not long after, things turn dramatically worse. While dining with other members of the crew, the previously injured man begins to choke. Then, in a ghoulish scene, a larger, more dangerous creature bursts from the man's body, killing him instantly. The frightening creature escapes into the crevices of the ship and the crew tries desperately to capture it.

As the film progresses, the creature grows and become more dangerous. The members of the crew, meanwhile, succumb to the creature's attacks, one by one. Ellen Ripley (played by Sigourney Weaver) emerges as one of the last survivors on the Nostromo. A strong and resourceful woman, she tries to figure out how to defeat the creature, which has grown even larger and more menacing. As she queries the vessel's computer for advice, she inadvertently learns of a "special order" that has been issued by the company that owns the Nostromo.

The special order is at the heart of *Alien*'s conspiracy narrative. As Ripley discovers, the company had already known about the wrecked spacecraft and about the dangerous creatures in the pods. They had instructed their onboard company representative, a science officer named Ash (played by Ian Holm) to make sure that one of the creatures was captured and returned to the company for testing and experimentation. The crew is expendable, and Ash had been informed that the mission must succeed at all costs.

When Ash learns that Ripley has uncovered the special order, they have a violent confrontation. Ash is about to kill Ripley when two other crew members stop him. Ash seemingly dies in the fight. At that moment, they realize that Ash is not human, but an android.

In the rest of the movie, Ripley and the other survivors desperately continue their struggle for survival against the creature, which travels through the vessel's extensive air duct system. Eventually, only Ripley and the creature are left, forcing Ripley to abandon the Nostromos in a small escape vessel. She is seemingly safe, though there is one more last-minute battle in the escape vessel.

Alien combines science fiction, horror, and conspiracy themes in a fast-paced, smartly directed package. But unlike earlier films, such as *Invasion of the Body Snatchers*, the threat faced by the humans is not only from an external enemy, but also from the crew's employers. Indeed, the story hinges on a conspiracy that exploits a human crew in order to advance the company's objectives.

As *Alien* demonstrated, by the late 1970s, a viewer could expect to encounter conspiracy angles in stories that were not really about conspiracies. When conspiracy appears, it is often not the centerpiece of the narrative, but rather an underlying element that is taken for granted. Increasingly, movies that touched on conspiracies and conspiracy theory were made with the assumption that audiences would understand and accept this part of the narrative without much explanation or convincing. The conspiracy theory mindset was, by this time, a readily understood way of thinking about the world.

END OF AN ERA

As the 1970s began, the United States was still engaged in the controversial war in Vietnam and had yet to fully process many of the social changes that had come to a boiling point during the previous decade. By mid-decade, the scene settled somewhat, but at a cost to the American psyche. The war had come to an unceremonious end, and its conclusion represented an unsettling loss for Americans, who were unaccustomed to anything but victory in military matters. And just as the country seemed to be extracting itself from the long and bitter war, the Watergate scandal generated a furor and brought down the presidency of Richard Nixon. Soon after, the economy turned for the worse. Events such as these contributed to the declining confidence that Americans had in their government and in the central institutions of their society.

Since the resurgence of conspiracy theory in United States during the early years of the Cold War, it had been a reliable barometer of public anxieties and apprehensions. That remained true in the 1970s, when the conspiracy theory theme reflected the growing lack of confidence that the nation had about itself. The importance of conspiracy theory in the 1970s, as in other decades, was not in the specific explanations it offered for certain events, therefore. Rather, its greatest importance was as a metaphorical representation of how people approached the world.

Indeed, a person did not need to take any specific conspiracy theory as literal truth in order to believe that the most powerful forces in society might not be trustworthy. Recent experience had demonstrated that. Rather, in an era of mistrust and diminishing national confidence, the thought that forces beyond the control of the individual pulled society's strings could be an easy explanation to accept. Of course, advocates of specific conspiracy theories continued to promote their beliefs as fact. It seems likely, however, that many people paid attention to the conspiracy theory theme not for what it said specifically about assassinations, UFO sightings, or other events, but because such theories drew on their own skepticism or disillusionments.

Thus, when conspiracy was represented on screen, it was increasingly portrayed as part of the fabric of society, not simply as an aberration. And this was the way in which conspiracy theory increasingly appeared in numerous dramas, action-oriented features, political thrillers, and science fiction movies. Such movies may not always have seemed very realistic, but they accurately reflected an underlying mood that had become prevalent in the United States. Indeed, in the mainstream of American life, the core idea of conspiracy theory—that unseen forces shaped, influenced, deceived, and exploited ordinary people—no longer seemed as unbelievable as it once did.

Vision and Re-Vision

The most obvious signal that American society was undergoing a change in 1980 was the spectacular success of Ronald Reagan as he marched toward his party's nomination and then victory at the polls in November. The worldview that the plain-talking Reagan effectively promoted was a simple one in which choices were clear and morality was unambiguous. He looked back at his country in the previous decade and saw the need for a new course, a way out of the discords and disaffections that had plagued America since the 1960s. With his election, voters seemed to be expressing a desire for their nation to return to traditional values and to a simpler view of life.

By 1980, however, the cultural phenomenon of conspiracy theory had become securely lodged in American popular culture. As such, it can be seen as a symbol, or perhaps a symptom, of the confusing, ambiguous complexity that Reagan wanted the nation to escape. After all, conspiracy theory in American culture at this time often implied the entire American system was suspect. Its central institutions—from the health care system to industry to the military to the government itself—often appeared as the villains in popular culture, particularly in the cinema. A restoration of the trust and righteousness that Reagan and his fellow neoconservatives desired therefore seemed to imply the opposite of everything the conspiracy theory worldview represented.

It would be a mistake to assume that Reagan and his followers were interested only in serious public discourse and not in how the popular culture represented American society. Reagan had been a successful Hollywood actor, but that was not the main reason he understood the importance that expressions of popular culture played in shaping and maintaining public perceptions.

A bigger reason was the emerging debate in American society that was later called the "culture wars." By the 1980s, the idea that popular culture—especially movies and television—affected how people perceived and reacted to life around them was a well-established proposition. (Indeed, had cultural elites not feared the corrosive influence of popular culture, there previously would not have been such an outcry against television, which some of its critics often called the "idiot box.")

Neoconservatives easily recognized the power of popular culture. Their objection was not that it was influential, however. Rather, their complaint was that it influenced with the wrong message. Thus, an underlying part of Reagan's plan of attack in the 1980s was a consistent effort to argue for different representations. It would seem that this would naturally have involved an effort to undercut the appeal of conspiracy theory messages, since conspiracy theory seemed now to represent a negative, critical stance toward much of American life.

Yet, it was not quite that simple. Perhaps the most obvious example of how thoroughly conspiracy theory thinking had infiltrated even the upper echelons of American politics was found in the new way that Ronald Reagan talked about the Vietnam War. It was a way of looking at things that argued for a more straightforward, accepting role of American nobility, seemingly the antithesis of what much conspiracy theory thinking implied at that time.

But his interpretation of how Americans had arrived at such negative feelings about the Vietnam conflict may have inadvertently paved the way for an even darker vision. Two examples of Reagan's rhetoric make this point. First, there is the famous statement from his first inauguration speech of January 20, 1980, in which he said, "Government is not a solution to our problem, government is the problem." An assertion that the federal government was at the root of the nation's malaise fits nicely with neoconservative doctrine, but it also reinforced the more negative idea that America's institutions had failed. And although Reagan clearly did not intend his words to be interpreted as a broad indictment of the American system, this statement was inadvertently congruent with a conspiracy theory mindset in which the system pervasively intrudes into personal life.

At the time, however, the darker way of thinking about Reagan's identification of government with "the problem" received little consideration. Throughout his presidency, Reagan's sincere and straightforward way of speaking charmed the nation, and as a result, the ambiguities in his some of his remarks tended to be overlooked. Of course, Reagan had separated the government as an ideal from the government as practiced. He wanted to set things straight, rescuing the practice of government, which he suggested was an overgrown, lumbering behemoth that sometimes was not too trustworthy. But while Reagan did not intend to undermine faith in American government or the central institutions of free enterprise, his declaration that "government is the problem," with its instant sound-bite nature, could be interpreted more cynically than he meant it to be.

In addition to this general theme of government—or big government, anyway—being a problem itself, a second, more specific theme, affirmed a distrustful interpretation of American experience in the very recent past. This was Reagan's new interpretation of the Vietnam War.

Like Gerald Ford and Jimmy Carter before him, Reagan knew that the ill-effects of the Vietnam War continued to dampen the national mood. Indeed, the turmoil about the war seemed to have spilled over beyond the end of that conflict, influencing the way Americans felt about their country in the years after that war. It is true, of course, that Americans seemed anxious to forget the war. But although peace had come, reconciliation among Americans who had argued about the war had not. Moreover, with the war's unsettling end, Americans now seemed reluctant to play a powerful role on the world stage. Reagan called this malaise the "Vietnam syndrome," and he wanted it to end.

One reason for his concern was the lessened influence that the United States seemed to exert on the rest of the world. Surely the controversies of the Vietnam War had not been confined to domestic American politics, but the place of the United States at the helm of the free world was equally damaged, in Reagan's view, by the fact that the nation seemed reluctant to remain engaged in complex international affairs. There was no doubt in Reagan's mind, then, that the Vietnam syndrome needed to be overturned so that the United States could reassume the rightful role that Reagan and others saw for it.

For Reagan, vanquishing the Vietnam syndrome meant a dramatic rethinking of the entire American experience in the Vietnam War. For him, this meant not seeing it as the war that America lost, but as a "war our government was afraid to let them [meaning the U.S. military] win," as he proclaimed in a 1980 campaign speech. Indeed, according to Reagan's interpretation, the government had tied the American military's collective hands, refusing to unleash the nation's awesome power and political will to finish the war with another American victory, rather than an ignoble defeat.

Reagan was undeterred by his understanding of these past events, however. He reasoned that although the Vietnam War ended badly and that the way the United States had acted damaged both America's perceptions of itself and the way the nation was perceived around the world, all was not lost. He asserted that Americans could overcome this unfortunate legacy by understanding the war in a different way. He argued that the Vietnam War should not be regarded as a quagmire or as an unwinnable or immoral military action. Instead, to escape from the malaise of the Vietnam syndrome, Americans needed to think about the Vietnam War in a wholly new way.

Accordingly, Reagan argued that "it's time that we recognized that ours was, in truth, a noble cause." Added to the fact that he believed the American military could have prevailed if it had been allowed to, he asserted that regardless of the unfortunate outcome, the war was something "noble." Americans had no reason to feel ashamed. If shame existed, in this view, it was reserved for those elements in government and society that had shackled the war effort. For everyone else—which Reagan apparently thought was a large proportion of the public—the way to escape the Vietnam syndrome was to recognize these reasons for the war's loss and correct them as the nation moved forward. There were, of course, very different ways of looking at the war, but Reagan's view resonated with many people.

The conspiracy theory thread in American thinking dovetailed conveniently with both of the important themes that Reagan had articulated. In terms of the general argument that the government is a "problem," this view had already become established in the way the popular culture represented the conspiracy theory theme. Movie articulations of this theme, in which the government was implicated in conspiratorial actions, had become especially prominent in the preceding years.

Meanwhile, Reagan's second theme, focusing on the Vietnam War, fit squarely with emerging conspiracy ideas regarding the fate of some Americans soldiers that had fought in that war. Specifically, Reagan's line of thinking, in which some part of government had refused to let the military win, coincided with the developing notion that the U.S. government had not revealed the truth, or the whole truth anyway, about the fate of American missing-in-action soldiers (MIAs) and those prisoners of war (POWs) whose fate remained unknown.

According to this way of thinking, some government officials, who already had betrayed missing American service personnel by not adequately supporting them in a time of war, had betrayed them again by abandoning them after they had gone missing. Now sweeping the whole matter under the carpet, the new conspiracy thinking about MIAs and POWs focused on the thought that perhaps, contrary to government assertions, there were still living American soldiers in captivity. Those holding this view began to think that a conspiracy of silence and cover-ups existed within some quarters of American government. According to this way of thinking, it was dedicated to suppressing knowledge rather than see the past misdeeds uncovered. It seemed like the stuff of conspiracy movies, and soon it was.

RAMBO-ERA FILMS

A group of films in the 1980s promoted these ideas about the government as a potentially malicious force that cared little for its military personnel. The movies that most captured these sentiments were *Missing in Action* and *Missing in Action 2*, featuring the martial artist-turned-actor Chuck Norris, and the widely popular *Rambo* movies that starred Sylvester Stallone, who already had risen to fame in the movie *Rocky*.

The first of these to appear was *First Blood*, director Ted Kotcheff's movie that introduced film audiences to fictional Vietnam veteran John Rambo.[1] In this 1982 outing, Rambo appears as a drifter, a man who is clearly still recovering from his experiences in the Vietnam War. An alienated loner, Rambo has an unfortunate encounter with law enforcement officials while passing through the American northwest. The movie does not necessarily imply a conspiracy theory reading at first glance, but its underlying narrative introduces, for a mass audience, the idea of the Vietnam veteran as the victim of secretive and malicious officials. This powerful cultural theme would develop into a more specifically conspiratorial narrative in several subsequent films.

The story of *First Blood* is that of an antihero, and on the surface it seems to be mostly an action-revenge drama. In the narrative, Rambo is the victim of a series of mistaken beliefs and misunderstandings, and he soon finds himself on the wrong side of the law. His biggest problem is with the local sheriff, Will Teasle (played by Brian Dennehy). The sheriff has little tolerance for people he regards as vagabonds and tries to run Rambo out of town. The movie shows the magnitude of Rambo's mistreatment by local law enforcement with a scene in which the hero is viciously beaten. Dazed from his mistreatment at the hands of people sworn to uphold law and order, all Rambo can manage is to escape into the wilderness that surrounds the town.

As audiences soon discover, Rambo is no ordinary veteran. Wrongly accused, he tries to disappear in the wilds of the countryside as he is pursued by an ever-increasing number of law enforcement personnel. Soon, the National Guard is called to assist with the pursuit of the hero, and Rambo must use his extraordinary cunning and superheroic combat skills to elude capture. This action takes up much of the movie.

As the dramatic incident becomes known, Rambo's former superior officer, Col. Samuel Trautman (Richard Crenna), arrives and tries to help. Knowing that Rambo possesses superior skills as a guerilla fighter from his days as a Green Beret, Trautman tries to convince the sheriff to back off, but to no avail.

In the end, the veteran-turned-vigilante hero escapes death several times. He causes much mayhem and destroys part of the sheriff's town. Just as Rambo confronts the sheriff, however, Trautman intervenes. It is clear that Rambo's freedom will come to an end.

Although billed primarily as an action movie, *First Blood* clearly pushed the conspiratorial idea that government misdeeds had obscured truths about the Vietnam War. As an emblem of the American soldier, Rambo's amazing physical prowess and fighting skills suggest that the American military was not the problem in Vietnam, reinforcing at some level the idea that Vietnam was a war that some power "did not let them win," as Reagan had said. Moreover, Rambo's mistreatment by the system can be interpreted as a symbol for the nation's poor treatment of all Vietnam War veterans, who, according to Reagan's re-visioning of the war, had been sent into harm's way by a government that had no real intention of supporting them during or after the fight.

This theme of the alienated-veteran-as-victim is developed into a narrative with more overt conspiracy theory underpinnings in movies that followed on the heels of *First Blood*. In these works, the stories depict malicious forces within government that explicitly have betrayed ordinary soldiers and that continue to use official authority to propagate lies and deception. The films show both conspiracies of silence and of immoral, maybe even criminal, action.[2]

The 1983 movie *Uncommon Valor*, for example, relied on a story line in which government officials actively worked against the interests of still-captive soldiers and worked aggressively to keep anyone from revealing evidence that some MIAs and POWs were still being held against their will. More blatantly, 1984's *Missing in Action*, the Chuck Norris vehicle, followed the exploits of fictional Col. James Braddock as he returned to Vietnam to find and free American compatriots still being held in wretched conditions by communist forces.

Making the biggest impact of any of these films, however, was the 1985 sequel to *First Blood*. The new movie, directed by George P. Cosmatos, was the hugely popular *Rambo: First Blood, Part II*, which usually was simply called *Rambo*. With a script that was written by returning star Sylvester Stallone along with James Cameron (later the director of such hit movies as *Terminator*, *Aliens*, and *Titanic*[3]), *Rambo* returns the hero to the scene of the original action in Vietnam.

According to the film's narrative, Rambo had been jailed as the result of earlier exploits that had been shown in *First Blood*. As the film begins, however, the government orders Rambo's release from prison in order to carry out a new mission, for which it is thought he is uniquely qualified. Rambo will be secretly taken back to Vietnam in order to covertly search for evidence that some American POWs are still being held captive. He is told that he is to gather such evidence, if any is to be found, and then bring it back for follow-up action. Rambo's former commander, the somewhat sympathetic Col. Trautman, is on hand, but he is not aware of all aspects of the mission. Instead, the operation is to be overseen by another officer, who has darker motives.

Indeed, though Rambo is under the impression that the mission is an indication that his government has finally come to see the importance of making a supreme effort to rescue any remaining POWs, those in charge of the operation actually wish for the mission to fail. They want to squelch any further investigations into matters they wish to remain obscured.

Rambo is unaware that he is expected to fail, however, and undertakes the mission vigorously. After he is secretly transported to a remote location in Vietnam, he begins his quest with the assistance of a Vietnamese woman named Co Bao. Before long, Rambo finds an encampment in which American soldiers are still held under barbaric conditions. Unable to tolerate the idea of merely bringing back evidence, Rambo springs into action and undertakes a rescue. Heroically, he manages to free one of the persecuted soldiers and prepares to rendezvous with the team that is to return him to safety.

At this point, things go awry for everyone concerned. The overseer of the operation, aghast that Rambo has not only found unexpected evidence but also plans to return with one of the captives, abruptly terminates the operation. He orders the destruction of all documentary evidence of the mission. Trautman is horrified but is powerless to change things. Rambo's rescue team is turned back, presumably to insure that Rambo and his evidence disappear forever. Indeed, Rambo is taken prisoner by hostile Vietnamese forces, and it is soon clear that his captors do not intend for him to survive.

Soon after he is taken prisoner, his captors subject Rambo to sadistic treatment. As he is tortured, his Vietnamese captors are aided by a cruel Soviet officer, who is inexplicably stationed in the remote Vietnam camp. As Rambo endures vicious and inhuman treatment, the prospects for his survival look dim.

Unexpectedly for his captors, however, Rambo soon manages to escape, thanks to the assistance of Co Bao. He does not plan to simply flee the area. Indeed, Rambo's wrath is accompanied by nearly superhuman vengeance. In the next sequence Co Bao dies, but Rambo continues to fight. He kills many enemy soldiers, eludes others, and destroys much of the countryside as he flees with POWs he has freed.

Making his way out of Vietnam, Rambo and the rescued soldiers are finally free. By then, it is clear that Rambo will expose the fraudulent mission if the overseers do not cooperate. And so in the end, it appears that Rambo will get the result that he was expecting all along. After his ordeal, Rambo's passion for his country is undiminished. All he wants, he says, is for his country to love him (and by extension, all Vietnam veterans) as much as he loves it.

Almost universally, movie critics panned *Rambo: First Blood, Part II*. This had little effect on audience enthusiasm, however. Indeed, *Rambo* was one of the most popular and financially successful films of the year, and its simple message resonated with many film-goers. In mainstream America, the movie was a hit, with its combination of simple patriotism and over-the-top action. Even Ronald Reagan, who could be an astute interpreter of mainstream American emotions, spoke positively about the film.

Although the conspiracy theory theme was not what drew Americans to *Rambo*—indeed, they may scarcely have noticed it—the idea that the government, or parts of it, had schemed to suppress and victimize brave members of the American military was an essential part of the plot. And so while audiences may have responded mostly to the clear-cut portrayals of good and evil and the numerous action sequences, *Rambo* was an effective vehicle for spreading and emphasizing the underlying conspiratorial narrative to a very wide audience. It was perhaps all the more effective in transmitting this theme since it was so plainly presented, as if it could be taken for granted that forces within the government would set up a hero and betray patriotic American soldiers. Indeed, the conspiracy element of Rambo is certainly far from the most unrealistic or outrageous element of the plot.

Movies such as *First Blood*, *Missing in Action*, and *Rambo* reveal the extraordinary level to which a line of conspiratorial thinking had penetrated into the American mainstream. These films, all quite popular in their day, channeled lingering anxieties about the way the United States had acted during the Vietnam War, and especially how it had acted from then until the present time with regard to its own military personnel. For a society that had often ignored or trivialized military service in the war, there may have been something cathartic in such movies. Yet, in telling the stories in the ways that they did—by choosing to tell stories in which elements of the American government itself were guilty of betrayal, serious misdeeds, and cover-ups— the film-makers played into cultural theme of conspiracy theory that had been evolving for several decades. Indeed, though the communist foes linger, sometimes in the background, as evil foes aiming to destroy America, it is clear that conniving elements within America's own government and military have equally contributed to the suffering of American soldiers. What is more, it is the conspiring Americans who keep the truth from being revealed, meaning a continuation of suffering for the forsaken Americans MIAs and POWs.

Conspiracy theory had long been present in some ways of thinking about the Vietnam War. (This was especially true after the publication of the Pentagon Papers, a secret document revealing government deceptions and misrepresentations about the conflict that was leaked to the press in 1971.) In the past, however, the conspiratorial interest usually focused on strategic aspects of the conflict and attempts to deflect public interest in policy matters. For example, a conspiratorial element seemed to lurk beneath the surface in some accounts of events such as the secret American incursion into Cambodia, which preceded the publicly acknowledged invasion in 1970. And then there was the government's apparent misrepresentation of the 1964 Gulf of Tonkin incident, the confusing event that triggered a massive increase in direct U.S. involvement in the war some years earlier.

What was different about the Reagan-era stories of conspiracy in the Vietnam War, then, was not that the conspiracy element was added to the ongoing national narrative about the war in public memory. Instead, the new twist was that the Rambo and Rambo-like stories focused not on a bending of the truth in a time of war, but the suggestion of a deep-seated betrayal of the American service personnel during and after the war.

In the political world of the day, Reagan argued that the conflict had been a "noble cause" that had gone bad, and the narratives of the new type of Vietnam War films provided underpinnings in the popular culture for such an interpretation. The war's bad result was now connected, in popular film fiction, with betrayal from within. In that way, defeat in Southeast Asia was not inflicted upon the nation, but the result of a self-inflicted wound. It was an easier way to think about things. It was fully consistent with the simpler view that America had simply not mustered the will to achieve a military victory. Conspiracy, even a fictionalized version, was a way to explain that failure to support the war effort was someone else's fault.[4]

CONSPIRACY IN OTHER GUISES

The conspiracy theory theme continued to occasionally appear in a relatively traditional and less politically cynical guise. Perhaps the most successful movie of the early 1980s to take this approach was director Brian DePalma's *Blow Out*. As the title suggested, it looked back to sources such as Michelangelo Antonioni's 1966 thriller *Blow-Up* as inspiration, as well as to *The Conversation*, which had pursued a similar theme and story line a few years earlier.[5] Yet, as much as it bears a surface resemblance to these two predecessors, *Blow Out* also follows in the tradition of Alfred Hitchcock with a narrative that focuses on a lone character's fear and desperation in the face of mysterious forces that seem to be working against him. And so unlike other conspiracy-themed movies of the era, DePalma does not deal with the theme by focusing on the decay of government and society as its source.

Blow Out stars John Travolta, the popular actor who at the time was still struggling to escape the typecasting that followed him on the heels of the phenomenally successful *Saturday Night Fever*. Travolta plays the part of Jack Terry, a run-of-the-mill sound engineer for a Philadelphia production company. One evening, while recording background sound effects for a movie, Terry witnesses a car wreck. Apparently, the tire on the car blew out just as it was crossing a bridge. Without hesitation, Terry attempts to rescue the occupants as the car sinks into the river. The driver is dead, but Terry manages to save the passenger, a young woman named Sally (played by Nancy Allen). Later, he learns that the driver of the car had been a rising political figure with aspirations for the White House.

Sometime after the accident, Terry realizes that as he was recording sound effects for his work, he inadvertently had also recorded the crash. When he listens carefully to the sounds on his tape, he is startled to hear what he thinks is a gunshot just prior to when the car careened out of control. He soon begins to wonder if the accident was an accident after all. Perhaps, he speculates, the sound of the blown out tire had obscured the sound of an assassin's bullet.

With his suspicions raised, Terry tries to discover more information about the incident. He stumbles onto a blackmail scheme, which seems to involve Sally. But it doesn't seem as though the potential blackmailers had murder on their minds, and so the truth seems hazier and more complicated than ever.

As with other movies of this type, the hero eventually tries to rally the interest of the authorities in the case, but to little avail. Terry thinks that the tape recording is compelling evidence that a gun was fired, but the authorities are not convinced. With officials uninterested in the case, the sound engineer-turned detective then tries to solve the mystery on his own.

Among DePalma's more successful movies, *Blow Out* is an effectively designed film that weaves a complicated story to entertaining effect. As a conspiracy theory film, its importance lies in two elements. First, *Blow Out* is further evidence that conspiracy theory, specifically political conspiracy theory, had reached a sufficient level of audience acceptance as a theme that it could be effectively used without much explanation. In the movie, the conspiracy is suggested, but the director never feels compelled to follow up with many details, or even to make the conspiracy the central theme. Instead, it is a conspiracy theory movie in which the conspiracy is simply there among other plot elements, somewhat similar to the way the theme was portrayed in *Chinatown*, which also had used the theme as one of many.

Second, in terms of furthering the evolution of conspiracy theory in film, *Blow Out* brings an earlier conspiracy theory element to new attention. This is the old idea that officials in the government (here represented by law enforcement) are unlikely to recognize a conspiracy even when they encounter it. In this respect, *Blow Out* calls to mind a wide range of predecessors, in such disparate movies as Hitchcock's *The Man Who Knew Too Much*, in which a lone man tries to bring attention to a conspiracy without much success, and even the two versions of *Invasion of the Body Snatchers* that had appeared to that date. This way of telling stories about conspiracy had received less attention in recent years, especially after the Watergate era, in which narratives often assumed that once evidence of conspiracy got into the hands of officials or news reporters, the story was essentially over. With *Blow Out*, the idea is reasserted that presentation of evidence might only mark the beginning of a struggle to uncover the truth. This theme would become a more essential component of populist conceptions of conspiracy theory in the coming years.

Other movies from the early 1980s also emphasized the institutional turn in conspiracy theory. Like *Rambo* and *Missing in Action*, they were more apt to represent certain elements within the nation's central institutions, particularly the government as the source of conspiracy. These movies also assumed that some parts of America's institutional landscape were still relatively pure, however, and so the stories assume that although conspiracy was lurking close to the surface of everyday American life, it could still be exposed simply by bringing evidence to the right people. In a way, then, the films tended to combine a sense of cynicism, which was a relatively recent development in the way such stories were told, with a more old-fashioned sense that certain parts of officialdom could still be trusted.

Some of the other conspiracy theory films of the era also resonated with political culture of the day, and specifically with Reagan's assertion that big government was the problem. Just as the new cinematic narratives about the Vietnam War fit squarely within Reagan's quest to reposition the whole war in American memory, movies of this era that focused on other kinds of stories sometimes picked up this theme. Probably in a way that would have met with Reagan's disapproval, however, Hollywood suspicions ran much deeper than simply the huge federal bureaucracy. Indeed, some movies continued to associate conspiracy with a more pervasively negative portrayal of the American way of life, with particular skepticism aimed at big business. Some prominent conspiracy theory movies of this time focus on themes of conspiratorial government and institutional complicity in actions that ran contrary to the interest of common people. In these films, like the popular Vietnam War films in the vein of *Rambo*, the broader portrayal of American institutions as conniving enemies of common people was perpetuated in more traditional conspiracy films of the era.

One such example was the 1983 film *Silkwood* from director Mike Nichols. Like *All the President's Men*, it was based on a true story, in this case the life and mysterious death of a woman who worked for the nuclear power industry. Yet, the story of whistle-blower Karen Silkwood called to mind more than events from the news.[6] The story of the film is reminiscent of the fictional *China Syndrome*, a 1979 movie about the cover up of an accident at a nuclear power plant.

Featuring an A-list cast headed by Meryl Streep in the leading role, *Silkwood* essentially embedded a conspiracy theory theme within a biographical portrait. In doing so, it implicitly indicted elements within the nuclear industry for her death. In some ways, *Silkwood* appears to begin as an ordinary depiction of life in American industry. As the story progresses, however, it is clear the movie is aiming to portray something much more sinister than this, and since the case on which the film is based was widely reported in the news of the day, most of the initial audiences knew where the movie was headed.

The audience is introduced to Karen Silkwood, an employee of a company that produces plutonium fuel rods for the nuclear power industry. While going about the routine duties of doing her job, Silkwood begins to worry. The materials that she and her fellow workers are handling are obviously very dangerous. She suspects that safety procedures have been intentionally compromised as the company takes cost-savings steps.

Silkwood files a complaint and soon the matter comes to public attention. The story is set in a time when there was widespread uneasiness about the nuclear power industry, and so not surprisingly, the press and politicians take almost immediate notice. Of course, some industry and company loyalists are deeply resentful of Silkwood's whistle-blowing and her accusations that the company is intentionally engaging in wrongdoing. It is easy to see that as her allegations attract more attention and she gains more notoriety, she has made many enemies.

The movie devotes much attention to the personal life of the main character, all of which has relatively little to do with the circumstances that have brought her to national prominence. In terms of conspiracy theory, it is the final chapter of Silkwood's life that holds the most significance. Indeed, as the complicated case continues to attract attention from the press, Silkwood agrees to provide a reporter from *The New York Times* with evidence to be used in the ongoing expose. In a sudden and tragic turn of events, however, her car crashes while en route to meet the reporter.

Silkwood did not survive the accident, and the strange coincidence of the accident and the meeting she had arranged with the reporter soon became fuel for conspiracy-minded people. By this time, of course, a substantial number of people had come to believe that American industry, or parts of it anyway, was secretly working against the public interest, sometimes with lethal results. It was a feeling that grew during the Vietnam War, in which some people felt military-related industries influenced war policy in order to maintain corporate profits, and then amplified by the shattering scandal of Watergate.

In addition to such movies, other films and television productions with apparently more escapist aims also used the conspiracy theory theme during the 1980s. Several examples illustrate this impulse. The 1981 film *Outland*, for example, links corporate greed to conspiratorial methods. This futuristic tale adds a science fiction flavor to the conspiracy theory theme by placing the action in a remote mining colony stationed on one of Jupiter's moons. In that story, a law officer (Sean Connery) is at first deceived by, and then menaced by, company agents who are trying to keep secret the illegal use of performance enhancing drugs by employees in company mines. In another manifestation of the conspiracy angle, the action-thriller *Blue Thunder* (1983) shows how a specialized high-tech helicopter, supposedly created for law enforcement operations, is actually being developed for more sinister purposes. In a somewhat similar vein, the narrative of the movie *RoboCop* (1987) shows how megalomaniac leaders of the future plan to use another new law enforcement innovation—in this case a powerful half-human, half-robotic creation—to further their own lust for power.

On television, series such as *Dallas*, *Knots Landing*, and *Dynasty* frequently resorted to conspiracy themes in their essentially soap-opera plots. Such shows, which focused on the bad behavior of the rich and powerful, were extremely popular in the 1980s. Their stories showed a world in which conspiracies were an integral part of business and politics.

Of course, sometimes the conspiracy theory theme continued to be depicted in a more intentionally serious way. The 1988 film *Betrayed*, for example, involves a murder investigation that leads to conspiracy. In the movie, director Costa Gravas follows the story of an undercover agent (portrayed by Debra Winger) as she tries to discover who is responsible for the murder of a prominent talk show host. As the plot unfolds, it becomes clear that the victim was targeted because he was Jewish and that the killers had bigger things than one simple murder on their minds. Indeed, to her horror, the agent eventually learns that a man she has befriended (a character played by Tom Berenger) is not an innocent man, but instead leads a violently militant white-supremacist conspiracy. This depiction of conspiracy deviated from what had usually been shown on screen, though it focused some attention on a facet of real-life conspiracy that had received only sporadic public attention. (The conspiratorial aspects of racial hate groups received much more public recognition within a few years. Awareness became especially pronounced after the deadly bombing of the federal building in Oklahoma City in 1995.)

THE ROSWELL EFFECT

Just as the beginning of the 1980s brought a change in the nation's political landscape, that time also saw another development in the evolving story of conspiracy theory in America. At first, it probably seemed to be an ephemeral development about a topic of little consequence. But it developed into an important narrative in popular culture within a few years.[7] This was the reemergence of an old news story, the supposed crash landing of a UFO in Roswell, New Mexico.

Although that event has caused a stir in the context of the UFO mania in the late 1940s, it mostly had faded from public memory soon thereafter. Indeed, although UFOs remained a popular topic of conversation and had attracted a cadre of committed enthusiasts, for three decades the Roswell incident was seldom mentioned.

Soon after the 1947 incident, the government declared that the reported crash was nothing more than a stray weather balloon. Officials produced material evidence that seemed to back up that claim. Other UFO accounts had less contrary evidence and seemed more open to interpretation for those wishing to believe, and so interest in the Roswell event had been overshadowed.

In the months before 1980, that situation began to change. Several people with a strong interest in UFOs, notably Stanton T. Friedman and William L. Moore, reexamined the strange reports from Roswell in 1947 and came away unconvinced of the official explanation that it was simply a government weather balloon.[8] Locating some of the people who claimed to have witnessed parts of the story thirty years earlier, the new investigators heard increasingly complicated accounts. After hearing these stories, the UFO investigators concluded that not only had a UFO crashed in New Mexico, but that alien occupants had been recovered. The details varied, but for UFO believers, it began to seem as though the Roswell incident had more to reveal than originally thought. Soon, new accounts of the event started to make the rounds. The stories were sufficiently interesting to attract a mainstream audience.[9]

One of the themes that emerged with the renewed attention to the Roswell incident was that of the government cover-up. Many committed UFO advocates believed not only that an extraterrestrial craft had crashed, but that it had been recovered with its occupants (in some accounts, several of the alien occupants were even alive to be captured). Of course, this meant that there needed to be an explanation about why such a monumental occurrence was not acknowledged by the government or by the leading institutions of society. The easiest reason seemed to be that the evidence was suppressed and that officials constructed an elaborate system of lies to hide the truth. Not surprisingly, then, for those persons who believed the fantastic accounts, a conspiracy theory element was a central and necessary part of the story.

But it was not only the firm believers who were attracted to the aliens-and-conspiracy story. Even those people for whom the Roswell story was mostly an entertaining speculation (rather than something that was literally true) were repeatedly exposed to the new version of the narrative. It continually surfaced in popular tabloids and magazines, movies, novels, and other forms of popular culture. With the attention that the Roswell story attracted, a conspiracy theory mindset was found in yet another strand of contemporary popular culture.

CLOSE ENCOUNTERS OF THE THIRD KIND

In fact, this blending of extraterrestrial-alien and conspiracy theory themes had already begun to surface, even as the reconsideration of the Roswell incident started to gain attention. Looking back, it is easy to see that fictional accounts with a similar theme and the purportedly new nonfiction accounts being produced by UFO advocates influenced each other. The 1977 release of the phenomenally popular movie *Star Wars* proved to Hollywood that the outer space theme had blockbuster potential. Yet, that film was essentially a futuristic version of a Western or perhaps war movie. Another movie from that year, though, replicated many of the UFO and conspiracy themes that were to be found in the reemerging Roswell story. This was director Steven Spielberg's *Close Encounters of the Third Kind.*

Close Encounters combines many elements from UFO narratives that had appeared in popular culture in the preceding quarter century. UFO sightings, alien abductions, cloaked government UFO research, hidden government installations—all prominently appear in the movie. The story follows the quest of ordinary people to meet up with aliens, to whom they feel strangely drawn. These people are not sure what force is causing this uncontrollable urge, but they independently make their way to a remote location, waiting for something to happen.

Upon nearing the location, however, they are turned back by military-looking government personnel, who concoct a cover story to clear the area. Undeterred, some of the people making the quest discover the ruse and sneak into the area. But they must avoid menacing helicopters, the occupants of which seem determined to keep them from completing their journey and thereby from discovering the truth. Indeed, according to the story, the government already has communicated with the aliens. They have arranged for a rendezvous at the secret site in order to effect what is essentially a friendly human-alien exchange program

Although the government has spent much of the film trying to cover up what was really going on, at the last moment officials have a change of heart concerning the two people who have slipped by all the security. Despite the government's initially ominous appearance, and its apparent willingness to use force in order to maintain the project's secrecy, the conspiracy in *Close Encounters of the Third Kind* appears to be essentially benevolent.

Overall, the story presented in *Close Encounters* is filled with hope and promise. Still, the lurking presence of a government scheming to withhold disclosure of a monumental development in human history adds another layer of meaning. As benevolent as the government's actions may appear by the end of the movie, the fact that the film's narrative relies upon a portrayal of the federal government as an entity that would go to extraordinary lengths to deny the truth inserts a less positive subtext to the story. Indeed, if the government's actions show an optimistic futurism, it is only after having resorted to lies, deceit, and intimidation that this result is obtained.

Perhaps at another moment in American history, the part of the story dealing with government secrecy and deception would appear to be benign or perhaps simple acts that were necessary for national security. Yet, *Close Encounters of the Third Kind* was released soon after the Watergate scandal, at a moment when government credibility was still under question. Coming to public attention in that context, therefore, some elements of the movie seemed connected to the larger impulse in American culture to find conspiracy riddled throughout modern life.[10]

E.T.: *THE EXTRA-TERRESTRIAL*

A few years later, Spielberg again addressed the theme of a dark, conspiratorial underside to government in the family-oriented movie *E.T.: The Extra-Terrestrial*. In many respects, this movie, released in 1982, tells a parallel story to that of *Close Encounters*. Again, Spielberg returns to the UFO theme, but here adds a human dimension to the tale. In fact, he relies on children to form the core of the narrative.

E.T. was an enormously popular film that further gilded Spielberg's golden reputation in Hollywood. It tells the story of Elliott (played by Henry Thomas), a lonely young boy who stumbles across a most remarkable discovery: a frightened, young alien, with an unearthly appearance and child-like innocence. As the audience knows, the strange creature had landed on earth in a spacecraft piloted by others of his kind. Unexpectedly, however, the craft was detected by humans, and it made an emergency take-off to avoid contact. In the rush to escape, however, the young extraterrestrial was accidentally left behind, alone and ill-equipped to fend for himself.

Elliott inadvertently discovers the alien, E.T., and befriends him. Elliott brings E.T. to his California home where he tries to figure out how to help his new extraterrestrial friend. Realizing that he must protect E.T., Elliott keeps his new friend a secret, hiding him in a closet where even his mother will not discover him. Yet, there is a much bigger problem. Government agents with questionable intentions seem to know that an alien is on the loose. As suburban Californian life goes on, they suspiciously comb the area in vans as they search for the scared alien creature.

Most of *E.T.* involves the adventures of the boy and his alien friend, as they slowly begin to learn about each other. Once they are able to communicate better, Elliott realizes that they must race against the clock. There is not much time for E.T. to arrange for the spacecraft to rescue him because soon it must leave for his home world, leaving E.T. behind if the rescue has not been made by then. In the end, of course, E.T. is rescued and Spielberg's story of innocence and friendship reaches a pleasant end.

Before this resolution, however, the parts of the story dealing with the pursuit of E.T. continue with the theme of a forbidding, conspiratorial government that Spielberg portrays in *Close Encounters*. Indeed, perhaps more than any other movie, *E.T.* brought the now familiar image of the conniving government and its faceless, apparently heartless agents to a massive film audience. And so while the government-as-conspirator theme had been in the air for some time, with the success of *E.T.* it moved beyond the adult-oriented paranoid thrillers and the mature stories of political intrigue. Now, the idea that the federal government could be assumed to be conspiratorial in nature was an idea packaged for the whole family.

Of course, like *Close Encounters*, the imposing federal agents who seemed both frightening and menacing were mostly serving the function of providing tension for the film's plot. In the absence of traditional villains, a plodding, scheming government was called to fill in temporarily. But also like *Close Encounters*, the ominous government agents are presented as less imposing than they appear. If anything, they symbolize a bureaucracy, the members of whom are simply going about their business, rather than people intentionally committing misdeeds. (Of course, this could also be read in a very negative way, since the theme of the uncaring bureaucracy is hardly one of the more uplifting notions in modern life.)

For ardent UFO advocates, movies such as *Close Encounters of the Third Kind* and *E.T.* held conflicting importance. On the one hand, the appearance of UFOs and alien life in mainstream movies brought new, respectable attention to their passion. It is likely that some people who had previously given the matter little thought may have left such films with enough sense of wonder to at least ask themselves about the possibility of such things. Yet, in another way, both these movies were successful as artifacts of popular culture that they could also draw ridicule to the subject of UFOs and extraterrestrial life. Providing easy reference points, well-known scenes from these movies could be used to make light of the whole topic, poking fun at the iconic movie moments that seemed so Hollywood they could hardly be reflective of something serious.

If, however, these movies are considered in relation to the new narratives about the Roswell incident that were emerging at the edges of popular culture, then something of more importance to the evolution of conspiracy theory becomes evident. In the accounts of UFO true believers and in the mainstream science fiction stories from Steven Spielberg, government conspiracy is not the object of attention, but it is nonetheless taken for granted. In fact, because the UFO theme is so attention-getting, by contrast the government conspiracy theme, whether intended as fact or fiction, seems so non-controversial that it hardly warrants additional thought. Indeed, little effort is made to persuade audiences that the government not only could, but would act in this way. Instead, it is simply assumed that this is business-as-usual.

The full importance of this turn in American conspiracy theory would not be seen for several years. Throughout the 1980s and into the 1990s, the Roswell story was to develop into a complex set of stories that increasingly involved elaborate efforts of government deception. As numerous commentators have noted, Roswell increasingly took on the character of a modern myth. By the end of the decade, the Roswell stories were so widely circulated in American popular culture that Hollywood grew increasingly drawn to them as readymade material. This impulse developed more fully in the following decade. And when it did, the conspiracy theory underpinnings of the story were even more prominent.

COMING OF A NEW ERA

As America entered the 1980s, leaders aimed to help it escape from the cynicism and divisiveness that had plagued the nation in the previous decades. The Vietnam War and Watergate were in the past, and now many people thought it was time to move forward in a more positive direction. In this context, Ronald Reagan brought an enthusiasm and directness to the American presidency that seemed to bring fresh air just as it brought a prominence for political conservatism.

Reagan's legacy was tarnished, for some people, by the Iran-Contra scandal.[11] Having conspiratorial overtones, this was the attempt to illegally funnel money to pro-democracy rebel forces known as the *contras* in Central America. The elaborate scheme, which skirted apparent Congressional prohibitions from directly funding the *contras*, began covertly in Reagan's first term. Oliver North, a Marine colonel serving as an aide to the National Security Council, arranged to illicitly move money to assist the *contra* cause without detection.

The plan worked until 1986, when a plane involved in arms smuggling was shot down over Nicaraguan air space. An American pilot was retrieved from the wreckage, and Nicaragua's leftist Sandinista government subsequently put him on display for the international news media. The news immediately brought public attention to the fact the United States had played a role in shipping arms to the *contra* rebels.

More revelations about the convoluted scheme slowly came to light, and Congress convened hearings about the affair the following year. Oliver North was called to testify and became simultaneously a cult hero for many conservatives and a villain in the eyes of many liberals. The Reagan-appointed Tower Commission issued its report in 1987, after which North and several top administration officials were indicted and convicted for wrong-doing. (The convictions were mostly overturned shortly thereafter.)

To some people, the Iran-Contra affair was reminiscent of Watergate a decade earlier. But many people did not object to what had been done, even if it was illegal. The idea of the U.S. government supporting a group that Reagan called "freedom fighters" did not seem criminal to them. Overall, the main effect of the Iran-Contra scandal was probably an increased sense of polarization in American politics. What one thought about it largely depended on one's ideological outlook. So while it resonated as a new conspiratorial event for some, it was little more than a politically motivated attack in the eyes of others. Although some people were suspicious that both the president and vice president were somehow involved, Reagan largely escaped unscathed by the affair. Indeed, Reagan remained popular among much of the American public until the end of his presidency.

Reagan's revolution was a comprehensive one, and although enormously popular among conservatives, the ideas he advocated often rankled liberals. Not surprisingly, therefore, during his time in office, the American political landscape became increasingly polarized along manifestly partisan lines.

Whatever other shortcomings some may have seen, by the time Reagan left office it was clear that the Cold War, which had dominated American foreign policy since the end of World War II, seemed to be ending. Although Reagan had talked tough about the Soviet Union during his years in office, he developed a personal rapport with Soviet leader Mikhail Gorbachev. The tense relationship between the two superpower nations soon thawed.

In 1988, George H.W. Bush easily won election as Reagan's successor. In many ways, this seemed to be a vote in favor of continuing with Reagan tradition. During Bush's single term, he saw the final collapse of the Soviet empire, the culmination of a process that had started while he was Ronald Reagan's vice president. This monumental occurrence seemed to herald the victory of democracy in many parts of the world. Although there were some setbacks, such as the failed Chinese uprising in Beijing's Tiananmen Square, the old, fearful world of the Cold War looked as though it was fast disappearing. Soon, the United States would be the world's only remaining superpower. Jubilant that the West had seemingly won the Cold War, there was soon enthusiastic optimism for a post–Cold War world. Rather than obsessing about foreign policy controversies of the past, now the discussion was how to spend the

"peace dividend" that resulted from a world that no longer seemed to require such extraordinary expenditures on war and defense. Soon, of course,
it was evident that this talk was premature.

The end of the Cold War was not enough to quell a polarization in American politics that seemed as pronounced as ever by the end of the 1980s.
The increasingly contentious nature of political rhetoric was given more fuel
by the escalation of the so-called "culture wars" that came to prominence
at that time. In widely debated works, such as *The Closing of the American
Mind*, the chasm dividing conservative and liberal American thought seemed
never to have been wider or deeper. Among a sizeable segment of the population, however, a main effect of the ongoing political fighting was disaffection.
From such a perspective, the government seemed far off and increasingly out
of step with the lives of ordinary people. This proved to be a fertile feeding
ground for the perpetuation of a conspiracy theory worldview, a perspective
that eyed the American political mainstream and other elites of society as
contaminated, self-interested in-groups. This impulse would become fleshed
out in the following decade.

A New Age of Conspiracy

For American movie-goers, the conspiracy theory theme rocketed to prominence with the emergence of the dangerous Cold War that followed World War II. Although the theme began to drift from these roots in later years, the Cold War backdrop provided a durable context that some filmmakers continued to explore even as the original paranoia of the 1950s and early 1960s was drifting into memory.

Early in the 1980s, Ronald Reagan expressed concerns of a renewed Soviet threat. His administration feared Soviet influence in Central America, which seemed to be spreading across the region. By the end of the 1980s, however, it seemed that whatever Soviet machinations had been at work earlier in the decade, these had been the last gasp of a now deflated empire. As George H. W. Bush assumed the presidency in 1989, the remaining remnants of the Cold War world began to disappear. Indeed, the world of global politics was in the midst of a radical transformation that would soon leave the world with a single superpower.

In some ways, it could have seemed that the quickly fading Cold War would render the whole conspiracy theory strand of moviemaking as a relic of the past. The conspiracy theme had originally been compelling largely because it related to the general mindset of fear and anxiety in the American public during the frightening years of that era. If this context was disappearing, one could ask if films with the theme would still seem relevant.

Yet, although the roots of conspiracy theory movies led back to the Cold War era, wrinkles in the context had weakened that connection over time. To a great extent, the external focus of the Cold War had long since turned inward. Although the Cold War still influenced the evolution of American political culture, over time political anxieties were just as likely to be caused by domestic factors as the specter of a lurking communist power. The upheaval caused by the Vietnam War, the Civil Rights Movement, the Women's Liberation Movement, and a host of other divisive social conflicts had ensured that. This change could be felt in the popular culture. It was reflected, for example, in many conspiracy-themed films of the 1970s and 1980s, which tended to be suspicious more of American government and institutions than of foreign enemies.

The shifting world order was poised to fundamentally change the global political landscape. This would change the context in which conspiracy theory would be interpreted in popular culture. To understand how the evolving political world affected moviemaking with this theme, then, it is necessary to recall some of the most important developments of the time.

The fall of the Berlin Wall during the first year of George H. W. Bush's presidency in 1989 symbolized the radical transformation that was underway in world politics. Although the final dissolution of the Soviet empire was not yet complete, this was clear evidence that the long struggle with what Ronald Reagan had once called the "evil empire" was now nearing resolution. In the following months, it seemed as though nothing could stop this march of progress. As the geopolitical context of world events rapidly changed, the conditions that had originally precipitated and exacerbated the growth of conspiracy theory culture in the United States seemed to be headed toward oblivion. The fear of global communism and mutual nuclear annihilation, which once had generated great fear and paranoia, increasingly seemed like the products of a bygone world.

Yet, unforeseen new political crises, both international and domestic, were about to play a part in regenerating and transforming the role of conspiracy theory in the cultural landscape. One source could be found in the Middle East and its environs, which had stubbornly inserted apparently unsolvable policy problems for the United States for many years. Within months a new situation in that region presented the president with a burgeoning new crisis. The situation reached the boiling point on August 2, 1990, when Iraq's renegade leader, strongman Saddam Hussein, ordered the invasion of the tiny neighboring state, Kuwait.

Bush and his advisors feared that Iraq had no intention of stopping with Kuwait, but actually had their eyes on the oil fields of nearby Saudi Arabia. Along with whatever other objections that the administration had about the invasion of Kuwait, the oil aspect of the situation held the potential to directly threaten American interests. Not surprisingly, therefore, the White House replied with a forceful response of its own. Within days, the United States dispatched troops to the region with the aim of preventing further Iraqi conquests. Soon, there was a dramatic gathering of American forces in the region in what was called Operation Desert Shield. As the American troop level grew to over 500,000 soldiers and military personnel, the administration negotiated with Saudi Arabia to allow the stationing of U.S. forces on their sovereign territory. (Much later, the presence of American troops on Saudi soil would be cited by Osama bin Laden as one of the primary reasons for his hostility toward the United States.)

The crisis continued for a period of months, during which the United States worked to secure United Nations approval for further action against Iraq. At the same time, administration officials courted sympathetic members of the international community and eventually succeeded in assembling a coalition of nations willing to contribute military personnel and other resources for actions against Iraq, should those become necessary.

Despite growing pressure and widespread condemnation from the international community, Saddam Hussein remained defiant. Thus, with an apparently rogue leader who refused to comply with United Nations mandates and with the successful building of a collation willing to work with the United States in any follow-up military action, Bush sought formal approval for such action from Congress in early January 1991. Once this approval was in hand, the American mission in the region changed. With open hostilities beginning to seem inevitable, Operation Desert Shield was renamed Operation Desert Storm.

As a showdown with Saddam Hussein approached, the president aimed to rally the nation. In his State of the Union speech in January 1991, he presented his vision of the future. In part, he focused on the brewing crisis at hand, saying:

> Halfway around the world, we are engaged in a great struggle in the skies and on the seas and sands. . . . For two centuries we've done the hard work of freedom. And tonight we lead the world in facing down a threat to decency and humanity.

As he continued, the president situated the current events in the pantheon of a bigger future. In his speech, the president continued:

> What is at stake is more than one small country, it is a big idea—a new world order, where diverse nations are drawn together in common cause to achieve the universal aspirations of mankind: peace and security, freedom, and the rule of law. Such is a world worthy of our struggle, and worthy of our children's future.

The president's words seemed innocent, even boldly optimistic. But to some people, these words suggested something else altogether. The words "new world order" captured the attention of some conspiracy theory enthusiasts residing beyond the bright lights of mainstream political thought. Some of these people thought they recognized a veiled reference to an ominous global conspiracy.

Indeed, the label "New World Order" was a powerful signal to a significant number of conspiracy theory advocates. A number of fringe groups, especially separatist militias and right-wing religious organizations, have at times subscribed to some version of this idea. To them, it signifies a dreaded one-world government, which would be headed by a secret cabal of elite persons. As conceived by conspiracy theorists, it is the antithesis of the American way of life. The conspiracy would install a dictatorial regime with harsh restrictions on personal freedom. According to some advocates of this conspiracy theory, opponents of the regime would be sent to concentrations camps that are in secret locations in the United States and elsewhere.

Most conceptions of this idea assert that the New World Order would be surreptitiously imposed by means that would seem innocent to ordinary people. According to this view, leaders of the New World Order would use groups such as the United Nations, the World Trade Organization, the International Monetary Fund, NATO, or other international and nongovernmental organizations to implement their plot.

Most people, of course, did not interpret the president's words this way. For the majority, the address affirmed that the president was resolute in his attitude about Saddam Hussein and Iraq and that the international situation was extremely grave. Indeed, within a few weeks, the waiting ended and the international coalition, led by the United States, took military action against the Iraqi forces that had invaded Kuwait some months earlier. A massive air campaign, complete with the latest war high-technology weapons and procedures, was unleashed, along with a lightning-fast ground strike. This all proved overwhelming for the Iraqi forces.

Although American officials had feared substantial casualties and a relatively long campaign prior to the beginning of hostilities, these fears were not realized. Instead, the Iraqi resistance quickly crumbled, and soon Kuwait was liberated. The American president issued a unilateral cease-fire order on February 27, 1991, and within a matter of weeks, the Iraqis agreed to meet the United Nations' demands and formally signed a cease-fire agreement.

The Gulf War came and ended quickly, but its effects lingered. Having achieved the initial objectives by freeing Kuwait, the Bush administration had abruptly terminated military action as soon as that result was achieved. And although Kuwait was freed and Iraq faced severe penalties and sanctions, Saddam Hussein remained in power, still presiding over his nation with an iron fist. As the world later realized, this result would have major consequences in the following decade.

The Gulf War was brief, but it caused an outpouring of American patriotism that had been unprecedented since the middle of the century. The war elicited little of the divisiveness and bitterness that had plagued the Vietnam War. Instead, during months before hostilities commenced many Americans were eager to support their country in a military operation against a clear aggressor. After the brief war, in some sense America seemed renewed to many people. The public was very pleased with the president, and at the time it seemed unimaginable that George Bush would not be returned to the White House for a second term. Yet, the tide quickly turned. Within months, the president's approval ratings dropped dramatically. When the election came, he was defeated by the Democratic governor from Arkansas, Bill Clinton.

After Clinton took office in January 1993, it was clear that the political landscape remained deeply polarized. The new president's initial priorities did little to reduce the divisive partisan divide. For example, Clinton's "don't ask, don't tell" policy regarding gays and lesbians in the military, which came early in his term, created a firestorm of controversy. It helped set the tone for the acrimony that was to come. Political rhetoric took an increasingly harsh tone, and the most ardent Republicans and Democrats missed few opportunities to characterize their political opponents in extremely derisive ways. Politics has always been a blood sport in the United States, but the bitter, invigorated partisanship of the 1990s, along with the burgeoning talk radio and cable news phenomena, now inserted it with full force into everyday American life.

These developments influenced the making of conspiracy theory movies in the new decade, sometimes in unforeseen ways. Rich new narrative strands were now in the air. They expanded the ways in which conspiracies were portrayed on screen in new and sometimes more extreme ways.

OLIVER STONE'S *JFK*

As the year of the Gulf War drew to a close, director Oliver Stone's film *JFK* was released. Appearing in American movie theaters in late December 1991, this new conspiracy theory movie would become the most influential and talked about film of its kind in many years.

Director Oliver Stone had already firmly established a reputation as a formidable director capable of first-rate filmmaking. A Vietnam veteran, Stone's impressive and varied credentials included directing such ground-breaking movies as *Platoon* and *Born on the Fourth of July*, both highly praised films that looked at the Vietnam War and its aftermath with intelligence and emotion.

Now the increasingly iconoclastic director aimed his sights not at the life of the assassinated president, but at the mysteries surrounding his death. As audiences discovered, Stone brought bravura and intensity to his subject. He regarded his project as more than simple entertainment, but as real history and politics. Putting his considerable filmmaking gifts to work, he projected a strong and highly controversial point of view into the topic.

As audiences soon discovered, Stone strongly believed that the assassination was the result of a conspiracy and that this alleged reality had been hidden from the public by a cover-up. Of course, by 1991 this was not a remarkable view. Some sources claimed that nearly 75 percent of the American public no longer believed the Warren Commission's conclusion that the president had been murdered by Lee Harvey Oswald alone. More startling than this, however, were the details of the plot that the movie seemed to suggest: that the assassination was the result of conspiracy that included highly placed government officials. Some viewers even believed that Stone had gone so far as to suggest that the vice president had been involved in the plot. Charges of these and other kinds had been circulating among assassination-conspiracy enthusiasts for some years, but now Stone brought them to wider public attention than ever before.

The significance of *JFK* was not simply that Stone had brought accusations of conspiracy to a wide audience, however. Just as importantly, it was the skill and artistry with which he presented the story that helped establish *JFK*'s influence. The director masterfully blended original footage with archival footage (including the famous home-movie of the assassination known as the Zapruder film, which at the time had seldom been seen by the American public) and faux archival footage. Audiences were thus confronted with a stew of traditionally staged material, actual historical evidence, and fake historical evidence, all mixed together in a compelling story. Indeed, even the film's critics nodded to Stone's successful assemblage of materials. In fact, some even feared that what he had done would be too persuasive and have the effect of confusing audiences about which parts were true and which were conjecture.

The movie prompted an unusually robust response in the mass media. Due to its highly charged political content, it attracted interest not only from movie and cultural critics, but also from political writers and columnists.

A review in *The Washington Post* aptly described *JFK* as "a riveting marriage of fact and fiction, hypothesis and empirical proof in the edge-of-the-seat spirit of a conspiracy thriller."[1] (The author apparently did feel obliged to add, "It's not journalism. It's not history. It is not legal evidence. Much of it is ludicrous."[2]) Still, this review, like many others, was quite positive overall. The trade paper *Variety*'s review was also laudatory. Capturing the essence of what it was about Stone's movie that resonated with audiences, it called the movie "[a] rebuke to official history" that "lays out just about every shred of evidence yet uncovered for the conspiracy theory surrounding the Nov. 22, 1963 assassination of President John F. Kennedy."[3] In the end, according to *Variety*, Stone dismissed official accounts as "a cover-up" and "a myth," and in its place he was "proposing a myth of his own."[4]

As a pivotal moment in American history, the assassination fascinated Stone. Like many others, he was skeptical of official accounts. He discovered two books on the subject that helped crystallize his thinking about alternative explanations. One of these, *Crossfire: The Plot that Killed Kennedy*, had been written by Jim Marrs, an experienced newspaper reporter and the author of works on a variety of conspiracy theory topics. The other book was *On the Trail of the Assassins*, written by a former New Orleans district attorney named Jim Garrison. It was this book that gave Stone not only a conspiracy-laden way of picturing the assassination, but also the real-life characters and narrative framework that he would use in *JFK*. Indeed, the final script features Jim Garrison (played in the movie by Kevin Costner) as the main character. Thus, the movie builds its conspiracy theory about the assassination by largely following the trail of Garrison's investigations.

And Garrison's story was unique. As district attorney, he once had the distinction of leading the only criminal prosecution directly related to the Kennedy assassination. He had brought to trial a local businessman named Clay Shaw in connection with the crime. Garrison believed that Shaw had been involved in an anti-Castro, right-wing conspiracy that was implicated in the assassination. The district attorney also thought this man had been involved in trying to make legal arrangements for Lee Harvey Oswald, the man identified by the Warren Commission as the lone gunman.[5] Federal prosecutors did not pursue the matter, but Garrison forged ahead.

Garrison brought Shaw to trial in 1969, but he was unable to persuade the jury, and Shaw was acquitted. Despite this setback, the district attorney's interest in the assassination, and in the conspiracy he thought was behind it, remained undiminished. Garrison maintained a strong interest in the matter, even after leaving the district attorney's office a few years later. A culmination of this interest was the book that had captured Oliver Stone's attention.

In most respects, Stone's treatment of the subject did not break new ground. Conspiracy theory buffs learned nothing new in the version of events that the director assembled for the film. But long before this time, much of the public had concluded that the single-assassin theory put forward by the Warren Commission could not be correct. Many books and articles had been published in the years since the president's murder. These writings contained an astonishing variety of hypotheses and suggested many possible suspects. Among the extremely varied group of alleged conspirators were foreign agents, corrupt American business executives, shifty public officers, elected officials, organized crime figures, pro-Castro agents, anti-Castro agents, and many others. Often in such accounts, the suspected people had supposedly worked in unusual combinations, against apparently opposite interests. As what was sometimes described as the crime of the century, the assassination continued to spark interest. Ideas about conspiracy were well, if sometimes vaguely, known even among those who did not have much familiarity with the specific writing from which some of the theories originated.

What is more, the picture of events that Stone presented was not dramatically different from some previous screen portrayals of the topic. For example, *Rush to Judgment*, the 1967 documentary from director Emil de Antonio that was written by assassination theorist Mark Lane, had asserted that the lone gunman idea was incorrect just a few years after the assassination. And in another example, the 1973 movie *Executive Action* had presented a thinly veiled version of an assassination conspiracy theory that had obvious similarities to the charges made in Stone's film.

Yet, by the time Stone's *JFK* appeared in 1991, the public was primed to take greater notice of charges about conspiracy and cover-up in the death of the president. General skepticism about government and the wide dissemination of conspiracy-oriented material (such as the many films, books, and articles about the subject) pushed the conspiracy theory perspective further into the mainstream of American thinking. In addition to the compelling subject matter, Stone's reputation assured that his ideas would receive substantial coverage in the press. And now Stone's remarkable filmmaking skills brought the story of assassination and conspiracy together in a way that would reach and resonate with a broad movie-going audience much more than previous film incarnations of similar ideas.

Indeed, *JFK* received much attention while it was still in production, and by the time it debuted in theaters, it had already aroused interest. Film critics often hailed the film as brilliant storytelling. Writers with more of an eye for history, however, often fretted about Stone's conspiracy theorizing, which was sometimes regarded as bad history and sometimes as outright propaganda. A review in *The Washington Post*, for example, judged that *JFK* was loaded with "absurdities."[6] *Newsweek* dubbed it "twisted history."[7] *USA Today Magazine* ran a major story that called the movie "Oliver Stone's big lie," claiming that the director's version of history was "distorted for the sake of propaganda."[8]

In general, then, writers did not debate whether or not Stone had produced an effective motion picture. While most movies are publicly judged with entertainment or aesthetic standards in mind, these were not foremost on the minds of many writers, especially among those who had a negative view of it. Instead, many writers objected not to the movie as a movie, but to the movie as history. Apparently, these writers feared that audiences would interpret Stone's film not simply as they would another trip to the movie theater, but as an experience that would educate people about a historical event. In this respect, they found *JFK* lacking. It did not conform to standard ideas about historical method, about measured interpretation based on cold, hard evidence.

A mass-marketed film has seldom been judged so much in terms of its historical accuracy. Hollywood has often used history as subject matter, and it frequently takes great liberties with generally accepted ideas about specific events and people from the past. Usually, this has been done without invoking the wrath of American columnists and pundits. *JFK*, however, was treated differently. By the early 1990s, Stone had become increasingly associated with a liberal worldview, and his choice of a highly charged subject matter attracted much attention from those wary that he would use his abilities to skew history for political effect.

The critical writers were right to fear the effect of Stone's production. It did seem to affect audiences in a more powerful way than would have been expected from a typical movie. Indeed, many people seem to have regarded it as a fairly faithful record of what happened in Dallas back in 1963, with perhaps only a few details remaining in the realm of conjecture.

Yet, although Stone may have had an influence on perceptions about the assassination, *JFK* can also be seen as a film that captured an already-existing public mood. In fact, for many years the American people had been skeptical of the lone-gunman account of the Warren Commission. The Gallup Organization, which occasionally asked about the public's beliefs in this matter in the years since 1963, reported that three-quarters of Americans believed a conspiracy was involved in this era.[9] In fact, by a wide margin, Americans had held this view about the assassination for many years. Yet, Stone's film made incendiary charges of complicity by American officials. *JFK* made the unofficial, conspiracy theory version of events more widely and more visibly available than ever before. For many people, then, Stone did not so much persuade them to accept the conspiratorial view as he provided an affirmation of what they already believed.

At the center of the controversy, Stone seemed to side with those who thought of the movie as history, or at least as a type of history. Indeed, in one interview, he was openly skeptical of how the story had been told in mainstream accounts. It was his view, he said, that "[t]he dirty little secret of American journalism . . . is that it's generally wrong. Sometimes a little, sometimes, a lot, but wrong."[10] On another occasion, he reported, "My name has become synonymous with lunatic conspiracy theory buff. However, the world is rooted in conspiracy. Every government in the world is rooted in conspiracy. . . . "[11] Yet, there was an irony in what Stone said. Perhaps the "lunatic conspiracy theory buff" was a populist way to think about those people who voiced an extreme and traditionally paranoid version of conspiracy.

Indeed, it is clear that by the early 1990s, conspiracy theory thinking had become an element of mainstream American thought. It was a strand of thinking that had moved in from the periphery and was now becoming as widespread as it was familiar. For many people, the charges in *JFK* no longer seemed shocking. The reported comments of one young man were perhaps reflective on many. Reflecting on the matter he said, "Of course that's what happened. We knew that. Why is this such big news?"[12]

A TURN FOR THE WORSE

With Bill Clinton's arrival in the Oval Office in January 1993, conditions for a major expansion of conspiracy theory thinking in American society were starting to take shape. Clinton was wildly popular with many people, but he was despised by many others. In the course of his two terms in the White House, national and international events called conspiracy to mind, at times with good reason.

Sometimes, dramatic events were involved. The 1993 plot to destroy New York's World Trade Center, for example, was the result of an actual conspiracy. The militant Islamist group that planned the attack failed to bring down the towers on this occasion, but 6 lives were lost and more than 1,000 people were injured as the result of the car bombing.

The specter of conspiracy also haunted two federal law enforcement operations in the 1990s. Incidents involving federal law enforcement officials in Ruby Ridge, Idaho, in 1992 and in Waco, Texas, in 1993 brought national attention to fringe groups espousing extreme views. Tragically, these later motivated the Oklahoma City bombing, one of the deadliest terrorist attacks in American history.

The Ruby Ridge incident came about when U.S. Marshals and FBI agents attempted to arrest Randy Weaver, a man wanted on weapons charges and for failing to appear for a court date. After a lengthy surveillance campaign, federal agents mounted an operation to arrest Weaver at his remote mountainside home in Idaho. Believing that Weaver was armed and could resist efforts to arrest him, agents made their way through the woods quietly, hoping to catch Weaver off guard. Unfortunately, the agents inadvertently encountered Weaver's teenaged son and a family friend, and in a confusing confrontation shots were fired. Weaver's son was dead.

From there, the situation spiraled out of control, and soon authorities faced a stand-off with Weaver and his family, who made a stand at their cabin. Surrounded by federal agents determined to bring the incident to a conclusion, Weaver and his group tried to hold off the authorities. Eventually, the authorities closed in, but not without more gunfire. Weaver's wife, who was standing in a doorway holding a young child, was fatally shot in the confusion.

Although federal authorities successfully arrested Weaver, the violence that preceded Weaver's custody reverberated through the many fringe groups. Beyond that audience, however, the extensive news coverage of the incident showed mainstream America a picture of federal law enforcement that was far from flattering. Even many of those who disapproved of Weaver and his politics were shocked at the chaos and resulting deaths at Ruby Ridge. Later, in a seeming rebuke to authorities, Weaver was tried and acquitted on the most serious charges. By then, however, Ruby Ridge had become a potent symbol of an untrustworthy government for members of the already alienated militia movement.

For people who already distrusted government, Ruby Ridge seemed to prove their point. In 1993, the federal siege of a Waco, Texas, compound housing members of the Branch Davidian group made matters substantially worse. In a televised stand-off with the group that lasted more than seven weeks, an operation to arrest Branch Davidian leader David Koresh went awry.

The Branch Davidians group had splintered from the Adventist faith earlier in the twentieth century. One of their most strongly held beliefs was that members of their group should live apart from the world of unbelievers.

The Branch Davidian group in Waco was regarded as much a cult as a simple sect by many on the outside. Koresh had assumed leadership of the group, proclaiming a direct connection with God. Under his leadership, the group increasingly lived in isolation from the world around them. Yet, some activities of Koresh and other group members aroused the concern of law enforcement officials. Now, he was wanted for stockpiling weapons and endangering the safety of children who lived in the compound.

Federal authorities decided that it was desirable to take Koresh into custody at the Waco compound. Realizing that a substantial cache of weapons was at his disposal and fearing that he might resist arrest, a contingent of federal agents assembled in preparation for the operation. They hoped for a swift operation and a peaceful conclusion.

When the agents finally began to move in, however, they came under fire. Four federal agents and six Branch Davidians were killed. Soon, it was apparent that what was planned as a quick action would turn into a lengthy siege.

Authorities tried several strategies to end the stand-off, but they were unsuccessful. Finally, a little more than seven weeks after the siege began, officials decided that the time had come to make another move before the besieged group could take drastic action that would lead to extensive loss of life. (People still remembered the 1978 mass suicide in Jonestown, Guyana.) Federal officials devised a plan. It involved the use of armored vehicles and the pumping of tear gas into the compound. Officials hoped that they would drive the barricaded Branch Davidians into the open.

The plan did not go as intended, however. Gunfire erupted, and the officials decided to increase the amount of tear gas. In addition, the compound building suffered some damage from the armored vehicles. It was a chaotic situation.

Despite the officials' efforts to induce the Branch Davidians to leave the compound, the sect members were apparently afraid to come out (or else were persuaded by Koresh not to). Donning gas masks, they retreated to sheltered areas. As the situation became ever more confusing, several fires broke out in the compound. Even then, however, only a few Branch Davidians fled to safety. Soon, the fires spread, creating a raging inferno. After the flames died down, authorities surveyed the carnage. In the end, eighty-five of the Branch Davidians died. At least seventeen children were among the deceased.[13]

In the aftermath of this incident, the credibility of federal law enforcement was damaged. The Bureau of Alcohol, Tobacco, and Firearms' own investigation judged that in Waco, "The decision to proceed was tragically wrong, not just in retrospect, but because of what the decision makers knew at the time."[14]

The Ruby Ridge and Waco incidents gave mainstream Americans reason to wonder about the effectiveness of federal law enforcement activities. At the same time, events such as these brought new attention to fringe groups whose activities had sometimes escaped public notice. Now, increased notice was taken of religious cults and white separatist groups.

The controversy took on a still greater importance among those who were less in the mainstream and more prone to strongly held conspiratorial world-views. To some of those sympathetic to such views, it seemed as though the authorities had gone too far. They were angry at the government for per-ceived abuses of power, and for some, resentment and hostility reached a boiling point. Two years later, an immense terror attack in America's heart-land showed how much some people resented their government.

The Oklahoma City bombing in 1995 also raised fears of conspiracy. The powerful blast destroyed much of a federal office building, resulted in almost 800 injured and the deaths of over 160 victims. Among those killed were nineteen children, many of whom were attending a day care center that was also housed in the building. In the immediate aftermath of the bombing, some media speculation focused on the possibility that the attack was part of a radical Islamist plot.

But it was nothing of the sort. Instead, Timothy McVeigh was arrested and charged with the crime. A former U.S. soldier, McVeigh was influenced by survivalist and white supremacist views and had come to view the United States government as an enemy. Apparently inspired by extremist material such as the novel *The Turner Diaries*, he was angered by the Ruby Ridge and Waco incidents He planned to avenge these events with the bombing in Oklahoma City.

In the months after his arrest, there was some speculation about whether a bigger conspiracy was involved. In the end, however, it was McVeigh and his immediate associates who were determined to have been at the root of the crime. McVeigh was convicted of the bombing in 1997 and his death sentence was carried out in June 2001. His accomplice Terry Nichols was convicted by state and federal courts and sentenced to life in prison without parole.

Thus, in the span of just a few years, intense and unexpected violence had made its mark on American perceptions, both about government and about the state of the world more generally. Ruby Ridge, the partially failed World Trade Center attack, the siege at Waco, and the horrific Oklahoma City bombing all cast a long shadow over the American mood. These incidents had different causes and resulted in different levels of death and destruction, but combined, they seemed to show a picture of government (in its law enforcement capacity, in any case) that was less than effective and that was prone to errors of judgment that had serious—and all too often, tragic—consequences.

The X-Files

As these conditions were developing, this profound lack of confidence was reflected in a televised screen production that perhaps represents the apex of post–World War II conspiracy theory. This was the Fox television series *The X-Files*, which, over the course of nine seasons, would bring together an astonishing number of strands of conspiracy theorizing. Indeed, *The X-Files* left few stones unturned in a continuing quest to layer as many variations of conspiracy theory on top of each other as possible.

Just two years earlier, Oliver Stone's *JFK* captured the public ongoing interest in conspiracy about the Kennedy assassination. But although Stone's movie was seemingly about that one event (and arguably events immediately surrounding it), the film also tapped into a more general mood, evident among many Americans, that conspiracy, or something quite similar to it, had penetrated far beyond that one event. In a way, Stone's *JFK* suggests a model for conspiracy more pervasive than one event, tragic though it was. Following the director's logic, then, conspiracy could be almost anywhere.

The X-Files, which originally aired from 1993 to 2002, brought the screen portrayal of conspiracy theory to a new level. The creation of executive producer Chris Carter, the show followed two FBI agents as they worked through cases that had been set aside because they seemed to defy rational explanation or contained deep mysteries that ordinary law enforcement methods could not solve. As viewers came to learn, this meant that most cases dealt with supernatural forces, extraterrestrial alien life-forms, or what were essentially the goblins and monsters of myth and superstition. Some of the stories, especially those concerning monsters and the supernatural, were self-contained. In contrast to these stand-alone episodes, however, there was another type of episode. These installments followed a long, convoluted, and conspiracy-laden story line involving UFOs, a secret cabal, and the disappearance of a young girl years earlier.

The missing girl was the sister of FBI agent Fox Mulder (played by David Duchovny), one of the show's main characters. Nothing about her disappearance was ordinary or, seemingly, explainable. Haunted by the mystery surrounding his sister's disappearance years earlier, Mulder is similarly fascinated with other unusual cases. After coming to work for the FBI, he began to delve into such cases, each involving some bizarre or reality-defying component. Labeled as "X-files," the unsolved mysteries were quickly forgotten by those in authority. Now, however, they had become a near obsession for Mulder. He vigorously pursues X-file cases, working doggedly out of his office in the basement of FBI headquarters. The stories of the series mostly follow Mulder's investigations into the bizarre cases in these files as he tries to discover the truth about his sister's disappearance.

Mulder is apparently a rather marginalized figure in the eyes of his superiors, however. They do not want him to make too much out of his investigations into paranormal and other unusual events. Therefore, FBI officials assigned him a partner, ostensibly to keep an eye on him. The woman assigned to work with Mulder is Dana Scully (played by Gillian Anderson). She is not only an FBI agent, but also a medical doctor. With her scientific background, Mulder's superiors hoped that she would bring a rational perspective to the investigations. Inclined to be skeptical of the paranormal and supernatural, the aim was for her to refute Mulder's conclusions when they seemed too out of the ordinary. As the series opens, Scully acts as voice of reason and thus provides a foil to Mulder's enthusiasm for seemingly outlandish theories. Or so it seems. As the series progressed, Scully and Mulder develop a close personal relationship. Eventually, she becomes increasingly likely to accept Mulder's conclusions about extremely unusual phenomena.

Although a conspiracy theory mindset informs the whole of the show, it is the ongoing story line that evolves from the mystery of Mulder's missing sister that fleshes out this theme most directly. For as it turns out, Mulder believes not just that his sister disappeared under mysterious circumstances. He thinks that she has been abducted by apparently hostile extraterrestrial aliens. This UFO angle provides a link that the show's writers used to construct a series-long story arc which, at its base, is perhaps the most complicated and sustained articulation of conspiracy theory that has appeared in any American screen production.

The conspiracy that is slowly laid out in *The X-Files* has breathtaking scope. As they developed the series' overarching conspiracy theory theme, the show's writers mined a vast range of material. The influence of such wide-ranging productions as *Invasion of the Body Snatchers, The Twilight Zone, All the President's Men, Three Days of the Condor*, and many others is at times quite evident. Writers also scanned fictional and purportedly non-fictional accounts of conspiracies that had appeared in books, articles, and other published materials. Indeed, many existing conspiracy theory ideas were incorporated into the scripts. Viewers can find evidence of everything from the Roswell incident to the Watergate affair scattered throughout many episodes.

By the time the whole conspiracy story of *The X-Files* is laid out, the mystery of Mulder's missing sister had led to a global—perhaps more accurately, interplanetary—conspiracy. It involves everything from extra-terrestrial invasion, mass killings, the secret control of American and international political events, the Kennedy and other assassinations, and more. Apparently nothing is beyond the interest of this conspiracy. Collusion with hostile extra-terrestrial aliens, manipulation of world governments, political assassinations (including the murder of John F. Kennedy) are all woven into the story line at various times. One episode even suggests that football's Super Bowl had been rigged by the conspirators.

Unlike the plots that are usually found in productions with conspiracy theory themes, the conspiracy in *The X-Files* is extraordinarily complicated. And although it is a core theme of the series, the conspiracy story line did not appear regularly. It was revealed in small pieces over a number of seasons. Sandwiched between stories involving such topics as ghouls, paranormal powers, and the supernatural, audiences were given pieces of the information about the conspiracy infrequently. Many episodes of *The X-Files*, in fact, make little or no reference to that theme. Still, the irregularly appearing conspiracy theory episodes—what producers and fans of the show called "mythology" episodes—drew much attention from the audience. Devoted fans of the show began to communicate via the Internet, a then-new innovation, to discuss their ideas about the conspiracy themes in the show.

One figure, more than any other, symbolized the ongoing conspiracy, and his appearance in an episode reminded viewers of this overarching theme. The mysterious Cigarette Smoking Man (played by William B. Davis) appeared infrequently and sometimes briefly, but his presence invoked the conspiracy. His appearance, or even the suggestion of it, signaled to viewers that something about a situation involved the overarching "mythology."

The Cigarette Smoking Man often literally lurks in the shadows. Early in the series, viewers realize that he has interest in Mulder's investigations, which he does not want to be continued, and that he also seems to exert influence over various officials in the FBI. Modeled on the Deep Throat of *All the President's Men* in some ways, the Cigarette Smoking Man appeared to be a government insider with some malevolent agenda. For a while, it was not clear what that agenda was.

The motivations and full extent of the Cigarette Smoking Man's involvement with the grand conspiracy and with Mulder are revealed slowly over many seasons (and in the 1998 theatrical movie *The X-Files: Fight the Future*). Eventually, viewers realize that extraterrestrial aliens had been involved in the disappearance of Mulder's sister years earlier, but that this had been part of a wicked deal made by a group of powerful humans. The Cigarette Smoking Man is apparently part of that cabal in some capacity. Regardless of his position within this syndicate, however, the Cigarette Smoking Man is in charge of implementing most of the group's convoluted schemes. He essentially directs the activities of what, by this time, had come to be known as a group of "men in black," mysterious, quasi-official men acting in a paramilitary capacity to keep the truth about UFOs and extraterrestrial life hidden from the public.

According to the story, the powerful conspirators had negotiated with some of the aliens (it turned out there were competing groups of aliens). In the mid-twentieth century, the group agreed to provide human captives—selected from their own relatives—in order to forestall a more complete invasion, or what they called a "colonization," that would not occur until later. Using their combined power and influence, the men had essentially formed a shadow world government, dictating the course of human events as they were supposedly preparing the world's human population for some diabolical fate.

The plot involves apparent cooperation with the would-be invaders. They aim to spread a virus-like substance throughout the human population by various means. The final effect would be to transform humans into virtual slaves of the alien beings. (This was a contemporary re-working of a theme that had appeared in earlier screen productions, such as *Invaders from Mars.*)

The human conspirators plan to double-cross the aliens, however. Although most humans would not be spared, they were determined to perfect a vaccine that would immunize them (and apparently some of their loved ones) from the ill-effects of the virus-like material. And so just as they fought to keep the existence of the aliens and the colonization plan a secret from the rest of humanity, their substantial efforts to develop the vaccine were conducted clandestinely so that the aliens would not be aware of their duplicity.

Beyond these conspiratorial elements, this complex story line required that the conspirators engage in many other schemes. Crossing international borders and spanning decades, the burden of keeping a huge conspiracy secret was challenging. The conspiratorial group infiltrated and subverted governments, eliminated people or groups who stood in their way, manipulated events, and influenced the perceptions of the masses of ordinary people who remained blissfully unaware that a colossal conspiracy jeopardized nearly all of human life.

Slowly but surely, agents Mulder and Scully uncover much of the truth. Sometimes this is the result of their careful and determined investigations. At other times, it is because of lucky coincidences. Still, as each new piece of the grand puzzle is revealed, the agents are not necessarily sure how it fits with what they already know—or what they think they already know. Over and over, the piecemeal approach that the show's writers took to divulging the scope and details of the conspiracy allowed for many false starts.

In the meantime, the series became an unexpected hit for the FOX television network. The show's many devoted fans, who often obsessed about what this or that new revelation meant in terms of the overarching mythology, brought increasing attention to the series. Eventually, the show began to attract ever more casual viewers, as well, and by the middle of its run, it achieved a level of popularity sufficient to ensconce the series in the mainstream of American popular culture.

By the end of the series, *The X-Files* had come to epitomize the idea of conspiracy theory in popular culture. It also served to demonstrate the different ways that this idea was represented in the contemporary culture. The series' main tagline "The Truth Is Out There," for example, was widely recognized both as a reference to the show and more generally as a marker for the whole idea of conspiracy theory. Indeed, this line could be taken in more than one way, with the different interpretations suggesting very different stances about the topic.

In one sense, "The Truth Is Out There" slogan recalled a way of thinking about conspiracy that was simple and straightforward. It suggested that the true state of affairs was presently hidden, and it strongly implied that it was hidden intentionally and with malice. This reading of the slogan, and of the series itself, therefore suggested a paranoid skepticism in which official accounts are fundamentally suspect. Like conspiracy theorizing in a much earlier era, this reading envisions a world in which life's events, big and small, are secretly directed by forces beyond the view of ordinary people.

As bleak as this outlook seems, however, the series suggests that the power of the individual can correct the situation. Mulder, and to some extent Scully, are potential antidotes. After all, it is through their individual efforts, rather than the efforts of the supposedly benevolent institutions of American society, that the truth is exposed. This view is well established in conspiracy theory thinking. It is a restatement of the idea that ordinary people are mostly ignorant about danger and that disaster can be averted only through the efforts of a few enlightened truth-tellers.

Yet, the series, like its tagline, can be read in an entirely different way, expressing an opposite worldview. Indeed, the mythology of *The X-Files* can be read as a narrative with much more ironic meaning, sometimes bordering on parody. From this perspective, the very phrase "The Truth Is Out There" is an inside joke. The words "out there" have a double meaning, one of which has pejorative overtones. Indeed, in some ways the series abounds with absurdities. The sheer complexity of the conspiracy, the inclusion of so many competing references from popular culture, and Mulder's tendency to immediately assume supernatural or extraterrestrial explanations all combine to stretch the limits of rationality.

By the late 1990s, then, conspiracy theory was thoroughly ingrained in the American imagination. But the cohesiveness of the idea as referring to something literal was starting to buckle under the increasing weight of decades of conspiracy-theorizing. The public's decades-long exposure to, and fascination with, the various forms of conspiracy theory had generated more confusion than clarity. There were many competing conspiracy theories about many topics, presenting a jumbled situation of many contradictions. As *The X-Files* showed, perhaps unintentionally, when one attempted to put a large number of these ideas together into one overarching conspiracy theory, the whole phenomenon could look unlikely, maybe even silly.

Depending on what attitude that a person took away after watching *The X-Files*, therefore, it could be either a reassertion of the idea of a fearful and paranoiac world of conspiracy or an entertaining but essentially ridiculous put-down of the whole idea. This was not unlike the situation of conspiracy theory in the wider culture of that time, of course. On one hand, a person did not need to believe in the details of the series story lines to believe that much of modern life was being influenced and dictated by forces that remained out of the limelight. If it is taken in a nonliteral way, this basic idea could be found throughout much of the series.

On the other hand, although people were perhaps more aware of conspiracy-theorizing as a cultural phenomenon than in preceding years, many seemed to think the conspiracy had limited application in the real world. Yes, perhaps some of what happened involved conspiring of some sort, but the big events of life had other, more obvious explanations. If the idea of conspiracy theory was taken too far, it seemed preposterous. The tendency to suspect conspiracy at every turn seemed to be interpreted as much an indication of a marginalized, fringe status in society as anything else.

The X-Files came to television at a particularly opportune moment. It captured and reflected back widespread disenchantment with official truth and packaged this mood with stories of monsters, UFOs, paranormal, and supernatural themes that had long been popular in American entertainment. Although the level of its success probably could not have been predicted, once the series became a hit, shows with similar themes were rushed into production. Although none had the success of *The X-Files*, these shows often did continue to push the fundamental idea that conspiracy was at the root of much modern experience.

Indeed, conspiracy theory reached a new level of saturation in American popular culture in this era. The screen entertainment business was soon littered with productions with similar themes. To some degree, these could be traced back directly to *The X-Files* and some of its precursors. This was especially true in television programming, which has always been a highly imitative business in the United States.

OTHER TELEVISION SERIES

The secret government operative and conspiracy theme, which had long roots in both film and television, was revived in the new interest in the conspiracy theme. One example was the NBC series *The Pretender*, which ran from 1996 to 2000 (and later in two made-for-television movies). It featured the story of a brilliant man named Jarod, who had been trained in near-isolation since boyhood by the sinister group that ran the Centre, an ultra-secret facility. This group had specially prepared Jarod, employing methods that veered toward brainwashing. For various nefarious purposes, they wanted him to use his intellectual genius to assume false identities to infiltrate settings of almost any kind.

Unfortunately for his captors, however, Jarod escapes from the Centre. He now uses his resources to avoid recapture, but along the way decides to use his special training to right injustices that he comes across. The series was formulaic in many ways, but it was well produced and featured appealing actors such as Michael T. Weiss, Andrea Parker, and Patrick Bauchau. Its success represented another way that the conspiracy theme was emphasized in the mainstream. Little about the story seemed shocking, however. Its story of a conniving cabal of influential people who seek to influence the course of current events was becoming almost pedestrian.

A similar theme was the basis for the series *La Femme Nikita*, which debuted on cable's USA Network in 1997. Inspired by two films—an original French production and an English-language American remake—the series told the story of an innocent woman, Nikita, who is framed by a secret organization and then trained to be an assassin-operative for its violent purposes. The organization uses fear and terror to compel her loyalty. Should she seek to escape or opt out of her assigned role, the consequences would be swift and severe. Only death would await her if she dared to defy the organization.

La Femme Nikita is an interesting fictional precursor of what would come after the real terror attacks of September 11, 2001. At times, the secret group that controls Nikita seems to harbor worthy goals. They are shown wanting to destroy evil plots, disrupt terrorist schemes, and maintain world order. Yet, the group does not appear to be tied to any particular government and it seems to believe that the ends justify any means to achieve them. As an innocent person drawn into their secretive world, the Nikita character shows how the group has descended into a world of moral ambiguity. Like so many screen portrayals of conspiracy before, *La Femme Nikita* ultimately is about an individual's confrontation with worldly powers that are beyond the ordinary person's control. The influence of the show was later seen in the series *Alias*, which explored many similar ideas.

Other television productions reflected an *X-Files*-like combination of conspiracy with paranormal, UFO, or supernatural themes. This angle was especially appealing to television programmers, and productions with this theme became an important part of TV schedules. From 1996 to 1999, Fox aired *Millennium*, another show from Chris Carter. It possessed the moodiness and secretive elements of his *The X-Files* series, and it added a gloom and doom theme with religious overtones, all related to the coming of the year 2000. Then there was the series *Roswell*, which ran on the fledgling WB network from 1999 to 2002. This show followed the story of aliens who had crash landed on earth in the Roswell incident. The twist to the story was that they were disguised as human teenagers and now attended a New Mexico high school.

Elsewhere on television, documentary-like programs also made use of the conspiracy theory theme. They often used loose standards of evidence and were prone to open-ended, leading lines of inquiry. Conspiracy theory was in many ways an ideal topic for such programs. Since so many of the most popular conspiracy theories (the Kennedy assassination and Roswell incident, for example) relied on suggestion, innuendo, and creative interpretation of insufficient evidence, such productions could coyly ask whether it could be proven that any given speculation was not true. This allowed for many entertaining, if logically questionable, speculations that took advantage of the public's heightened interest in conspiracy theory.

Some of these, for example, reflected a perception that the public was more willing to believe extreme allegations of conspiracy regarding human contact with extraterrestrial beings. Soon, quasi-documentary productions with this theme helped fill the rapidly expanding world of cable television, which had a continuing need for new content. Probably the most notorious of such productions was a highly touted program in 1995 that was supposedly a documentary about an alien autopsy. At the core of the show was footage that allegedly recorded a secret dissection of a humanoid extraterrestrial life form. The producers secured the services of actor Jonathan Frakes to host the program. (Frakes had costarred in television's *Star Trek: The Next Generation*.) The production marginally addressed the question of whether the autopsy film was authentic as it presented various theories about a recovered alien. Not surprisingly, most informed viewers regarded the footage as a badly staged hoax.

CRISIS IN THE WHITE HOUSE

As conspiracy theory achieved mainstream status in popular culture, the travails of the Clinton White House followed suit. This became especially pronounced after the Republican revolution of 1994, which brought a solid Republican majority to Congress. On the heels of their self-professed "Contract with America," the Republicans soon waged battle with the president in an ideological struggle for the soul of the United States. Emboldened by their stunning success at the polls, the energized Republicans were not shy about expressing their disdain for the Democratic president. More than simple disputes about the shape and direction of policy, many of the Republicans took issue with Bill Clinton the man. The perceived shortcomings of the president and his inner circle were soon talking points for conservatives, who seldom failed to take advantage of opportunities to reiterate their ideas for the public.

Already, the death of deputy White House counsel Vince Foster in 1993 had provided an early opportunity to raise questions about the White House and First Lady Hillary Rodham Clinton. Some conservative critics were skeptical about accounts of Foster's death and the official ruling that it was a suicide. Foster had worked with the First Lady early in her career at the Rose Law firm in Arkansas, and some people suspected that his files contained material about Mrs. Clinton that might be incriminating. (The First Lady had been the target of accusations in the Whitewater scandal, which involved financial improprieties in a development deal years earlier and about the unrelated, but controversial firing of staff members in the White House travel office in 1993.) Soon, some political enemies of the White House came to believe that the alleged files had been stolen after Foster's death to cover up any incriminating evidence. Others went further. They thought that Foster's death was actually a murder disguised as suicide and that the White House had been involved.

Eliciting even more controversy than these events were accusations that became known in early 1998. At that time, the rumblings about an inappropriate relationship in the Oval Office began to be widely circulated. Although the president had long been the target of suggestions that he had extra-martial affairs with various women, the new accusation involved a young White House intern. When the accusations attracted the attention of the mainstream news media, it resulted in a scandal of major proportions.

The president firmly denied that anything inappropriate had occurred. In a television appearance, he resolutely declared that he had not had sex with "that woman."[15] Those who believed him—a group that initially included his wife—were indignant at what they perceived as a smear campaign that was being mounted for partisan reasons.

Appearing on NBC's popular *Today Show* as the controversy escalated, the First Lady defended her husband. It was in this venue that she made the famous statement, "The great story here for anybody willing to find it, write about it and explain it is this vast right-wing conspiracy that has been conspiring against my husband since the day he announced for president." Indeed, she seemed to view the matter in a much broader context, adding, "Bill and I have been accused of everything, including murder, by some of the very same people who are behind these allegations. So from my perspective, this is part of a continuing political campaign against my husband."[16]

The charges of the president's inappropriate relationship with the intern later proved true, which deepened the crisis at the White House. After a special prosecutor investigated the matter, Bill Clinton faced impeachment on charges of perjury and obstruction of justice. Although he was acquitted in a close, mostly party-line vote, the bitter and embarrassing episode seriously weakened him politically.

Controversies such as these emphasized the polarization in American politics. For committed partisans—a group that included both supporters, and opponents of Clintons—these events provided evidence that their party's perspective was correct. For many other people, however, the continuing ideological wrangling in Washington was alienating. Perhaps more than ever, politics seemed to be a spectator sport. This climate was well suited to the continuing growth and evolution of conspiracy theory in popular culture.

CONSPIRACY ON THE BIG SCREEN

The 1990s resurgence in the conspiracy theory theme was also evident in major feature films. In these movies, the subject took on several different forms, exhibiting decidedly different interpretations of the theme.

CONSPIRACY THEORY
Perhaps the most obvious of such movies was *Conspiracy Theory*, a 1997 film directed by Hollywood veteran Richard Donner. A psychological drama

with comic and romantic overtones, it followed the story of a man named Jerry Fletcher (played by Mel Gibson). An otherwise unremarkable taxi driver in New York City, Fletcher has two notable characteristics. He deeply distrusts the government and he thinks he sees conspiracy almost everywhere he looks. Seemingly paranoid and prone to credulity-stretching speculation, the story takes a turn when it appears that he has stumbled onto a real conspiracy and has seemingly been marked for death.

The breadth of the conspiracies that are the object of Donner's interest is huge, but those that attract most attention involve CIA mind-control, malevolent use of NASA technology to trigger seismic events, and a plot to assassinate the president.

A marginalized figure, few people notice Donner or take him seriously. That changes when two murders bring him to the attention of officials. One victim is a NASA scientist. The other turns out to be the father of an assistant district attorney (played by Julia Roberts). As she looks into her father's death, she realizes that Donner is somehow involved. Further investigations suggest that Donner has been subjected to mind-control techniques in an effort to turn him into an unwitting assassin. (This element of the plot is very similar to *The Manchurian Candidate*.)

MEN IN BLACK

A completely different response to conspiracy theory in the 1990s is found in *Men in Black*. This 1997 comedy from director Barry Sonnenfeld makes light of the entire UFO conspiracy phenomenon. The movie mocks many stereotypical features of conspiracy theory that by then had become well-worn facets of popular culture. The idea that aliens had been discovered by the government and were engaged in schemes to take control of earth, for example, is treated as a pedestrian affair. They appear to be incompetent buffoons, not dangerous invaders, and nothing about the aliens seems to present a serious threat. The government agents leading the battle, meanwhile, are caricatures of the men in black from popular culture. But they are hardly ominous soldiers of a conspiring government. Instead, they are light-hearted action heroes who view their job as just another day at the office.

The overall effect of *Men in Black* is one that mocks conspiracy theory culture and plays it for laughs. The most ominous and fearful aspects of conspiracy seem silly as they are taken to extreme form and caricatured in the movie. *Men in Black* is not laughing with conspiracy theory advocates. It is laughing at them. And its enormous box-office success is one indicator that although conspiracy theory was widely visible in popular culture of the day, this did not necessarily mean that it was always taken to heart.

In some screen incarnations, then, conspiracy theory was not simply a topic *for* entertainment. It *was* an entertainment. For many people, it was something that was interesting, perhaps even fun to watch, but it was not necessarily anything that seemed real. Some segment of the population, of course, continued to take conspiracy theory seriously, just as had been true for a very long time. Yet, even for these people, it seems reasonable to believe that the enormous proliferation of conspiracy theory—both as a set of propositions and as a popular culture phenomenon—influenced how literally the idea was interpreted. As a general mood or inclination, one that vaguely suggested that larger social and political forces exerted unrealized influence on the lives of mainstream America, conspiracy theory may have seemed plausible, even commonplace. As a set of literal propositions, it may have seemed less so.

THE TRUMAN SHOW

Taken to the extreme, conspiracy theory can encompass nearly all of human experience. After all, if conspiracy is pervasive enough, it might dictate every facet of a person's life. Although it is often not regarded as an expression of conspiracy theory at all, the 1998 movie *The Truman Show* contains, perhaps, the most comprehensive, all-encompassing version of conspiracy to appear on screen. The film is a dark comedy, set in the glare of a beautiful, if artificial, light.

Director Peter Weir's film tells the story of Truman Burbank (played by Jim Carrey). He is a naïve young man who has been sheltered from the outside world, although he does not know this. Since birth, Truman has been raised as the unwitting star of a global television reality series. He thinks he is leading an ordinary life, but his every move is actually recorded by secret cameras for live television transmission. Without his knowledge, his every move is watched by legions of devoted viewers around the globe.

Although Truman's experiences seem authentic to him as he grows up, everything and everyone else around him are not what they seem. Truman appears to live in an idyllic seaside town name Seahaven, but the town is the world's largest television studio, housed under a huge dome in which even the weather is artificially created. More than this, however, everyone except Truman is an actor; there are no "real" people.

The television series is a huge success, and seemingly the whole world watches him grow up, have his first kiss, go to work, and get married. But all these events are staged by the show's dictatorial producer, Christof (played by Ed Harris), who watches and organizes Truman's experiences like a god.

As the film opens, Truman is all grown up, though his sheltered life has given him an aura of sweetness and innocence. Through a series of small missteps by those around Truman, however, cracks begin to appear in his artificial world. Slowly, he begins to suspect that things are not as they seem.

Much of the narrative deals with Christof's attempts to keep Truman from learning the truth. Christof increasingly appears intoxicated not only by the phenomenal popularity and financial success of his show, but also by his nearly complete power over Truman. As a result, he takes increasingly drastic steps to make sure Truman does not learn the real story of his life.

In short scenes that are intercut throughout the movie, however, it is clear that it is not only Christof who wants the charade to continue. Viewers from around the world have become fixated on Truman, and the thought that Truman might discover the deception and end the show is met with anxiety. Indeed, as these scenes make clear, the show's viewers enable Christof's manipulation of Truman. It is their fanatical loyalty to the show, to the artificial reality that it represents, that is the source of Christof's power.

By the end of the film, Christof's attempts to conceal the truth fall apart. Truman manages to solve the mystery of his own life and prepares to escape across the huge artificial sea housed within the dome. Truman nears the horizon, but even that is fake. Truman discovers a previously unseen stairway, at the top of which is a door leading to the outside world.

As Truman begins to climb the stairs, Christof makes one last, desperate attempt to convince him that he should stay in Seahaven. In a booming voice emanating from hidden speakers, he tries to convince Truman that life in the artificial world is better, that he will be happier and safer if he stays. Truman stops and thinks, but not for long. Acknowledging the audience, he exits through the door, bringing an end to the fake reality that previously characterized his life.

Aided by Jim Carrey's star power, *The Truman Show* was an international success. The story of an innocent man overcoming extraordinary attempts to manipulate and control him appealed to many people. *Variety's* review noted that despite the serious themes of manipulation, control, and authority, the film was notable for its "lightness, its assumption that modern audiences are just as savvy about the media as are its practitioners and don't need to have lessons hammered home."[17]

The Truman Show offers wry commentary about television and the media world. It is more than that, however, even if it is not immediately obvious. On the surface, the deception of the show may not seem like a conspiracy of the sort that had made such a forceful presence in popular culture of the preceding years. Yet, in some ways, *The Truman Show* is the epitome of conspiracy theory. It tells the story of a secretive scheme that intrudes into one person's life in almost every way, manipulating that person's perceptions of reality and constantly using him for their own purposes without his knowledge. It may not be a plot to overtake the world, but it is a plot to completely take over the life of an innocent victim, which is exactly how Truman is portrayed throughout the film.

Beyond this, one aspect of the film makes an especially important comment on conspiracy theory culture. This is in the nature of the conspiracy itself, which is unlike previous incarnations of the theme in movies or television. While portrayals of conspiracy theory had occasionally shown large-scale conspiracies involving a substantial number of people, *The Truman Show* goes much further. Its story reveals that nearly the whole world is part of the conspiracy. In fact, although some characters sympathize with Truman, everyone other than Truman either is part of the deception or an accomplice to it. Indeed, Truman is betrayed and exploited in some way by virtually everyone he has ever known, all for the organized purpose of keeping the show on the air. Thus, *The Truman Show* takes the idea of conspiracy theory to a logical extreme, beyond which it would seem the idea would fall apart: It is a conspiracy with one victim, with the rest of the world part of the conspiracy.

Indeed, where could conspiracy theory go from here? *The Truman Show* is in some respects the end of the line for one way of thinking about conspiracy theory since there appears to be no way to have fewer victims or more conspirators. In some ways, then, *The Truman Show* shows the limits of global conspiracy theory. Because it is a conspiracy in which almost everyone takes part, the conspirators, rather than the victim, are the ones who seem to be detached from reality. As willing observers of massive deception, moreover, the television show's audience appears to understand less about their existence than Truman comes to learn of his.

The Truman Show is an instructive metaphor for the evolution of conspiracy theory in popular culture of the 1990s. During a decade in which the political world became mired in acrimony and the entertainment world found willing audiences for portrayals of massive deception, duplicity, and conspiracy, ordinary people might well have identified with the plight of hapless Truman Burbank, a character who had little control or understanding of his own life.

Many viewers seemed to identify with Truman in some way. It is probably safe to say that Truman's plight resonated with many Americans who had become jaded about politics and the media. By the end of the 1990s, they were less surprised when official accounts did not hold up under scrutiny, or when the declarations of their leaders turned out not to be true. If they were not conspiracy theorists in the literal sense, many people nonetheless harbored increasingly cynical and skeptical views about many of the central institutions of their society. The alienating, and alienated, underpinnings of conspiracy theory had become a prominent feature of mainstream popular culture and of mainstream thought.

Belief and Disbelief

The early twenty-first century brought events that thrust the world into a far-reaching and new kind of global conflict, the War on Terrorism. In the months before the new millennium approached, however, there was little that foreshadowed the changes to come. Americans worried about politics and the economy, as they always did.

There was one new worry, however, which was the so-called "Y2K problem." This was the name given to the discovery that widely used computer programs had not adequately included provisions for the change from 1999 to 2000. Computer programs mostly had coded calendar dates using only the last two digits of the year. Therefore, unless programs to correct this technical issue were prepared and installed, computers could interpret the year 2000 as the year 1900 and so forth. Far from a minor glitch, the fear was that the date problem would wreak havoc with financial and business systems—potentially jeopardizing national security and global banking—as well as causing major headaches for ordinary computer users. Since American life had grown dependent on computers and the Internet, some people also feared that the Y2K issue could be exploited by malicious computer hackers and criminals to intentionally stage a massive attack on the computers used for finance and government.

The approach of the year 2000 was a subject of much interest for many people in the United States for other reasons, as well. For example, the very designation of the year 2000, a reckoning of time based on the Christian calendar, suggested religious dimensions about the event to some people.

The end of the millennium indicated to some Christian groups that important prophesized occurrences, perhaps apocalyptic in scale, could be fast approaching. To those holding such views, the new millennium meant far more than simply turning the page on a calendar, then. It was the herald of a major moment in history that seemed imminent. Such ideas directly emanated from the Christian traditions that have always informed much of American culture.[1]

Thus, for these and other varying reasons, some groups viewed the approach of the new millennium with apprehension. This sometimes prompted intense feelings of anticipation and anxiety. Frequently, it seemed that the people with the strongest, most apocalyptic beliefs regarding the subject were associated with groups that much of the public viewed as religious fringe groups or organizations with far-right political aspirations.

Interestingly, in the popular imagination, such groups often had been associated with various forms of conspiracy. This continued to be a frequent theme on screen and throughout popular culture. But even as the year 2000 came closer, the combination of millennial and conspiracy themes did not seem to excite the general population. In the United States, people seemed more worried about how they would celebrate the arrival of the new millennium.

The approaching event also did not elicit much interest from film-makers and television producers. Perhaps emblematic of this was the fate of the television series *Millennium*, which had been created for the FOX television network by Chris Carter. (He had also created their *The X-Files* series, which by then had also peaked in popularity.) Despite the apparently timely combination of millennial and conspiracy themes that ran throughout the *Millennium*'s narrative, the series soon floundered. It was cancelled by the network in 1999.

AMERICAN POLITICAL SCENE

The year 2000 signaled the coming of the next presidential election in the United States. The polarizing figure of Bill Clinton, having survived two terms, would be ineligible to run. And so the prospect of a wide-open field of candidates from both the Democratic and Republican parties generated widespread anticipation and speculation well before the beginning of 2000. When the primary season was over, the conventions of the two major parties anointed their candidates. Vice President Al Gore received the Democratic nomination and Texas governor, George W. Bush, was selected by the Republicans.

Gore and Bush conducted vigorous, hard-fought campaigns in a close contest. But when the November election finally came, it produced results of historic ambiguity. At first, however, this was not apparent. Soon after the polls closed, some news organizations announced that Al Gore would win the contest, basing this prediction on exit polls. Within hours, such predictions seemed premature. As more tallies became available, it appeared that the vote in Florida (the governor of which was the brother of the Republican candidate) would determine the final outcome. The Florida numbers were very close, but by the early hours of the next morning it appeared that Bush, rather than Gore, had carried the state.

When the official vote was finally recorded, therefore, it seemed that George W. Bush had defeated Al Gore in Florida, apparently settling the matter. But to Gore's supporters, the results did not seem correct, especially in three counties that usually voted Democratic. Further investigation revealed issues with vote counting procedures and, indeed, with the ballots themselves. The Gore camp requested a recount. It was a lengthy and tortuous path from that point forward.

A series of legal challenges led all the way to the Supreme Court. Indeed, though there was apparently dissension within the Court, America's highest judicial authority entered the fray and ultimately made the final decision about how to interpret the results of the election, and hence who would assume the Oval Office. The Supreme Court issued its 5-to-4 decision in mid-December, finally settling the matter. Despite some public apprehension about the legitimacy of the vote, George W. Bush was sworn into office on schedule in January of 2001. In the early months of his term, American politics seemed poised to return to relative calm.

SEPTEMBER 11 AND THE WAR ON TERRORISM

Whatever sense of calmness emerged in the first eight months of that year was shattered by the horrifying events of September 11. When hijacked planes were piloted into the Twin Towers of the World Trade Center in New York and the Pentagon just outside the nation's capital, the world changed. By mid-morning of that fateful day, it was clear that the attacks were the greatest tragedy in at least a generation. The death and destruction stunned and traumatized the nation, deeply scarring the American people.

In the wake of 9/11, the president solemnly announced that the attacks had constituted an act of war against the United States. He promised that swift and forceful justice would be carried out against the perpetrators of the catastrophe. Although the hijackers had died along with their victims in the attacks, officials soon determined that a known, but previously shadowy Islamist terrorist organization was behind the plot. Calling itself Al-Qaeda, the terrorist group seemed to be taking refuge in Afghanistan. Al-Qaeda's leader, a Saudi national named Osama bin Laden, soon became America's most hated and most wanted man.

The 9/11 attack was a genuine conspiracy of international proportions, and it brought the world to a dangerous new level of fear and hostility. When, immediately after the attack, the president framed the traumatic event as an act of war, however, the conspiracy aspect of the event seemed almost incidental to the greater threat. The newly recognized enemy was not feared primarily because it was a conspiracy, even though it was on a grand scale. Instead, it caused fear and anger because of its terrorist goals and methods.

Thus, in post-9/11 rhetoric, Al-Qaeda was cast more in the role of a traditional enemy than a conspiratorial one. The conditions were seemingly ideal for the growth of conspiracy fears, however. Like the situation a half-century earlier, the September 11 attacks presented Americans with an external threat emanating from people who espoused beliefs that were highly dissonant with American ideals. Five decades earlier, the threat that global communism posed to the American way of life fueled fear and paranoia about conspiracy in the nation's midst. Now it was the threat of Islamist extremism. And just as there had been constant efforts to identify hidden enemies in the Cold War era, after 9/11 there were constant struggles to identify hostile persons and sleeper cells in the United States.

But unlike the case in the Cold War, in the wake of 9/11 there was little public concern that "ordinary" Americans might be involved in such treachery. Instead, in the public's mind, the threat mostly remained external. Of course, in the aftermath of the attacks, Americans did become much more cautious and suspicious. And some people were leery of anyone who appeared "foreign" or who seemed to be Islamic. To be sure, Americans remained apprehensive, resigning themselves to a new era of color-coded terrorism alerts and increasingly pervasive security measures in everyday life.

All of these anxieties did relatively little to evoke a widespread conspiracy theory interpretation of the frightening new situation, however. Indeed, by the early 2000s, America's ideas about conspiracy and conspiracy theory had undergone a dramatic transformation from the early Cold War, and whatever intense emotions the terrorist attacks elicited, fear and paranoia about the threat as a conspiracy *per se* were not foremost among them.

And so the United States began its military campaign against terrorism. Afghanistan was identified as the first target since Al-Qaeda seemed to be based there, and it seemed to be receiving support from the ruling Taliban, which was already known for its anti-Western views. That military action included a hunt for Osama bin Laden. But although the Taliban was quickly driven from power, bin Laden proved to be a wily and resourceful enemy. Despite numerous attempts to locate him, he managed to avoid death or capture, apparently escaping to the rugged region along the Afghan-Pakistani border.

WAR IN IRAQ

Soon after its initial success, the United States successfully assembled a group of willing nations to assume most of the security support for Afghanistan, as a new regime tried to rebuild the Afghan nation. Now largely freed from tending to the situation of Afghanistan, the president and his advisors considered the theaters of war they thought should follow Afghanistan in the global war on terrorism. The administration set its sites on Iraq. With increasing confidence, White House officials declared that Iraq, a nation with which the United States had tangled in the Persian Gulf War a decade earlier, had harbored and aided terrorists and that it was somehow implicated in the September 11 attack.

The administration aggressively promoted the idea that Iraq was linked to the 9/11 attacks and that it was a dangerous terrorist state with weapons of mass destruction (nuclear, chemical, and biological weapons). They argued that Iraqi dictator Saddam Hussein would surely make such weapons available to terrorist groups and perhaps even use them himself. In the wake of the horror of September 11, it was too dangerous to let this situation stand, according to administration officials. "Regime change" in Iraq was clearly their goal.

Many White House officials saw the case against Iraq to be compelling in its own right and felt there was little need to obtain the approval from the United Nations before taking swift action. The most visible holdout to this view within the administration was Secretary of State Colin Powell. He strongly advocated that the matter be taken to the UN for their approval, and eventually this course of action was taken. Thereafter, in late 2002, the UN approved such a resolution. It demanded that Iraq give up any weapons of mass destruction it had stockpiled and that it promptly terminate any programs aimed at producing such weapons.

The Iraqis did not comply with weapons inspections to the satisfaction of the United States, and a few months later, in February 2003, Secretary of State Colin Powell was dispatched to the UN to call for swift follow-up action. In his speech to the world body, Powell spoke authoritatively about evidence he said the United States had assembled. This compelling evidence, he declared, demonstrated that Saddam Hussein's regime already harbored a vast stockpile of weapons of mass destruction, and it defiantly maintained an aggressive program to produce or acquire nuclear weapons. (These assertions were in line with previous declarations from the Bush White House and its close ally, the administration of British Prime Minister Tony Blair.) Therefore, the United States requested the UN to support a resolution that specifically authorized the use of force to compel Iraqi compliance with the previous resolution. There was substantial opposition from other UN member states, however, and the proposal was withdrawn.

In March 2003, the White House announced that diplomatic efforts to secure Iraqi compliance had failed. Shortly thereafter, the United States and allies commenced the war in Iraq, which it called Operation Iraqi Freedom. The conflict initially went well for the United States and its allies. Baghdad soon fell. Saddam Hussein fled from the capital and went into hiding. (He was not captured until December.)

In May 2003, with the regime toppled, George W. Bush made a dramatic announcement on the flight deck of a U.S. naval aircraft carrier that was at sea off the coast of San Diego. He declared to Americans and the world, "Major combat operations in Iraq have ended." That assessment, however, would not turn out to be accurate.

Before the war, administration officials apparently believed that when the fighting concluded, the victorious Americans would be welcomed with open arms by a grateful Iraqi people. Although many Iraqi citizens were undoubtedly overjoyed to see the despotic regime of Saddam Hussein vanquished, the security situation in Iraq soon descended into chaos. Before long, it started to become clear that although Saddam Hussein had been driven from power, the United States would now face a violent and stubborn insurgency.

It was a development for which the administration was ill prepared. Over the coming months, it led to a much less secure Iraq and many more American casualties than had been anticipated. As the violence raged and as American troop deployments to Iraq involved more call-ups from the National Guard and longer tours of duty, public opinion polls showed Americans increasingly disapproved of the war.

Public approval of the war dropped precipitously as the conflict dragged on. But the war continued even as American support of it declined. Opponents of the war started to reassess the circumstances that led up to it. They began to look at how the nation had ended up in this troubling situation.

Despite confident predictions from administration officials before the Iraq war, when American and allied troops took control of Iraq, they were unable to locate weapons of mass destruction. Since the existence of these weapons had been the primary justification for launching military action, opponents of the war became suspicious. Many were angered by what they saw as a deliberate deception on the part of the administration, though the White House argued that it had acted on the basis of the best information that was available at the time. Furthermore, administration officials said, Saddam Hussein presided over an evil regime, and Iraqis were surely better off now that he had been removed from power.

Many war opponents were not persuaded by such arguments, however. They focused on the thought that the administration had decided to go to war with Iraq whether or not there was supporting evidence to justify such action. Indeed, some members of the administration, especially Vice President Richard Cheney and Deputy Secretary of Defense Paul Wolfowitz, had long advocated for the Saddam Hussein's removal from power. One of the chief architects of the administration Iraq war policy, Wolfowitz had previously championed the idea of preemptive strikes against hostile regimes.[2]

Moreover, before 2001, influential conservative voices had also argued for broad American intervention in the Middle East and around the globe. The neoconservative think tank Project on the New American Century, for example, had described a scenario much like the administration's Iraq war policy. That group, which included leading neoconservatives William Kristol and Robert Kagan, issued a report entitled *Rebuilding America's Defenses: Strategies, Forces, and Resources for a New Century* in 2000. It laid out a vision of a unipolar world in which the United States would be the only superpower. Accordingly, the document presented the following:

> America has a vital role in maintaining peace and security in Europe, Asia, and the Middle East. If we shirk our responsibilities, we invite challenges to our fundamental interests. The history of the 20th century should have taught us that it is important to shape circumstances before crises emerge, and to meet threats before they become dire. The history of the past century should have taught us to embrace the cause of American leadership.[3]

Such information fueled the growing skepticism about the administration's war policies for some people. As the war had become unpopular, critics increasingly examined what had come before. They scrutinized the justifications that the White House had offered for taking bold military action in the first place. The administration had made Iraq's alleged weapons of mass destruction the centerpiece of their argument for war, but weapons of mass destruction had not been found. The administration claimed that faulty intelligence had led to erroneous predictions, but that they had otherwise acted in good faith. It later became clear that important voices in and near the administration had desired American intervention in the region before the 9/11 attacks had even occurred, however. Critics therefore wondered if this is all there was to the story. Many war opponents thought that the administration had deliberately manipulated the intelligence information in order to justify an action that the White House had already decided to take. The resulting controversies over this question raged on.

FAHRENHEIT 9/11

These suspicions and more appeared in a new documentary film from director Michael Moore in 2004. Entitled *Fahrenheit 9/11*, Moore's new film assailed the president and his actions in the wake of the terrorist attacks. As the director lays out his version of the full story in the period of time before and after September 11, an extremely unflattering picture of the president emerges. The film implies that the Bush administration had been less than forthright about many things, especially regarding supposedly mysterious dealings with Saudi oil interests. According to Moore's argument, the president's agenda was already formed prior to September 11, and the terrorist attacks were used as a pretext to carry out goals that had already been established. The wars in Afghanistan and Iraq were not, then, the spontaneous decisions they appeared to be, but were instead part of a bigger master plan.

Moore's thesis was similar to an incarnation of conspiracy theory that had come to cultural prominence in the preceding years. It suggested that powerful people and institutions could not be trusted and that major events could be manipulated to further an unseen agenda. Such ideas had frequently appeared in fictional films and among committed conspiracy theorists. Moore, a polarizing director with a high public profile, now suggested that one such scheme had actually been carried out. He did not make these claims from an obscure Internet Web site or underground newspaper or in a film that would be seen only by a few people. Instead, his version of history appeared in mainstream movie theaters across America, often playing to large audiences. By the end of 2004, *Fahrenheit 9/11* reportedly had grossed near $120 million, a huge sum for a documentary film.

Fahrenheit 9/11 prompted vocal reaction. The response from film reviewers and political columnists was especially strong. Reaction was mixed and often partisan. For example, writing for *The Hollywood Reporter*, Kirk Hunnicutt reported, "Michael Moore drops any pretense that he is a documentarian to pull together from many sources an angry polemic against the president. . . . There is no debate, no analysis of facts or search for historical context. Moore simply wants to blame one man and his family for the situation in Iraq the United States now finds itself in."[4] *The Chicago Tribune*'s Michael Wilmington also noted the one-sided approach of the film, but judged that it was "among the movies everyone should see this year."[5]

Moore's film was provocative, indeed. It was especially despised by the president's supporters. It was an incendiary film and pushed the political limits of what would be accepted in mainstream movie theaters. Yet, it was far from the most extreme version that this line of thinking produced. Indeed, lurking within the story that leads from September 11 to the war in Iraq were the makings of a more shocking and more explicit new conspiracy theory. Focusing on the 9/11 attacks that triggered subsequent events, the theory suggests a radically different interpretation of these events than what appeared in mainstream news accounts and official pronouncements. Although the majority of citizens seemed not accept the new theory as of 2007, the theory's ideas gained much publicity and notoriety.

OTHER SCREEN TREATMENTS

There are many incarnations of this new variant of conspiracy theory, but they share a focus on the events of September 11, 2001. The various versions agree that the attacks of 9/11 were not what they seemed. Indeed, the central allegation is a jolting rejection of standard accounts of the attacks. The 9/11 conspiracy theorists claim that American interests and U.S. government officials were the masterminds behind the attacks. According to this view, the events of 9/11 were staged by the conspirators in order to make it appear that an outrageous act of war had been committed against the American people. The magnitude of the event would then provide justification for bold American military responses in the Middle East and elsewhere.

To many Americans, such claims were and remain an outrage. Yet, a report published in 2006 indicated that 36 percent of Americans thought that it was "'very likely' or 'somewhat likely' that government officials either allowed the attacks to be carried out or carried out the attacks themselves."[6] Some of these people are very committed to the view, and they assume that even a nonexpert could determine the truth of these claims with a close look at the evidence. (Skeptics of the 9/11 conspiracy theory obviously disagree and generally think that the theorists are seriously misreading the evidence.)

The Internet has been an especially powerful tool in promoting variations of a 9/11 conspiracy theory. Public awareness of the claims has also been heightened by outspoken media celebrities, who have used their fame to call attention to the supposed discrepancies in standard accounts of the attacks.

Indeed, the 9/11 theory makes grand claims about the attacks. Most versions question official explanations about the way in which the World Trade Center towers collapsed, suggesting that the standard account is impossible and that the buildings must have been rigged with explosives. Some accounts do not believe that the occupants of the towers died, but that they were taken away in advance. Others suggest that the Pentagon attack, in which a jetliner flew directly into the building, did not really involve an aircraft at all and that the entire event was staged. In the many versions of the theory, an astonishing array of claims is put forward.

An amateur film called *Loose Change* pulled together footage and material relating to the 9/11 attacks. It purported to demonstrate flaws in the description of the attacks that appears in standard accounts. It suggests, for example, that the damage from the jetliner crashes appears inconsistent with what is known about such crashes. *Loose Change* assembles photographs, eyewitness accounts, and other material to make the case that the official story must be wrong.[7] The film was widely circulated among members of the 9/11 Truth Movement, a group promoting September 11 conspiracy theory ideas and facilitating the distribution of new material that supports this cause.

Even the stalwart British Broadcasting Corporation forayed into the controversy with a television program called *9/11: The Conspiracy Files*. Although its producers claimed that its purpose was to thoroughly investigate the 9/11 conspiracy claims in order to distinguish fact from fiction, it was not fully successful in achieving this aim. It provocatively presented the ideas and seemed to encourage advocates of the theory. It was widely circulated among people interested in 9/11 conspiracy theory.

To skeptics, the central claims of 9/11 conspiracy theory appear to be ridiculous. Indeed, vigorous efforts to debunk such claims emerged as the public's awareness of them grew. But such refutations seem to have little effect on committed advocates of this theory. Indeed, the multitude of variations and the constant shifts in what is claimed in the 9/11 conspiracy theory make complete refutation difficult to achieve.

From one perspective, the determined advocacy of 9/11 conspiracy theorists appears to be the result of something more than only the events of September 11, 2001. Indeed, in some ways that 9/11 conspiracy theory can be seen as a new stage in the decades-long evolution of conspiracy theory in American popular culture. It continues the tradition of conspiracy theory in the political realm—the realm that generated conspiratorial explanations for the AIDS epidemic, the assassination of a president, and many more real events.

But in other respects, the 9/11 conspiracy theory has strong similarities to more obviously fictional sources from the screen. The most obvious point of comparison is with the film *Capricorn One*, which had depicted how a NASA mission to Mars, complete with three astronauts, could be convincingly faked. Similarly, the 9/11 conspiracy theory suggests although the World Trade Centers towers were destroyed and the Pentagon was damaged in a massive explosion, the jetliners did not cause these results. Instead, according to the theory, the buildings were rigged in advance, as if a special effects scene from an elaborate movie production. Like a number of political conspiracy screen productions—*Seven Days in May*, *The Parallax View*, and *The X-Files* among them—the 9/11 conspiracy theory suggests that dramatic events can be created and manipulated through massive efforts of deception and subterfuge. Of course, such themes have been present in the writings of theories of various extremist and fringe groups at least since the nineteenth century. But in recent years, with the explosion of conspiracy theory themed productions in popular culture media, such ideas have also been circulated widely in the general population.

In the United States, the prolonged Iraqi insurgency generated political upheaval in the United States. As the perception that the war had stalled grew, public confidence in the administration's Iraqi policy declined. The 2004 elections yielded a reelection victory for George W. Bush, but it also resulted in Democratic control of Congress. Unsurprisingly, Washington politics became more rancorous, especially with regard to the war in Iraq.

SYRIANA

The 2005 film *Syriana*, which was directed by Stephen Gahan, was released in this context. *Syriana*'s executive producer was George Clooney, who also starred in it along with Matt Damon, Jeffrey Wright, and Amanda Peet. Clooney's association with the project probably brought the political underpinnings of the story more partisan attention than it might otherwise have received. A popular actor who often appeared on the cover of weekly entertainment magazines and tabloids, his outspoken endorsement of liberal political causes was also well known.

The story in *Syriana* was reflective of the confusing and sometimes perplexed mood of American voters. Indeed, one reviewer noted that it "is the kind of serious-minded project one is predisposed to embrace, especially those who believe the U.S. government is engaged in a devious partnership with conglomerates to dominate the world."[8] Clooney plays CIA agent Bob Barnes, who becomes entangled in a complicated story involving the intersection of political intrigue, corrupt oil business, and terrorism. Barnes is an experienced agent and believes in the importance of his work for the intelligence agency. He uncovers massive corruption and deception—some of which even emanates from the White House—and is even tortured by men who had once been allies. Still, he cannot quite believe it when his CIA superiors abandon him.

The narrative of *Syriana* has many ambiguous and inconclusive elements. It is far from a clear-cut story. But rather than a filmmaking deficiency, here the element of uncertainty and the muddled portrayal of global politics are consistent with the film's overall purpose. *Syriana* is a metaphor for the real world of global politics, which, for much of the general public, often seems to be no more comprehensible. The Bob Barnes character, in this reading of the film, is in some respects a surrogate for the average person. He has trusted the goals and motives of his country and thought that the world of oil and politics was essentially as it appears. He finds it difficult to accept that he has been deceived or that his country, represented here symbolically by various officials and agencies.

Syriana is not so much a movie depiction of conspiracy theory as the representation of the world that conspiracy has created. Conspiracy theory in this film—like conspiracy theory that had been seeping into the mainstream of American consciousness for several decades—is not a function or reflection of fear and paranoia only.

CONSPIRACY THEORY AND DISAFFECTION

Upon examining the ways that conspiracy theory has been represented since the tragedy of September 11, it is clear that the concept has changed since its use during the Cold War. In popular culture forms (such as film and television) and in the realm of mainstream American politics, the proliferation of conspiracy theory that came about with the emergence of the Cold War was almost always associated with the fear and anxieties of those times. With the seeming political paranoia of the McCarthy era, the connections between conspiracy theory and the broader political environment became unmistakably clear. For a long time thereafter, standard interpretations of conspiracy theory, as a cultural phenomenon, continued to stress that it was largely the manifestation of this underlying mood.

Critics of conspiracy theory often complain of its potentially damaging and corrosive influences on society. One scholarly view is that "social scientists scorn conspiracy theory—big time. Likewise, they scoff at the conspiracy politics in popular films."[9] Another scholar suggested, "The greatest danger we face in taking the risks of conspiracy theory seriously is a divisive, society wide paranoia."[10] Comments such as these probably represent the mainstream of academic thinking about conspiracy theory as something that is detached from reality and that represents an interpretation of world events that is highly unlikely, and sometimes absurd.

A common view, then, is that the spread of conspiracy theory is detrimental because it could cause the public to become paranoid, fearful, or some similar state. But this idea is based on assumptions that may no longer be accurate. If the record of conspiracy theory in the popular cultural media of film and television is any indication, over recent decades the concept has often drifted quite far from its Cold War-era fear-and-paranoia origins.

Indeed, while conspiracy theory with such underpinnings has occasionally resurfaced, in recent decades conspiracy theory often appears to have different underpinnings. It is disaffection, not paranoia, which appears most prominently. Instead of an expression of fear, this disaffection suggests varying degrees of alienation from some aspects of contemporary life.

PARANOIA, CYNICISM, AND DISAFFECTION

As found in American popular and political cultures since the late 1940s, the conspiracy theory theme has passed through at least three evolutionary stages. At first, the theme emerged from the paranoia, fear, and anxiety that are so often mentioned. The external threat of the Soviet Union and the prospect of nuclear annihilation found expression in a vein of conspiracy theory that represented this widespread interpretation of the world. On screen, this articulation of conspiracy theory can be found in *Big Jim McLain*, *Invasion of the Body Snatchers*, *The Manchurian Candidate*, or any of a host of other movies in which the theme was represented.

A second stage of evolution saw the conspiracy theory theme transform from an expression of fear and paranoia to one that reflected cynicism. This came about as the focus of conspiracy theory changed from a foreign, external threat to one that was a domestic, internal threat. The enemy was no longer from the outside; it came from the inside. And with this change in focus, the underpinning of fear and paranoia was slowly replaced by one of increasing cynicism.

The film *Seven Days in May* foreshadowed some of this change with its story of a government takeover plot originating in the Pentagon. The threat was relocated to within the American system, but the film did not exude the degree of cynicism that would be found a decade later. In the end, the system works and can mostly be trusted. By the mid-1970s, a film such as *All the President's Men*, which repeated the true story of Watergate, more overtly reflected the cynical streak that had become a regular feature of American politics. The film showed that the government—or some of it, anyway—could be very untrustworthy, but at the same time showed that Americans institutions, in this case the news media, were still reliable. Later in 1970s, the fictional narrative of *Capricorn One* went much further in portraying a conspiracy theory based on cynicism. Its story showed government agencies that would engage in massive public deception and resort to the use of unwarranted deadly force in order to maintain the secrecy of its scheme. Here, though the news media has not lost all of its luster, it is easily fooled and does not, for most of the film, seem up to the task of shining a light on the true inner workings of a government that could veer into conspiratorial actions.

During the 1980s, conspiratorial thinking became more overtly directed at the heart of American institutions, which were frequently shown as untrustworthy, ineffective, occasionally criminal, and prone to covering up their misdeeds. The theme was widely scattered across a wide array of screen productions. It appeared prominently in movies as varied as *Rambo*, *Silkwood*, and *Close Encounters of the Third Kind*.

By the 1990s, the cultural representation of conspiracy theory reflected not only cynicism, but also a strong sense of disaffection from at least some parts of the American society and its politics. This is not really a surprising development in most respects. There had been many indicators, after all, that a substantial segment of the population had become disengaged in civic participation. Voter apathy in the United States has been a persistent problem, for example. And by the 1990s, there was a widespread sense that there is not much use in engaging with the institutions of society since they do not seem to reflect the interests of ordinary people anyway.

On screen, such productions as *JFK*, *The X-Files*, and *The Truman Show* mostly took for granted the cynical side of conspiracy theory. Many other films, such as 1999's *The Matrix*, wove themes with conspiracy theory origins into their narratives that focused on other topics. Their portrayals of conspiracies of enormous scale and complexity suggest not only that some parts of society should not be trusted, but that engaging with them at all is almost pointless. Once the scale reaches mammoth proportions, only luck and good fortune will save a person.

Some people may always be attracted to conspiracy theory as a literal way of explaining parts of their lives or the events in the world around them. In some matters, such theories may even turn out to be true. But the pervasiveness of conspiracy theory in contemporary American culture seems to reflect something more than attempts to provide comprehensive explanations of these sorts.

Taken as a metaphor, rather than as literal truth, however, conspiracy theory can be a powerful lens. For those looking through it, this lens can make sense of a world that is ambiguous and often confusing and cruel. Indeed, as it has become a pervasive feature in modern life, the example of conspiracy theory suggests that belief can precede experience. The conspiracy theory lens stands as a readymade template through which to interpret troubling or otherwise inexplicable events. One does not examine evidence and then construct a theory of conspiracy, therefore. Through the conspiracy theory lens, one sees that a person has little power or influence in the face of much greater forces, seen and unseen.

But in the world of the twenty-first century, it is no longer shocking to suggest that complex forces, which sometimes remain unidentified, influence and shape the world and individual lives. In its metaphorical sense, conspiracy theory is a way of talking about these forces.

A CHANGING METAPHOR

Conspiracy theory is still a shorthand way to see the world, but it has been so frequently invoked that its power as an explanation has become diluted. For those people seeking to sound an alarm bell about what they think is an actual large-scale conspiracy, the very label "conspiracy theory" chips away at credibility. Now interpreted as a metaphor, the suggestion of conspiracy theory as a literal phenomenon often receives little consideration.

Conspiracy theories about many different subjects abound. They offer explanations about the coordinated scheming of mysterious forces that try to control worldly affairs. But the cultural idea of conspiracy theory, as a metaphor for the world of experience, has largely replaced these more literal ideas. Indeed, frequent and casual use of the label has stripped the idea of most of its literal meaning. Still, it has been a durable concept in popular culture and politics. Undoubtedly, future screen productions will continue to reflect changes in ideas about conspiracy theory. How it will be incarnated in the future remains to be seen.

Notes

PREFACE

1. Peter Knight, *Conspiracy Culture: From Kennedy to "The X-Files"* (New York: Routledge, 2000), p. 2.

2. See a discussion of this topic in Jane Parish and Martin Parker, eds., *The Age of Anxiety: Conspiracy Theory and the Human Sciences* (Oxford: Wiley-Blackwell, 2001), pp. 1–16.

CHAPTER 1: CONSPIRACY THEORY IN THE AMERICAN IMAGINATION

1. Daniel Pipes, *Conspiracy: How the Paranoid Style Flourishes and Where It Comes From* (New York: The Free Press, 1997), p. 20.

2. Ibid., p. 21.

3. See, for example, Robert Alan Goldberg, *Enemies Within: The Culture of Conspiracy in Modern America* (New Haven, CT: Yale University Press, 2001).

4. Many works catalogue the wide variety of conspiracy theories that appear in American culture, ranging from mass market paperback books such as Kate Tuckett, ed., *Conspiracy Theories* (New York: Berkley Books, 2005) to more serious works such as Peter Knight, *Conspiracy Theory in American History: An Encyclopedia* (Santa Barbara, CA: ABC-CLIO, 2003).

5. See Timothy Melley, *Empire of Conspiracy: The Culture of Paranoia in Postwar America* (Ithaca, NY: Cornell University Press, 2000) and Peter Knight, *Conspiracy Nation: The Politics of Paranoia in Postwar America* (New York: New York University Press, 2002).

6. See, for example, Mark Fenster, *Conspiracy Theories: Secrecy and Power in American Culture*, (Minneapolis, MN: University of Minnesota Press, 1999); George Marcus, *Paranoia Within Reason: A Casebook as Explanation* (Chicago: University of Chicago Press, 1999); Shane Miller, "Conspiracy Theories: Public Arguments as Coded Social Critiques," *Argumentation and Advocacy* 39 (2002), pp. 40–56; Jane Parish and Martin Parker, eds. *The Age of Anxiety: Conspiracy Theory and the Human Sciences* (Oxford: Wiley-Blackwell, 2001); and Harry G. West and Todd Sanders, *Transparency and Conspiracy: Ethnographies of Suspicion in the New World Order* (Durham, NC: Duke University Press, 2003).

7. Ted Goertzel, "Belief in Conspiracy Theories," *Political Psychology*, 15, no. 4 (1994), pp. 731–742.

8. See Elizabeth A. Klonoff and Hope Landrine, "Do Blacks Believe That HIV/AIDS Is a Government Conspiracy against Them?" *Preventive Medicine* 28, no. 5 (May 1999) pp. 451–457.

9. Ibid.

10. Richard J. Hofstadter, "The Paranoid Style in American Politics," *Harpers Magazine*, November 1964, pp. 77–86.

11. Ibid.

12. Ibid.

13. Bennett Kravitz, "The Truth Is Out There: Conspiracy as a Mindset in American High and Popular Culture," *Journal of American Culture*, 22 (Winter 1999), pp. 23–29.

14. Ibid., p. 21.

15. Frank P. Mintz, The Liberty Lobby and the American Right: Race, Conspiracy, and Culture (Westport, CT: Greenwood, 1985).

16. See Melley, *Empire of Conspiracy.*

17. See Ray Pratt, *Paranoia: Conspiratorial Visions in American Film* (Lawrence, KS: University of Kansas Press, 2001).

18. See Peter Knight, *Conspiracy Culture: From the Kennedy Assassination to The X-Files* (New York: Routledge, 2000).

19. Dan Nimmo and James E. Combs, *Mediated Political Realities* (New York: Longman, 1983), pp. 72–73.

20. See Stephen J. Whitfield, *The Culture of the Cold War* (Baltimore, MD: Johns Hopkins University Press, 1991).

21. For a brief overview of this subject, see "Project Paperclip: Dark Side of the Moon" by Andrew Walker, *BBC News*, http://news.bbc.co.uk/2/hi/uk_news/magazine/4443934.stm (accessed April 28, 2008).

22. See David M. Oshinsky, *A Conspiracy So Immense: The World of Joe McCarthy* (New York: Oxford University Press, 2005).

23. Ibid.

24. Steven J. Ross, *Movies and American Society* (Malden, MA: Blackwell, 2002), p. 201.

CHAPTER 2: THE RED MENACE AND ITS DISCONTENTS

1. See Michael Rogin, "Kiss Me Deadly: Communism, Motherhood, and Cold War Movies," *Representations*, 6 (Spring 1984), pp. 1–36.

2. Review of "*Conspirator*" (Motion Picture), *Monthly Film Bulletin*, 16(181/192) (1949), p. 136.

3. "The New Pictures: In the Good Old Summertime" [reviews several films, including *The Red Menace*], *Time*, July 18, 1949.

4. Review of "*I Was a Communist for the F.B.I.*" (Motion Picture), *Monthly Film Bulletin*, 18(204/218) (1951), pp. 324–325.

5. Review of "*My Son John*" (Motion Picture), *Monthly Film Bulletin*, 20(228/239) (1953), pp. 69–70.

6. "The New Pictures," *Time*, April 7, 1952.

7. Review of "*Invasion U.S.A.*" (Motion Picture), *Monthly Film Bulletin*, 20(228/239) (1953), pp. 84–85.

8. Bosley Crowther, "The Screen in Review: *Big Jim McLain*, Film Study of Congressional Work against Communism" (Motion Picture), *The New York Times*, September 18, 1952.

9. Review of "*Big Jim McLain*," *Variety*, August 27, 1952.

10. See Thomas Rosteck, *See It Now Confronts McCarthyism* (Tuscaloosa, AL: University of Alabama Press, 1994).

11. Bosley Crowther, "The Screen Review: Sinatra in *Suddenly* at the Mayfair," *The New York Times*, October 8, 1954.

12. Ibid.

13. Review of "*Suddenly*" (Motion Picture), *Variety*, September 8, 1954.

14. University of Colorado (Boulder campus) and Edward Uhler Condon, *Final Report of the Scientific Study of Unidentified Flying Objects* (New York: Dutton, 1969).

15. See Stuart Samuels, "The Age of Conspiracy and Conformity: Invasion of the Body Snatchers (1956)," in John E. O'Connor and Martin A. Jackson, eds., *American History/American Film: Interpreting the Hollywood Image*, rev. ed. (New York: Continuum, 1989), pp. 200–215.

16. A. H. Weiler, "Passing Picture Scene," *The New York Times*, March 23, 1958.

17. Ray Pratt, *Projecting Paranoia: Conspiratorial Visions in American Film* (Lawrence, KS: University of Kansas Press, 2001), pp. 32–33.

18. A. H. Weiler, "Screen: Hitchcock Takes Suspenseful Cook's Tour," *The New York Times*, August 7, 1959.

CHAPTER 3: CONSPIRACY IN THE NEW FRONTIER

1. Eric Louw, *The Media and the Political Process* (Thousand Oaks, CA: Sage, 2005), p. 154.

2. See Don Munton and David A. Welch, *The Cuban Missile Crisis: A Concise History* (New York: Oxford University Press, 2007).

3. See Graham T. Allison, *Essence of Decision: Explaining the Cuban Missile Crisis* (Boston: Little, Brown, 1971).

4. Review of "*Advise and Consent*" (Motion Picture), *Variety*, May 23, 1962.

5. "The Milieu Is the Meaning," *Time*, June 8, 1962.

6. *Peyton Place* was later the basis for a popular television series. It aired between 1964 and 1969.

7. George Axelrod, quoted in Hal Hinson, twenty-fifth anniversary review of "The Manchurian Candidate" (Motion Picture), *The Washington Post*, February 13, 1988.

8. Hinson, "The Manchurian Candidate."

9. Ray Pratt, *Paranoia: Conspiratorial Visions in American Film* (Lawrence, KS: University of Kansas Press, 2001), pp. 91–93.

10. George Axelrod, quoted in Hinson, "The Manchurian Candidate."

11. Ibid.

12. Ibid.

13. Ibid.

14. Review of "*Dr. No*" (Motion Picture), *Variety*, October 17, 1962.

15. Henry Cabot Lodge, quoted in Maurice Isserman and Michael Kazin, *America Divided: The Civil War of the 1960s*, 3rd ed. (New York: Oxford University Press, 2008), p. 101.

16. John F. Kennedy, quoted in Isserman and Kazin, *America Divided*, p. 102.

17. United States, Warren Commission, *Report of the President's Commission on the Assassination of President John F. Kennedy* (Washington, DC: Government Printing Office, 1964), pp. 2–4.

18. Ibid., p. 374.

CHAPTER 4: SHOCK AND UPHEAVAL

1. See Jeremy Black, *The Politics of James Bond* (Westport, CT: Praeger, 2000).

2. Other considerations are discussed in Henry F. Salerno, "Politics, the Media and the Drama," *Journal of American Culture*, 1 (1978), pp. 189–194.

3. Review of "*Seven Days in May*" (Motion Picture), *Variety*, February 5, 1964.

4. *The Twilight Zone* episode entitled "The Monsters Are Due on Maple Street" was first broadcast in March 1960.

5. In addition, both series spawned remakes. *The Twilight Zone* was the basis of an ill-fated movie in 1983 (perhaps more famous because TV star Vic Morrow died in a helicopter accident during production than because of its relative merits) and attempts to revive it as a televised series in the 1990s and 2000s. It was difficult for these productions to match the formidable reputation and expectations raised by the original series, however. *The Outer Limits* was more successfully revived in the mid-1990s as a series for the popular cable network Showtime, with episodes also syndicated to broadcast stations. Production of the show eventually moved to the Sci-Fi Channel. Although production terminated in 2002, it continued to be aired after that date.

6. Mark Lane, quoted in Bob Callahan, *Who Shot JFK?: A Guide to the Major Conspiracy Theories* (New York: Simon & Schuster, 1993), p. 17.

7. Mrk Lane, *Rush to Judgment: A Critique of the Warren Commission's Inquiry into the Murders of President John F. Kennedy, Officer J. D. Tippit, and Lee Harvey Oswald* (New York: Holt, 1966).

8. Bernard Weiner and Emile de Antonio, "Radical Scavenging: An Interview with Emile de Antonio," *Film Quarterly*, 25, no. 1 (Autumn 1971), p. 8.

9. Review of "*Rush to Judgment*" (Motion Picture), *Variety*, June 7, 1967.

10. For a general discussion of these programs, see Wesley Britton, *Spy Television* (Westport, CT: Praeger, 2004).

11. See Chris R. Tame, *Different Values: An Analysis of Patrick McGoohan's "The Prisoner"* (London: Libertarian Alliance, 1983).

12. An example of critical opinion of the film can be found in Robert B. Frederick, review of "*2001: A Space Odyssey*" (Motion Picture), *The Washington Post*, April 3, 1968.

CHAPTER 5: SCANDAL AND SKEPTICISM

1. Review of "*Executive Action*" (Motion Picture), *Variety*, November 7, 1973.

2. Toni Mastroianni, "*Executive Action* Filled with Subtle Drama," *Cleveland Press*, November 15, 1973.

3. Roger Ebert, review of "*Executive Action*" (Motion Picture), *Chicago Sun-Times*, November 20, 1973.

4. Richard Schickel, review of "*The Conversation*" (Motion Picture), *Time*, July 8, 1974.

5. Richard Schickel, review of "*The Parallax View*" (Motion Picture), *Time*, July 8, 1974.

6. Ian S. Scott, "'Either You Bring Water to L.A. or You Bring L.A. to Water': Politics, Perceptions and the Pursuit of History in Roman Polanski's *Chinatown*," *European Journal of American Studies*, 2 (2007). [Online resource]

7. It was adapted, with a superfluous title change, from James Grady's novel *Six Days of the Condor*.

8. Roger Ebert, review of "*Three Days of the Condor*" (Motion Picture), *The Chicago Sun-Times*, January 1, 1975.

9. Review of "*All the President's Men*" (Motion Picture), *Variety*, March 31, 1976.

10. Michael Schudson, *Watergate in American Memory* (New York: Basic Books, 1992).

11. This phenomenon is commented upon in David Bowdley, "Hollywood Goes to the Moon: The Greatest Hoax of Them All?" *Physics Education*, 38 (2003), pp. 406–412.

CHAPTER 6: VISION AND RE-VISION

1. The movie was based on a novel of the same name by David Morrell.

2. See Gordon Arnold, *The Afterlife of America's War in Vietnam: Changing Visions in Politics and on Screen* (Jefferson, NC: McFarland, 2006), pp. 81–84.

3. The script was based on a story by Kevin Jarre.

4. Arnold, *The Afterlife of America's War in Vietnam*.

5. Roger Ebert, review of "*Blow Out*" (Motion Picture), *Chicago Sun-Times*, January 1, 1981.

6. Review of "*Silkwood*" (Motion Picture), *Variety*, December 14, 1983.

7. For a thorough discussion, see Jodi Dean, *Aliens in America: Conspiracy Cultures from Outerspace to Cyberspace* (Ithaca, NY: Cornell University Press).

8. See Karl T. Pflock, "The Young Mortician On Call That Night," *Omni Magazine* (Fall 1995), pp. 100–105.

9. Among the best-known publications that raised public awareness of the old story was Charles Berlitz, *The Roswell Incident* (New York: Grosset & Dunlap, 1980).

10. See Michael Barkun, *A Culture of Conspiracy: Apocalyptic Visions in Contemporary America* (Berkeley, CA: University of California Press, 2003), p. 30.

11. See Arnold, *The Afterlife of America's War in Vietnam*, pp. 102–105.

CHAPTER 7: A NEW AGE OF CONSPIRACY

1. Desson Howe, review of "*JFK*" (Motion Picture), *The Washington Post*, December 20, 1991.

2. Ibid.

3. Review of "*JFK*" (Motion Picture), *Variety*, January 20, 1992.

4. Ibid.

5. Gordon Arnold, *The Afterlife of America's War in Vietnam* (Jefferson, NC: McFarland, 2006), pp. 143–144.

6. These statements are recorded in Arnold, *The Afterlife of America's War in Vietnam*, p. 145.

7. Ibid.

8. Bruce Loeb, "Kennedy, Vietnam, and Oliver Stone's Big Lie," *USA Today Magazine*, May 1993.

9. Reported in a transcript of *NewsHour*, the PBS public affairs program, on November 20, 1993.

10. Oliver Stone, as quoted in Peter Travers, "Oh What a Tangled Web," *Rolling Stone*, January 23, 1992.

11. Oliver Stone, as quoted in Gregg Kilday, "Oliver Stoned," *Entertainment Weekly*, January 14, 1994, pp. 28–33.

12. See H. Johnson, *Divided We Fall: Gambling with History in the Nineties* (New York: Norton, 1994), p. 48.

13. Howard Chua-Eoan, "Tripped Up By Lies," *Time*, October 11, 1993.

14. Ibid.

15. Peter Baker and John F. Harris, "Clinton Admits to Lewinsky Relationship, Challenges Starr to End Personal 'Prying,'" *The Washington Post*, August 18, 1998.

16. Hillary Rodham Clinton, quoted in "Excerpts of Mrs. Clinton Interview," *The Washington Post*, January 27, 1998.

17. Todd McCarthy, "*The Truman Show*" (Motion Picture), *Variety*, April 27, 1998.

CHAPTER 8: BELIEF AND DISBELIEF

1. Mervyn F. Bendle, "The Apocalyptic Imagination and Popular Culture," *Journal of Religion and Popular Culture*, 11 (Fall 2005). [Online resource]

2. Seymour Hersh, "Annals of National Security: Selective Intelligence: Donald Rumsfeld Has His Own Special Sources: Are They Reliable?" *The New Yorker*, May 12, 2003, p. 44.

3. *Rebuilding America's Defenses: Strategies, Forces, and Resources for a New Century*, Washington, DC, Project for the New American Century, 2000.

4. Kirk Hunnicutt, review of "*Fahrenheit 9/11*" (Motion Picture), *The Hollywood Reporter*, May 18, 2004.

5. Michael Wilmington, review of "*Fahrenheit 9/11*" (Motion Picture), *The Chicago Tribune*, June 25, 2004.

6. Lev Grossman, "Why the 9/11 Conspiracy Theories Won't Go Away," *Time*, September 3, 2006, p. 46.

7. Ibid.

8. Ruthe Stein, "The International Battle for Oil Has Rarely Seemed So Confusing," *San Francisco Chronicle*, December 9, 2005.

9. John S. Nelson, "Conspiracy as a Hollywood Trope for System," *Political Communication*, 20 (2003), p. 499.

10. Lee Basham, "Malevolent Global Conspiracy," *Journal of Social Philosophy*, 34(1) (Spring 2003), p. 101.

Bibliography

"Advise and Consent" (Film review). *Variety*, May 23, 1962.

Allison, Graham T. *Essence of Decision: Explaining the Cuban Missile Crisis*. Boston: Little, Brown, 1971.

"All the President's Men" (Film review). *Variety*, March 31, 1976.

Arnold, Gordon. *The Afterlife of America's War in Vietnam: Changing Visions in Politics and on Screen*. Jefferson, NC: McFarland, 2006.

Baker, Peter and John F. Harris. "Clinton Admits to Lewinsky Relationship, Challenges Starr to End Personal Prying." *The Washington Post*, August 18, 1998.

Barkun, Michael. *A Culture of Conspiracy: Apocalyptic Visions in Contemporary America*. Berkeley, CA: University of California Press, 2003.

Basham, Lee. "Malevolent Global Conspiracy." *Journal of Social Philosophy*, 34(1) (Spring 2003): 91–103.

Bendle, Mervyn F. "The Apocalyptic Imagination and Popular Culture." *Journal of Religion and Popular Culture*, 11 (Fall 2005). http://www.usak.ca/relst/jrpc/art11-apocalypticimagination.html (Accessed on June 22, 2008)

Berlitz, Charles. *The Roswell Incident*. New York: Grosset & Dunlap, 1980.

"Big Jim McLain" (Film review). *Variety*, August 27, 1952.

Black, Jeremy. *The Politics of James Bond*. Westport, CT: Praeger, 2000.

Bowdley, David. "Hollywood Goes to the Moon: The Greatest Hoax of Them All?" *Physics Education*, 38 (2003): 406–412.

Britton, Wesley. *Spy Television*. Westport, CT: Praeger, 2004.

Callahan, Bob. *Who Shot JFK?: A Guide to the Major Conspiracy Theories*. New York: Simon & Schuster, 1993.

Chua-Eoan, Howard. "Tripped Up By Lies." *Time*, October 11, 1993.

"Conspirator" (Film review). *Monthly Film Bulletin*, 16(181/192) (1949): 136.

Crowther, Bosley. "The Screen in Review: Big Jim McLain, Film Study of Congressional Work against Communism" (Film review). *The New York Times*, September 18, 1952.

―――. "The Screen Review: Sinatra in Suddenly at the Mayfair" (Film review). *The New York Times*, October 8, 1954.

Dean, Jodi. *Aliens in America: Conspiracy Cultures from Outerspace to Cyberspace.* Ithaca, NY: Cornell University Press, 1998.

"Dr. No" (Film review). *Variety*, October 17, 1962.

Ebert, Roger. "Executive Action" (Film review). *Chicago Sun-Times*, November 20, 1973.

―――. "Three Days of the Condor" (Film review). *Chicago Sun-Times*, January 1, 1975.

―――. "Blow Out" (Film review). *Chicago Sun-Times*, January 1, 1981.

"Excerpts of Mrs. Clinton Interview," *The Washington Post*, January 27, 1998.

"Executive Action" (Film review). *Variety*, November 7, 1973.

Fenster, Mark. *Conspiracy Theories: Secrecy and Power in American Culture.* Minneapolis, MN: University of Minnesota Press, 1999.

Frederick, Robert B. "2001: A Space Odyssey" (Film review). *The Washington Post*, April 3, 1968.

Goertzel, Ted. "Belief in Conspiracy Theories." *Political Psychology*, 15(4) (December 1994): 731–742.

Goldberg, Robert Alan. *Enemies Within: The Culture of Conspiracy in Modern America.* New Haven, CT: Yale University Press, 2001.

Grossman, Lev. "Why the 9/11 Conspiracy Theories Won't Go Away." *Time*, September 3, 2006.

Hersh, Seymour. "Annals of National Security: Selective Intelligence: Donald Rumsfeld Has His Own Special Sources: Are They Reliable?" *The New Yorker*, May 12, 2003.

Hinson, Hal. "The Manchurian Candidate" (Film review). *The Washington Post*, February 13, 1988.

Hofstadter, Richard J. "The Paranoid Style in American Politics." *Harpers Magazine*, November 1964, 77–86.

―――. *The Paranoid Style in American Politics and Other Essays.* New York: Knopf, 1965.

Howe, Desson. "JFK" (Film review). *Washington Post*, December 20, 1991.

Hunnicutt, Kirk. "Fahrenheit 9/11" (Film review). *The Hollywood Reporter*, May 18, 2004.

"Invasion U.S.A." (Film review). *Monthly Film Bulletin*, 20(228/239) (1953): 84–85.

Isserman, Maurice and Michael Kazin. *America Divided: The Civil War of the 1960s.* 3rd ed. New York: Oxford University Press, 2008.

"I Was a Communist for the F.B.I." (Film review). *Monthly Film Bulletin*, 18(204/218) (1951): 324–325.

"JFK" (Film review). *Variety*, January 20, 1991.

Johnson, H. *Divided We Fall: Gambling with History in the Nineties.* New York: Norton, 1994.

Kilday, Gregg. "Oliver Stoned." *Entertainment Weekly*, January 14, 1994, 28–33.

Knight, Peter. *Conspiracy Culture: From the Kennedy Assassination to 'The X-Files.'* New York: Routledge, 2000.

————. *Conspiracy Nation: The Politics of Paranoia in Postwar America*. New York: New York University Press, 2002.

————. *Conspiracy Theories in American History: An Encyclopedia*. Santa Barbara, CA: ABC-CLIO, 2003.

Kravitz, Bennett. "The Truth Is Out There: Conspiracy as a Mindset in American High and Popular Culture." *Journal of American Culture*, 22 (Winter 1999): 23–29.

Lane, Mark. *Rush to Judgment: A Critique of the Warren Commission's Inquiry into the Murders of President John F. Kennedy, Officer J. D. Tippit, and Lee Harvey Oswald*. New York: Holt, 1966.

Loeb, Bruce. "Kennedy, Vietnam, and Oliver Stone's Big Lie." *USA Today Magazine*, May 1993.

Louw, Eric. *The Media and the Political Process*. Thousand Oaks, CA: Sage, 2005.

Marcus, George. *Paranoia Within Reason: A Casebook on Conspiracy as Explanation*. Chicago: University of Chicago Press, 1999.

Mastroianni, Toni. "Executive Action Filled with Subtle Drama" (Film review). *Cleveland Press*, November 15, 1973.

McCarthy, Todd. "The Truman Show" (Film review). *Variety*, April 27, 1998.

Melley, Timothy. *Empire of Conspiracy: The Culture of Paranoia in Postwar America*. Ithaca, NY: Cornell University Press, 2000.

"The Milieu Is the Meaning," *Time*, June 8, 1962.

Miller, Shane. "Conspiracy Theories: Public Arguments as Coded Social Critiques." *Argumentation and Advocacy*, 39 (2002): 40–56.

Mintz, Frank P. *The Liberty Lobby and the American Right: Race, Conspiracy, and Culture*. Westport, CT: Greenwood, 1985.

Munton, Don and David A. Welch. *The Cuban Missile Crisis: A Concise History*. New York: Oxford University Press, 2007.

"My Son John" (Film review). *Monthly Film Bulletin*, 20(228/239) (1953): 69–70.

Nelson, John S. "Conspiracy as a Hollywood Trope for System." *Political Communication*, 20 (2003): 499–504.

"The New Pictures." *Time*, April 7, 1952.

"The New Pictures: In the Good Old Summertime." *Time*, July 18, 1949.

NewsHour (PBS public affairs radio program). Broadcast of November 20, 1993.

Nimmo, Dan and James E. Combs. *Mediated Political Realities*. New York: Longman, 1983.

Oshinsky, David M. *A Conspiracy So Immense: The World of Joe McCarthy*. New York: Oxford University Press, 2005.

Parish, Jane and Martin Parker, eds. *The Age of Anxiety: Conspiracy Theory and the Human Sciences*. Oxford: Wiley-Blackwell, 2001.

Pflock, Karl T. "The Young Mortician on Call That Night." *Omni Magazine*, Fall 1995, 100–105.

Pipes, Daniel. *Conspiracy: How the Paranoid Style Flourishes and Where It Comes From*. New York: The Free Press, 1997.

Pratt, Ray. *Paranoia: Conspiratorial Visions in American Film*. Lawrence, KS: University of Kansas Press, 2001.

Project for the New American Century. *Rebuilding America's Defenses: Strategies, Forces, and Resources for a New Century*. Washington, DC: Project for the New American Century, 2000.

Rogin, Michael. "Kiss Me Deadly: Communism, Motherhood, and Cold War Movies." *Representations*, 6 (Spring 1984): 1–36.

Ross, Steven J. *Movies and American Society*. Malden, MA: Blackwell, 2002.

Rosteck, Thomas. *See It Now Confronts McCarthyism*. Tuscaloosa, AL: University of Alabama Press, 1994.

"Rush to Judgment" (Film review). *Variety*, June 7, 1967.

Salerno, Henry F. "Politics, the Media and the Drama." *Journal of American Culture*, 1 (1978): 189–194.

Samuels, Stuart. "The Age of Conspiracy and Conformity: Invasion of the Body Snatchers (1956)." In John E. O'Connor and Martin A. Jackson, eds. *American History/American Film: Interpreting the Hollywood Image*. Rev. ed. New York: Continuum, 1989.

Schickel, Richard. "The Conversation" (Film review). *Time*, July 8, 1974.

———. "The Parallax View" (Film review). *Time*, July 8, 1974.

Schudson, Michael. *Watergate in American Memory*. New York: Basic Books, 1992.

Scott, Ian S. "'Either You Bring Water to L.A. or You Bring L.A. to Water'." http://ejas.revves.org/document1203.html (Accessed on June 22, 2008) *European Journal of American Studies*, 2 (2007).

"Seven Days in May" (Film review). *Variety*, February 5, 1964.

"Silkwood" (Film review). *Variety*, December 14, 1983.

Stein, Ruthe. "The International Battle for Oil Has Rarely Seemed So Confusing." *San Francisco Chronicle*, December 9, 2005.

"Suddenly" (Film review). *Variety*, September 8, 1954.

Tame, Chris R. *Different Values: An Analysis of Patrick McGoohan's "The Prisoner."* London: Libertarian Alliance, 1983.

Travers, Peter. "Oh What a Tangled Web." *Rolling Stone*, January 23, 1992.

Tuckett, Kate, ed. *Conspiracy Theories*. New York: Berkley Books, 2005.

United States, Warren Commission, *Report of the President's Commission on the Assassination of President John F. Kennedy*. Washington, DC: Government Printing Office, 1964.

University of Colorado (Boulder campus) and Edward Uhler Condon. *Final Report of the Scientific Study of Unidentified Flying Objects*. New York: Dutton, 1969.

Walker, Andrew. "Project Paperclip: Dark Side of the Moon." *BBC News*, http://news.bbc.co.uk/2/hi/uk_news/magazine/4443934.stm (accessed on April 28, 2008).

Weiler, A.H. "Passing Picture Scene." *The New York Times*, March 23, 1958.

———. "Screen: Hitchcock Takes Suspenseful Cook's Tour." *The New York Times*, August 7, 1959.

Weiner, Bernard and Emile de Antonio. "Radical Scavenging: An Interview with Emile de Antonio." Film Quarterly 25, no. 1 (Autumn 1971), 3–15.

West, Harry G. and Todd Sanders. *Transparency and Conspiracy: Ethnographies of Suspicion in the New World Order*. Durham, NC: Duke University Press, 2003.

Whitfield, Stephen J. *The Culture of the Cold War*. Baltimore, MD: Johns Hopkins University Press, 1991.

Wilmington, Michael. "Fahrenheit 9/11" (Film review). *Chicago Tribune*, June 25, 2004.

Index

Adams, Don, 77
Advise and Consent (film), 45–48, 63
Alien autopsy, 152
Alien (film), 109–10
Allen, Lewis, 26
All the President's Men (film), 102–4, 146, 147, 170. *See also* Watergate scandal
Al-Qaeda, 161–62
Anderson, Gillian, 146
Andress, Ursula, 56
Antonioni, Michelangelo, 92, 121
Arness, Jim, 24
Arnold, Kenneth, 30–31
Atomic bomb, 13–14
Axelrod, George, 49

Bauchau, Patrick, 150
Bay of Pigs invasion, 44, 63
Beatty, Warren, 94, 95
Bernstein, Carl, 102
Betrayed (film), 124
Big Jim McLain (film), 24–25, 170
Bin Laden, Osama, 161–62
Black helicopters, 106–7
Blair, Tony, 163

Blow Out (film), 121–22
Blow-Up (film), 92, 121
Bond, James, 54–58, 63, 66–67
Branch Davidians, 142–43
Brooks, Mel, 77
Burr, Raymond, 21
Bush, George H.W., 134–37
Bush, George W., 160–61, 168

Cambodia, incursion into, 85–86, 120
Cameron, James, 118
Capricorn One (film), 105–8, 168, 170
Carrey, Jim, 155
Carroll, Leo G., 39, 78
Carter, Chris, 145, 160
Castro, Fidel, 40, 44
Censorship in films, 22
Central Intelligence Agency, 44
Cevic, Matt, 21
Cheney, Richard, 164
China, 16, 17
China Syndrome (film), 123
Chinatown (film), 90, 97–100
Clarke, Arthur C., 83
Clinton, Bill, 10, 137, 141, 152–53, 160
Clinton, Hillary Rodham, 3, 152–53

Clooney, George, 168
Close Encounters of the Third Kind (film), 126–28, 171
Closing of the American Mind (book), 131
Cold War, 11–18, 40–42, 60, 63, 73–74. *See also* Domino Theory; McCarthy, Joseph; Union of Soviet Socialist Republics; Vietnam War
Coma (film), 108
Combs, James E., 10
Connery, Sean, 124
Conspiracy theory: Bill and Hillary Clinton and, 152–53; disaffection and 169–72; as a general phenomenon, 1–6; global conspiracy, 8–9; government secrecy and, 83–84, 86, 91; history and, 140–141; in 1970s, 89–90, 104, 108, 110–11; in 1980s, 123, 133–34; in 1990s, 151–52; Joseph McCarthy and, 25–26; as metaphor, 4, 171–72; Oliver Stone's views of, 140; rise in American culture, 9–10, 20; traditional views of, 6–7; Vietnam War and, 119–20; widespread belief in, 4. *See also* Cold War; Kennedy, John F., assassination; McCarthy, Joseph; Union of Soviet Socialist Republics; Watergate scandal
Conspiracy Theory (film), 153–54
Conspirator (film), 19–20
Contras, 129–30
The Conversation (film), 92–94, 100, 121
Coppola, Francis Ford, 92
Cosmatos, George P., 118
Crenna, Richard, 117
Crichton, Michael, 108
Crossfire: The Plot That Killed Kennedy (book), 138
Cuba, 40, 59
Cuban Missile Crisis, 44–45, 63
"Culture wars," 114

Damon, Matt, 168
The Day the Earth Stood Still (film), 31–33

De Antonio, Emil, 75–76, 90, 139
Dennehy, Brian, 117
DePalma, Brian, 121
Destination Moon (film), 31
Domino Theory, 17, 36
Donner, Richard, 153
Double Indemnity, 11
Douglas, Kirk, 68
Dr. No (film), 54–58
Dr. Strangelove (film), 82
Duchovny, David, 145
Duvall, Robert, 93

E.T.: The Extra-Terrestrial (film), 127–29
Eisenhower, Dwight D., 17, 43–44
Executive Action (film), 90–92, 93, 139

Fahrenheit 9/11 (film), 165–66
First Blood (film), 117–18. *See also* *Rambo*
The Flying Saucer (film), 31
Fonda, Henry, 45
Ford, Gerald R., 60, 102
Foster, Vince, 152
Frakes, Jonathan, 152
Frankenheimer, John, 48, 52, 68, 70
Freed, Donald, 90
Freemasons, 5, 8
Friedman, Stanton T., 125
From Russia with Love (film), 66
Fuchs, Karl, 14

Gahan, Stephen, 168
Garrison, Jim, 139
Gates, Nancy, 27
Geer, Will, 90, 91
Get Smart (television series) 77–78
Gibson, Mel, 154
The Girl from U.N.C.L.E. (television series), 77
Goldfinger (film), 66, 67
Gold, Harry, 14
Goldman, William, 102
Goldwater, Barry, 65
Gorbachev, Mikhail, 130
Gore, Al, 160–61

Grant, Cary, 39
Gravas, Costa, 124
Gregory, James, 49
Gulf War, 136–37

Hackman, Gene, 92
Harris, Ed, 155
Harvey, Laurence, 49
Hayden, Sterling, 27
Hayes, Helen, 22
Heflin, Van, 22
Henry, Buck, 77
Hitchcock, Alfred, 39–40, 121, 122
HIV/AIDS conspiracy theory, 4
Ho Chi Minh, 17
Hoffman, Dustin, 102
Hofstadter, Richard J., 5, 6
Holbrook, Hal 103, 105
House Un-American Activities Committee, 15, 24
Humphrey, Hubert H., 84
Hussein, Saddam, 134–36, 163–64
Huston, John, 98

Illuminati, 5
I Married a Monster from Outer Space (film), 37
Invaders from Mars (film), 33–34, 52, 148
The Invaders (television series), 74
Invasion of the Body Snatchers (film), 1956 version, 33, 34–37, 38, 146, 170; 1978 remake, 108
Invasion U.S.A. (film), 23
Invisible Invaders (film), 37
Iran-Contra scandal, 129–30
Iraq, crisis of 1991, 134–37
Iraq War, 163–65
I Was a Communist Spy for the FBI (film), 21

Jagger, Dean, 22, 23
Jesuits, 5
JFK (film), 90, 137–41, 171
Johnson, Lyndon Baines, 44, 65–66, 80–82, 84

Kennedy, John F., assassination of, 6, 10, 26, 53, 58–62, 67, 91. *See also JFK* (film); *Rush to Judgment* (film)
Kennedy, Robert F., 79–80
Kent State University shooting, 86
Khrushchev, Nikita, 25, 41, 45
King, Martin Luther, 79–80
Korean War, 16, 17, 25–26. *See also The Manchurian Candidate* (film)
Koresh, David, 142–43
Kotcheff, Ted, 117
Kubrick, Stanley, 82

La Femme Nikita (television series), 151
Lancaster, Burt, 68, 71, 90
Lane, Mark, 75, 90, 139
Lansbury, Angela, 49, 50
Laughton, Charles, 46
Leigh, Janet, 49
Lodge, Henry Cabot, 58
"Lone gunman" theory, 61–62. *See also* Warren Report
Loose Change (film), 167
Lost in Space (television series), 73
Lucas, George, 109

The Manchurian Candidate (film), 26, 48–54, 63, 70, 96, 170
The Man from U.N.C.L.E. (television series), 39, 77–78
Manhattan Project, 14
The Man Who Knew Too Much (film), 39, 122
Mao Zedong, 16
Marrs, Jim, 138
The Matrix (film), 171
McCarey, Leo, 22
McCarthy, Joseph, 4, 15, 25, 26, 28
McCarthy, Kevin, 35
McGoohan, Patrick, 79
McVeigh, Timothy, 144
Men in Black (film), 154–55
Menzie, William Cameron, 33
Millennium (television series), 160
Miller, David, 90
Mintz, Frank P., 8
Missing in Action (film), 116, 118, 122

Mission Impossible (television series), 78–79
Moon landing, as hoax, 107
Moore, Michael, 165–66
Moore, William L., 125
Motion Picture Association for the Preservation of American Ideals, 24
Murrow, Edward R., 26
My Son John (film), 22–23

Napier, Alan, 24
Neal, Patrica, 32
New World Order, 135–36
Ngo Dinh Diem, 58. *See also* Vietnam War
Nichols, Mike, 123
Nicholson, Jack, 97
Nimmo, Dan, 10
9/11 terrorist attacks, 161–62, 165–68; skepticism of, 167–68
9/11: The Conspiracy Files (film), 167
Nixon, Richard M., 44, 84–87, 89, 91, 102. *See also* Watergate scandal
North by Northwest (film), 39–40
North Korea, 16, 17
North, Oliver, 129–30

Oklahoma City bombing (1995), 144
One World Government, 5
On the Trail of the Assassins (book), 138
Operation Desert Shield, 134
Operation Desert Storm, 135
Operation Iraqi Freedom, 163
Oswald, Lee Harvey, 54, 59–62, 68, 75; portrayal of in *JFK* (film), 138. *See also* Warren Report
The Outer Limits (television series), 72–73, 74
Outland (film), 124

Pakula, Alan J., 94, 102
The Parallax View (film), 90 94–97
"The Paranoid Style in American Politics" (essay), 5
Parker, Andrea, 150
Peet, Amanda, 168
Persian Gulf War, 136–37

Pidgeon, Walter, 46
Pipes, Daniel, 1, 8
Point of Order (film), 76
Polanski, Roman, 97
Pollack, Sydney, 100
Powell, Colin, 163
Powers, Francis Gary, 41
Pratt, Ray, 38
Preminger, Otto, 45, 48
The Pretender (television series), 150
The Prisoner (television series), 79
Project on the New American Century, 164–65

Rambo (film series), 116, 122, 171. *See also First Blood* (film)
Rambo: First Blood, Part II (film), 118–20
Reagan, Ronald, 113–15, 130, 133–34

Redford, Robert, 100, 102
The Red Menace (film), 19–20
Rennie, Michael, 31
Robertson, Cliff, 100
Roddenberry, Gene, 73
Rosenberg, Ethel, 14
Rosenberg, Julius, 14
Roswell, New Mexico, UFO incident, 31, 125–26
Roswell (television series), 151
Ruby, Jack, 59–60
Ruby Ridge incident (1992), 142, 144
Rush to Judgment (film), 75–76, 90, 139
Ryan, Robert, 90, 91

See It Now (television series), 26
Sellers, Peter, 82
September 11, 2001 terrorist attacks. *See* 9/11 terrorist attacks
Serling, Rod, 71–72
Seven Days in May (film), 68–71, 170
Siegel, Don, 34
Silkwood (film), 123–24, 171
Sinatra, Frank, 26–28, 49, 53
Sonnenfeld, Barry, 154
Soviet Union. *See* Union of Soviet Socialist Republics

Spielberg, Steven, 126–27
Stallone, Sylvester, 116, 117, 118
Star Trek (television series), 73, 74
Star Wars (film), 109
Stone, Oliver, 90, 137–41
Streep, Meryl, 123
Suddenly (film), 26–28, 54
Syriana (film), 168–69

Taylor, Elizabeth, 19
Thinnes, Roy, 74
Thomas, Henry, 127
Three Days of the Condor (film),
    100–101, 146
Thunderball (film), 66
Tonkin Gulf incident, 120
Tonkin Gulf Resolution, 65
Travolta, John, 121
The Truman Show (film), 155–57, 171
The Turner Diaries (book), 144
The Twilight Zone (television series), 72,
    73, 146
2001: A Space Odyssey (film), 82–84

Uncommon Valor (film), 118
Unidentified Flying Objects (UFOs), 9,
    29–31, 125–26, 128–29; Kenneth
    Arnold report of, 30–31; in science
    fiction, 145–50. *See also* Roswell, New
    Mexico
Union of Soviet Socialist Republics,
    13–14, 25, 37–38, 41, 44–45, 59, 74
United Nations, 16–17
USSR. *See* Union of Soviet Socialist
    Republics
U-2 crisis, 41

Vietnam War, 17, 26, 58, 65, 74,
    79–81, 84–85, 101; national memory
    of, 114–21, 122. *See also Missing in
    Action* (film); *Rambo* (film)

Waco, Texas incident (1993), 142–43
War of the Worlds (film), 37
War of the Worlds (radio production),
    29–30
War on Terrorism, 162–63. *See also*
    9/11 terrorist attacks; Iraq War
Warren Report, 60–62, 67, 74, 75–76,
    94, 138. *See also JFK* (film); Kennedy,
    John F.; *Rush to Judgment* (film)
Watergate scandal, 4, 86–87, 89, 91,
    130. *See also All the President's Men*
    (film)
Wayne, John, 24–25
Weaver, Randy, 142
Weaver, Sigourney, 109
Weir, Peter, 155
Weiss, Michael T., 150
Welles, Orson, 30
The Whip Hand (film), 21
Winger, Debra, 124
Wolfowitz, Paul, 164
Woodward, Bob, 102
World Trade Center: 1993 bombing of,
    142; 2001 terrorist attack on, 161–62.
    See also 9/11 terrorist attack

The X-Files: Fight the Future (film), 147
The X-File (television series) 9, 103,
    145–50, 171

Y2K problem, 159

About the Author

GORDON B. ARNOLD is Professor of Liberal Arts at Montserrat College of Art in Beverly, Massachusetts, where he has taught courses in film, media, and politics for many years. He was previously a reference librarian and library director at public and academic libraries. His publications include the book *The Politics of Faculty Unionization* (2000), as well as articles in *Library Journal*, *Change*, and *Labor Studies Journal*.